Rethinking Rufus

GENDER *AND* SLAVERY

Rethinking Rufus

SEXUAL VIOLATIONS OF ENSLAVED MEN

Thomas A. Foster

The University of Georgia Press
ATHENS

Athens, Georgia 30602
www.ugapress.org

Set in Garamond Premier Pro by Graphic Composition, Inc. Bogart, GA.

Most University of Georgia Press titles are
available from popular e-book vendors.

Printed digitally

Library of Congress Cataloging-in-Publication Data

Names: Foster, Thomas A., author.
Title: Rethinking Rufus : sexual violations of enslaved men / Thomas A. Foster.
Other titles: Sexual violations of enslaved men
Description: Athens, Georgia : University of Georgia Press, [2019] | Series: Gender and slavery ; 2 | Includes bibliographical references and index.
Identifiers: LCCN 2018049578| ISBN 9780820355214 (hardcover : alk. paper) | ISBN 9780820355221 (pbk. : alk. paper) | ISBN 9780820355207 (ebook)
Subjects: LCSH: Slaves—Abuse of—United States—History. | Slaves—United States—Sexual behavior—History. | Slaves—Family relationships—Southern States—History—19th century. | Male sexual abuse victims—United States—History—19th century. | Male rape victims—United States—History—19th century. | Male rape—United States—History—19th century. | Slave trade—United States—History. | Slaveholders—United States—Sexual behavior—History. | Plantation life—Southern States—History—19th century.
Classification: LCC E443 .F675 2019 | DDC 306.3/620973—dc23
LC record available at https://lccn.loc.gov/2018049578

For Marlon

CONTENTS

ILLUSTRATIONS

ACKNOWLEDGMENTS

I first became acutely aware of the gendered gap in our understanding of sexualized violence under slavery in my history of sexuality course at DePaul University. It was with those undergraduate students and repeated discussions of the interview with Rose Williams and the existing scholarship on the sexual assault of enslaved women that I began to suspect that we were not thinking about the complete story—and that the interview might also be able to help us ponder Rufus's experiences. That I studied the topic at all is largely due to conversations with Marlon Henry in which he expressed his belief that enslaved men were exploited and assaulted by enslavers. His conceptualization of the sexual violence of slavery was not represented in the extant scholarly literature and derived from his understanding of slavery and human nature. I decided to see if contemporary fictionalized instances of sexual violence against enslaved men could be found in historical accounts.

My research was initially published as an exploratory article in a special issue for the *Journal of the History of Sexuality*, edited by Ramón Gutiérrez. I am indebted to Ramón and the participants of the conference related to that special issue for their suggestions on that essay. That article would not have become a book had it not been for the encouragement of Daina Berry and participants in two related conferences, "Sexuality and Slavery: Exposing the History of Enslaved People in the Americas" (University of Texas at Austin, 2011) and "Working Group on Slavery and Freedom" (Humanities Institute, CUNY Graduate Center, 2012). It was in those forums that I first became motivated to attempt to expand the initial article.

I could never have managed to handle the administrative duties as a department chair and continued to make progress on this book without the support of research assistants. They kept the project moving along even when I could not turn to it on a daily basis. I am indebted to the careful and dogged research over the years of a small army of undergraduate and graduate students at DePaul University, including Felipe Agudelo, Callie Bretthauer, Nathan Christensen, Ramiro Hernandez, Scott Jones, Kristen Masterson, and Kasia Szymanska. Daina Berry's graduate students, Nakia "Nikki" Parker and Signe Peterson

Fourmy, tracked down what little we could find in records about Rufus in Texas after emancipation.

A number of historians gave freely of their time to share feedback on earlier drafts of chapters or to share relevant archival cases, including Sharon Block, Trevor Burnard, Frances M. Clarke, Jim Downs, Marisa Fuentes, Leslie Harris, Martha Hodes, Vanessa Holden, Jessica M. Johnson, Jen Manion, Seth Rockman, Joshua D. Rothman, Honor Sachs, John Saillant, James Schuelke, Loren Schweninger, David Shields, Terry Snyder, Christine Walker, Emily West, Lisa Ze Winters, and Betty Wood. I would also like to thank the talented staff at the University of Georgia Press, the anonymous external reviewers, and the editors for the series Gender and Slavery, Daina Berry and Jennifer Morgan.

I am also thankful for the very helpful staff at the History Society of Pennsylvania, the Kentucky State Archives, the Library of Congress, the Library of Virginia, the National Archives, the New York Public Library, and the North Carolina State Archives. I'm also grateful for the speed with which various permission holders processed rights to use their images and for high-resolution files (see individual images for details).

Conference participants and audience members at a number of conferences helped me develop, test, and hone my arguments and analysis in ways that they could never imagine. I am grateful to those individuals, to the organizers, and to DePaul University and Howard University for support to travel and participate in the following conferences: "Male Bonds in Nineteenth-Century Art" (Ghent University, Museum of Fine Arts, May 2018); "QP7" (Grand Cayman, June 2016); "Gay American History @40" (Humanities Action Lab at the New School for Public Engagement, CLAGS: The Center for LGBTQ Studies at CUNY Graduate Center, and OutHistory.org, May 5–6, 2016); "Sexual Violence: An Interdisciplinary Conference" (Virginia Tech, April 2016); "Historicising Rape Conference" (University of Cardiff, July 2015); "American Circuits, American Secrets" (University of Alberta, Banff, Canada, September 2014); "New Directions in the Humanities" (University of San Pablo CEU, Madrid, June 2014); "Working Group on Slavery and Freedom" (Humanities Institute, CUNY Graduate Center, October 4–6, 2012); and "Sexuality and Slavery: Exposing the History of Enslaved People in the Americas" (University of Texas at Austin, November 11–12, 2011).

An adapted version of chapter 2 appeared as "'No Man Can Be Prevented from Visiting His Wife': Henry Butler and Enslaved Manliness in Family and Intimacy," in *Rethinking America's Past: Voices from the Kinsey African American Art and History Collection*, ed. Timothy Gruenewald (Cincinnati, Ohio: University of Cincinnati Press, 2019). A version of material included in chapter 5, "'Till

I Had Mastered Every Part': Valets, Vulnerability, and Same-Gender Relations under Slavery," has been previously published in Bee Scherer, ed., *Queering Paradigms VII* (Oxford: Peter Lang, 2018).

Equally important to my progress was the encouragement that came from invited lectures. I thank the organizer for those important visits at Yale-NUS College; Lawrence Henry Gipson Institute for Eighteenth-Century Studies, Lehigh University; Hong Kong University, January 2017; Canterbury Christ Church University, Canterbury, UK; and the Cambridge University American History Seminar, Cambridge, UK, October 11, 2016.

Discussions via Skype with graduate and undergraduate students at several universities also nurtured my thinking about the ways that enslaved men were sexually violated, including T. Hasan Johnson's undergraduate seminar AFRS 139: The Black Male Experience, California State University at Fresno, February 2018; Catherine Jacquet's undergraduate seminar WGS 4500: Gender, Violence, & Resistance, Louisiana State University, January 2017; and Daina R. Berry's graduate course HIS 392: Gender, Slavery, & Sexuality, University of Texas at Austin, March 2015. In-person visits to the Pembroke Center at Brown University, thanks to Seth Rockman, and Cornelia Dayton's graduate seminar at the University of Connecticut were also very helpful.

For funding, I would like to thank the Council of Independent Colleges and the Gilder Lehrman Institute of American History Summer Institute, Slave Narratives, Yale University, July 2015 (and David Blight and the participants, especially Martha Eads and Kevin McGruder, for their comments regarding Giles's narrative). The Graduate Research Assistant Program, Social Science Research Center, Undergraduate Research Assistant Grants, College of Liberal Arts, and the Competitive Research Grants Program, University Research Council, all at DePaul University, provided much-needed funding for conference travel and research.

For key visual culture sources, I am extraordinarily grateful to David Bindman and Henry Louis Gates Jr. for their research and invaluable insights in their multivolume set, *The Image of the Black in Western Art* (Cambridge, MA: Belknap Press, 2011).

Rethinking Rufus

INTRODUCTION

The Rape of Rufus?

Sexual Violence against Enslaved Men

Rufus landed hard on the dirt floor. Rose's kick had caught him off guard when she fought him. He had wanted to lie down. He was exhausted. The Texas sun had drained his energies. He now knew that Rose and he wouldn't sleep together that night, but he knew they would eventually have to. It was how things worked under slavery. Some called him a bully, but he knew who held the real power. Days before, his master, Hall Hawkins, told him that it was time for him to make babies. Hawkins told him to pair up with Rose. He didn't know her well but had seen her around, working. Not who he would have picked. He liked another young woman, but in this life you did as you were told or you paid the consequences. Rufus was no stranger to being told what to do with his body. Lift this. Carry that. Sleep here. Move now. Sleep with her and make babies. He hated Hawkins for telling him whom to have sex with, but he knew he had no choice. He'd been poked, prodded, stripped, whipped, leered at, and now mated. At times he wondered if they even knew he was a man. Life with Rose would work out. It was better than getting lashed for resisting, and he had wanted to have children someday and head a household. But for now, he found himself on a dirt floor, tasting blood and faced with a woman wielding a fireplace poker. Tonight, he would sleep outside.

Rufus was enslaved in Texas in the nineteenth century, but we know few other biographical details about him. We do not know his last name or where he lived after slavery ended. What we know about Rufus's own experiences during slavery comes to us from an interview with Rose Williams that took place in the early twentieth century with a representative of the federal Works Progress Administration. She characterized Rufus as a "bully" and described resisting him as he attempted to crawl into her bed. Rose's interview has been often reprinted and is well known as a vivid account of the sexual coercion of enslaved women. By imagining their clash from Rufus's perspective, we can begin to see that our current understanding of sexual violence under slavery is limited. A generation ago, Wilma King noted that discussion of Rose's experiences took place "without raising questions about its impact on her spouse."[1] This is the first study to respond to that observation with a focus on Rufus and enslaved men.

Rethinking Rufus examines the sexual conditions that slavery produced and that enslaved men lived within, responded to, and shaped. To tell the story of men such as Rufus, this book queries the range of experiences for enslaved men. Although focused on the United States, it employs a broad chronological and geographic scope. It uses a wide range of sources on slavery—early American newspapers, court records, slave owners' journals, abolitionist literature, the testimony of former slaves collected in autobiographies and in interviews, and Western art—to argue that enslaved black men were sexually violated by both white men and white women. *Rethinking Rufus* is a history of how the conditions of slavery gave rise to a variety of forms of sexual assault and exploitation that touched the lives of many men, their families, and their communities.

The topic of sexual violations of enslaved men has long been in cultural circulation and is not unfamiliar. As the evidence examined here shows, in a variety of ways, enslaved people referenced sexual abuse of enslaved men in their accounts of slavery produced before and after emancipation. Through the twentieth century and right up to the present day, fictionalized accounts of slavery have contained references to men sexually accosted by enslavers, men and women, and forced to reproduce.

But the academy has been slow to produce studies that verify oral traditions that include sexual violence against enslaved men. Through their painstaking research in slave records, scholars have shown that the sexual abuse of enslaved women was ubiquitous.[2] Establishing this now widely accepted conclusion was itself a challenge, for historians had to argue against deep-rooted racist depictions of enslaved women as hypersexual. This book does not equate the sexual assault of women with that of men.[3] Turning to the sexual abuse and exploitation of enslaved men builds on the perspective of this recent literature to more fully understand how sexual violence affected all members of the community.

In their scholarship on the sexual violations of enslaved girls and women, a few scholars have noted that enslaved men were almost certainly also victimized.[4] King noted that a broader scholarship on sexual exploitation was needed, especially on "illicit activities between white women and enslaved men."[5] Martha Hodes's examination of relations between white women and black men in the nineteenth century included several examples of enslaved men as victims of assertive white women.[6] More recently, Daina Ramey Berry has postulated regarding the coerced coupling of enslaved people: "Because it is not clear whether bondmen consented to these recurring acts of intercourse, one could argue that bondmen who were forced to participate in sexual relationships with women who did not give their consent were by definition victims of rape."[7] No studies have a sustained focus on the sexual violations of enslaved men.

Some scholars raise the issue of sexual violations of enslaved men but diminish it or complicate it without further examination. Presumably drawing the conclusion from the absence of scholarship on the topic, bell hooks asserted that the "sexism of colonial white patriarchs spared black male slaves the humiliation of homosexual rape and other forms of sexual assault." Hooks did not consider the position of men in her examination of "breeding."[8] In her groundbreaking book, Saidiya Hartman argued that castration should be examined as "sexual violation because enslaved men were no less vulnerable to the wanton abuses of their owners." Still, her analysis stopped short with the concession that "the extent of their sexual exploitation will probably never be known."[9] More recently, Sasha Turner has acknowledged that "forced unions victimized both enslaved men and women," but she frames the gendered imbalance of power in a way that leads her to emphasize the role of men in these unions in the subordination of women: "To what extent were enslaved men collaborators in the subordination and the sexual abuse of enslaved women?" Turner rightly notes that enslaved men "exerted physical and sexual power over black women through rape and domestic violence."[10]

The study of enslaved men has not covered sexual assault not only because of the legacy of slavery, which characterized black men as hypersexual (and therefore always willing sexual participants) but also because of the historical and enduring understandings of sexual assault.[11] For centuries, our culture has tended to view rape in archetypal ways as the violent sexual assault of a white woman by a stranger, most often a man of color and/or lower status. The early American legal system established sexual assault as a gendered crime, one that by definition covered only free women. In application of the law, its coverage was even narrower, with biases, especially along lines of race and status, influencing outcomes. As Sharon Block has shown, early American print depictions of rape most often highlighted the male guardian as the victim of the male perpetrator.[12] In her study of changing conceptions of rape, historian Estelle Freedman has shown how the "meaning of rape is . . . fluid, rather than transhistorical or static," how "its definition is continually reshaped," and how its history is largely about changing understandings of "which women may charge which men" with the crime.[13] In the era of slavery, Anglo-American culture already embraced a message about black men as particularly sexual, prone to sensual indulgence, and desiring white women. In the late nineteenth century, activists argued for a broadened understanding of rape, one that included sexual assault of African American women but still did not consider the inclusion of men as potential victims.

By the time of the mid-twentieth-century women's movement, feminist theory had shifted the cultural understanding of rape from a crime of passion, usually committed against women who bore responsibility for their victimization, to an expression of violent power, specifically as a tool of the patriarchal oppression of women. This conceptualization has successfully allowed us to better understand sexual assault and rape as a display of power rather than of sexual desire. It does not, however, help us fully understand sexual assault. Even a cursory consideration of sexual assault today can readily point to examples of abuse of power that do not include the shoring up of patriarchy. Sexual assault also happens to boys and men: dependent elderly men who are assaulted by caregivers; incarcerated men by inmates and male and female guards; boys and men in war; prisoners of war or "enemy combatants"; boys and underage youth by male and female teachers, ministers, babysitters, coaches, senior teammates, senior fraternity members—the list is long.

Using the term "rape" to describe sexual violations of men only in the title to this introduction, and even there only hesitatingly posed in question form, signals that the work does not radically revisit or reclaim the word. It may well be too entrenched in historical roots to recover and be useful today for both men and women. But *Rethinking Rufus* does argue that the peculiarities of slavery meant that enslaved men were victimized and sexually assaulted in complex ways and in a manner that may only best be thought of and called rape, even if our available vocabulary remains insufficient for such a study.

This book is indebted to feminist theory of sexual assault as an expression of power and employs the conceptual framework applied to the study of sexual violence in early America. Sharon Block's work is especially useful for scholars of slavery because it "analyzes the gap between the personal coercion of sex and the public classification of rape."[14] Block also builds on feminist conceptualizations of sexual violence as existing along a range of actions and experiences. Examining sexual coercion of enslaved men on a continuum allows recognition of the power at work in a wide range of interactions beyond the narrowly defined legal framework of rape. It is also a useful way to think of the range of sexually abusive situations that enslaved people navigated and the chaotic and unstable nature of interpersonal interactions with enslavers. The continuum, however, must not be seen as a hierarchy of abuses or traumas. Daily objectification, for example, might be as influential as a single physical penetrative assault. As Hartman has shown, "terror of the mundane and quotidian" must also be understood and grappled with to fully see what was slavery.[15]

Rethinking Rufus takes as a starting point the basic recognition that enslaved men could not consent to sexual intimacy with enslavers because of their legal status as property and because of their vulnerability as enslaved people within the hierarchical ordering of society. As Hartman reminds us, the "crime of rape relies upon the capacity to give consent or exercise will."[16] Early Americans centered consent in their understanding of rape. The law assumed that marriage, for example, signaled consent, and so the law could not conceive of the idea of rape within marriage. The legal system acknowledged that children could not consent; therefore, the law presumed that sexual contact under the age of ten qualified as assault. Although early Americans excluded enslaved people from those who could not consent, we would be remiss to repeat their conceptualizations. This book, therefore, follows Block's approach to examining "early American systems of power without replicating the perspective of those systems."[17]

As a study of enslaved men, this book has important implications for our understandings of how sexual vulnerability figured in developing concepts of masculinity for enslaved people. The scholarship on gender and enslaved people has recently started to explore masculinity in more complex ways than the abolitionists' original emphasis on enslaved men as frustrated patriarchs, a concern illustrated, for example, in Richard Ansdell's painting *The Hunted Slaves* (fig. 1). As bell hooks has argued, "To suggest that black men were dehumanized solely as a result of not being able to be patriarchs implies that the subjugation of black women was essential to the black male's development of a positive self-concept, an ideal that only served to support a sexist social order."[18] Rebecca Fraser and others have noted that the nineteenth-century models of manhood emphasized independence, genteel patriarchy, and the ability to provide for and protect dependents and loved ones. These white middle-class ideals, the hegemonic models for gender, transitioned in this period from emphasizing independence and self-reliance to the model of the self-made man with market successes and individual achievements.

FIGURE 1. Richard Ansdell's *The Hunted Slaves* (1861) captures the linkages between physique, sexual potency (via the red sash he is wearing), and the role of protector for the idealized model of enslaved manliness. Courtesy National Museums Liverpool, Walker Art Gallery.

For enslaved men, other models of masculinity were also in play, including admiration for successes and achievements in areas in which enslaved men were allowed to participate: hunting, fishing, work, courtship, physical competitions among men. Masculinity also figured in some areas in which enslaved men were not allowed and that countered slavery, including literacy, protection of loved ones, defiance of masters, and other manners of "expressions of masculinity" that forged a "group solidarity" among enslaved men.[19] David Doddington has argued that enslaved men competed with one another in ways that informed their identities as men: "Although enslaved men supported one another against the oppression of slavery, they also viewed, judged, and ranked one another in order to validate their gendered sense of self." Competitiveness took place in sports and games, as well as economically and in terms of productivity.[20] Sergio Lussana's work has explored the subculture of enslaved men and contexts in which male bonding and homosocial and homoerotic spaces and activities could forge ties among men in the community, as well as reinforce their identities as men.[21]

Sarah N. Roth has argued that silences in the abolitionist literature reveal that depictions of black masculinity changed dramatically over time. By the 1840s the abolitionist literature had placed a comfortable (and comforting) distance between black men and violence or revenge against whites. As she notes, it was necessary to portray slaves in a manner that did not threaten sympathetic white audiences, and so black authors intentionally sought to instill in white readers a sense of pity by highlighting appropriate sufferings.[22] Running away could be an acceptable response to slavery, but violent resistance would alienate readers. Roth concludes that this approach succeeded in attracting a larger white audience to abolitionist literature than the more radical themes addressed in the 1830s and 1850s, when violent resistance was more frequently highlighted.

Roth's point that abolitionist literature was crafted in a way to elicit sympathy has deep implications for the extent to which it could address the sexual assault of enslaved men and helps us understand why many accounts do not contain explicit descriptions of this type of abuse. Graphic stories of abuse would elicit revulsion, not sympathy. In some cases, these stories could also raise the specter of culpability, given prevailing norms of the day that assumed black men were hypersexual and white women were passive. In the case of same-sex sexual assault, such literature would have immediately conjured up guilt by association.

In many ways, we have maintained the gendered division of abuses most often circulated by nineteenth-century abolitionists. The early nineteenth-century painting *Virginian Luxuries*, for example, carefully depicts gendered differences by portraying the intimate violation of an enslaved woman and the whipping of an enslaved man (fig. 2). This painting echoes the nineteenth-century discussions of gendered abuses within slavery as those of "violence against black men" and "sexual exploitation of enslaved women," still most commonly considered.[23] *Rethinking Rufus* contends that we view such images with fresh eyes as illustrations of specific examples, but examples that should not be understood to represent the full range of abusive experiences of enslaved men and women.

In five chapters this book attempts to understand the possibilities of Rufus's experience by examining and listening to the experiences and tellings of a wide range of enslaved people. Chapter 1 focuses on the bodies of enslaved men. Although men's bodies figure throughout the book, this chapter pays particular attention to the ways that dominant American culture denigrated, celebrated, and damaged the bodies of enslaved men. But whites' sexual attraction to black men did not lead to their sexual assault. Black men were sexually violated and exploited because those actions served the racial hierarchy and subordination of black men under slavery.[24] Chapter 1 also posits that enslaved men used their bodies for pleasure and resistance, and they shared publicly their resentment at the abuses they endured.

Chapter 2 historicizes relational standards of masculinity that were culturally present during the height of slavery. Men like Rufus valued autonomy in intimate aspects of life. The ability to choose and then protect one's loved ones was paramount. Chapter 2 examines these ideas and the ways that enslaved men found

FIGURE 2. *Virginian Luxuries*, 1825. This abolitionist painting by an unidentified artist exemplifies nineteenth-century depictions of the different violations suffered by enslaved men and women. These gendered portrayals have largely continued unquestioned. The Colonial Williamsburg Foundation. Museum Purchase.

themselves frustrated and violated in various parts of their lives. Although this book has wide-ranging implications for our understanding of the history of sexuality in America, it does not purport to be a history of sexuality for enslaved men. Rather, it is a history of the particular topic of sexual violence against enslaved men. Study of this topic necessitates some broader examination and contextualization that touch on understandings of enslaved male sexuality, but it is not to be taken as a complete history in that area. As Treva B. Lindsey and Jessica Marie Johnson remind us, we must continue to complicate our understandings of sexuality for enslaved people: "To have erotic sensations was to steal bodies back from masters. . . . [T]o search for [erotic sensations] in chattel slavery . . . allow[s] for the interior lives and erotic subjectivities of enslaved blacks to matter."[25] Abuse and violation here are not meant to define enslaved men's sexuality, although for some they may well have done so.

Chapter 3 looks at the widespread practice of forced reproduction and coerced coupling. Rufus enters Rose Williams's narrative because the two were told to set up a household and produce children for their master's financial gain. A wide range of sources document that reproduction was expected and that coupling was often guided and directed. While chapter 2 shows how men complained that such interference stymied their masculine independence, chapter 3 examines more deeply the broader implications for this interaction between master and enslaved men and how it affected understandings of manliness and positions within families and in the community.

Chapter 4 takes up the issue of white women's relationships with enslaved men and the various other ways that white women violated and exploited enslaved men. It posits that the well-documented incidents of relations between enslaved men and white women suggest that more was at work than simply attraction that boldly flew in the face of prohibitions. Indeed, viewed within the context of power and abuses of enslaved men, the number of such connections suggests that accessibility and exploitation would also be at work in such cases.

Chapter 5 focuses on the experiences of enslaved men as they encountered sexual exploitation directly at the hands of white men. This included but was not limited to same-sex sexual behavior. It also included the complex ways that white men violated and exploited enslaved men in their intimate lives. The chapter focuses on the particularly vulnerable position of enslaved valets. It also underscores the bonds of intimacy that were forged between enslaved men in the context of enslavement.

The book ends, as it began, with Rufus. The conclusion includes the full interview with Rose Williams because the sexual abuse and exploitation of enslaved men affected not only individual men but also their spouses, families, and communities.

Not all enslaved men would have experienced their identities in relation to the experience of sexual assault or even the perceived threat of it. Some men would have had little exposure or given much thought to it. Some might have even considered access to white women as a marker of their prowess.[26] Others might have experienced sexual pleasure, better lives, or even emotional connections from sexually exploitative situations with those who held power over their well-being, their lives. But many experienced direct assault, and most, if not all, experienced the type of sexual violations that devalued and objectified the men, underscoring their status as enslaved men. The point of this book is not to heal the traumas of the past; indeed, for some, telling these stories may inflict more violence. Toni Morrison, bell hooks, and others have grappled with the harming and healing powers that sharing such stories hold.[27] The literature on trauma that limits itself to historical and collective memory, specifically, historical atrocities, has also probed these questions extensively.[28] This book is not the story of how all enslaved men were subjected to violent and traumatic sexual assault, but it is a history of the peculiar conditions that enslavement established, nurtured, and expanded—conditions that enabled those in power to dominate many enslaved men in part through sexual violence.

CHAPTER I

"Remarkably Muscular and Well Made" or "Covered with Ulcers"

Enslaved Black Men's Bodies

> I puts de feet 'gainst him and give him a shove and out he go on de floor 'fore he know what I's doin'. Dat nigger jump up and he mad. He look like de wild boar. He starts for de bunk and I jumps quick for de poker. It am 'bout three foot long and when he comes at me I lets him have it over de head. . . . Dat night when him come in de cabin, I grabs de poker and sits on de bench and says, "Git 'way from me, nigger, 'fore I busts yous brains out and stomp on dem." He say nothin' and git out.
>
> —ROSE WILLIAMS

When Rufus attempted to lie down in his and Rose's bunk for the first time his body paid a price. Rose used physical violence to discourage Rufus from crawling into bed with her, giving him a shove with her feet and hitting him in the head with a metal rod. The account as told by Rose rightly positions her as a victim, but we should not overlook that Rufus was also placed in a position that made him vulnerable to his enslaver. He had been kicked, hit over the head, sent out of his cabin, and violently threatened. All this occurred because the people who held legal rights to his body determined that he should reproduce by setting up a household with Rose. In the eyes of the society, his body was theirs to control. They commanded both his labor and his intimate life, as countless masters and mistresses had done to enslaved men for generations.

His enslaver's decision to place Rufus in this situation held important meaning for Rufus as an enslaved man. Scholars have shown that the bodies and the physical capabilities of many enslaved men held important meaning for norms of masculinity. The body was central for understandings of masculinity. Kathleen Brown argues that because they were denied other means of propertied manliness, "the bodies of enslaved men—or, more precisely, the social persons rooted in those bodies—were more crucial to the meanings and experience of their manhood than was the case for other men."[1] Other scholars have similarly found specific areas in which enslaved manliness was expressed through physicality. The bodies of enslaved men were controlled by enslavement, but they also held keys to manliness. This chapter argues that enslaved men's bodies were symbols of enslaved manhood and sites of violation. Enslaved men were poked and prodded on the auction block; objectified in various cultural forms, including abolitionist literature; and scrutinized, vilified, and tortured by masters and mistresses.

The 1797 portrait of Jean-Baptiste Belley, a formerly enslaved captain in the Haitian Revolution and member of the National Council in France, captures Western cultural adoration of black masculinity (fig. 3). Painted by Anne-Louis Girodet de Roussy-Trioson, Belley stands in full formal uniform as a representative of Saint-Domingue to the French Convention. A landscape, presumably Haiti, is visible in the distant background. He leans against a marble pedestal, on top of which is a bust of philosopher and abolitionist Guillaume-Thomas Raynal. The painting, done in the style that was popular for prominent politicians and military leaders at the time, illustrates the power of presence associated with men of African descent. Scholars have noted that the image is remarkable for its presentation of a new French subject—a black man—painted as refined and in honorable dress and a classical pose.

The portrait also captured the culture's positive assessment of black male sexuality as potent and desirable. Some art historians have even speculated that the artist must have been attracted to Belley, or at least admired him, as his genital outline is so undeniably present and further highlighted by the positioning of his hand and the sumptuously painted fabric of his pants.[2] It is not possible to know if the artist enhanced what he saw to underscore his depiction of Belley's virility. Belley may well have played upon the culture's fascination with black men and their sexuality by wearing his pants in a manner that was more revealing than concealing, refusing to be ashamed of his manhood and employing the provocative power that it carried.

Belley's portrait was unusual for the period. Few black men were the subject of such paintings, but it was typical of cultural representations of enslaved men, who were at times described in terms that emphasized idealized male power. John Saillant's work on the eroticization of the black male body in early U.S. abolitionist literature shows that whites found sexual appeal in black male bodies. He notes that this literature idealized black male bodies in a manner that included an unusual focus on height, musculature, and skin color. Accounts in late eighteenth-century and early nineteenth-century American publications like the *American Universal Magazine* and the *Philadelphia Minerva* described black male characters as "the blackest, the best made, the most amiable," "beautiful in

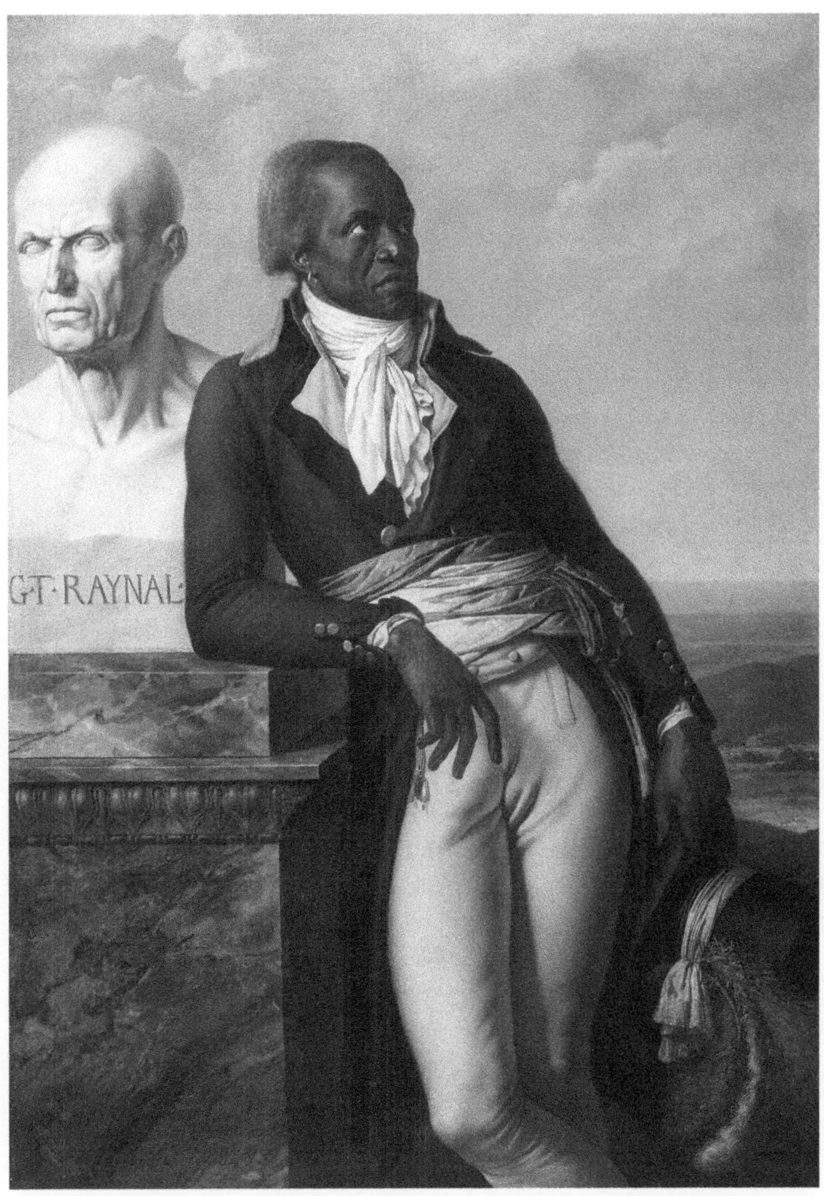

FIGURE 3. Anne-Louis Girodet de Roussy-Trioson, *Portrait of Jean-Baptiste Belley, Deputy of Santo Domingo to Convention of France*, 1797. The portrait of Captain Belley, hero of both the American and Haitian revolutions, celebrates the accomplishments of a formerly enslaved man while also undercutting them by depicting him in a manner that uses sexuality to signal that black men were inherently uncivilized. Photo: Gérard Blot. © RMN–Grand Palais / Art Resource, N.Y.

shape as the Apollo of Belvedere," and "tall and shapely."[3] Numerous abolitionist images fixated on the black male body as perfection, highlighting muscular bodies and, in almost pornographic detail, exposed buttocks enduring unjust abuse and degradation. Black abolitionist publications also described men's bodies in prose that evoked sympathy. The *Colored American*, for example, included this description of an enslaved man: "Jack knelt down—not a muscle of his countenance quivered—he was entirely naked, and was a remarkably muscular and well made man. He looked like a fine bronze statue."[4] Another account, this one included in Frederick Douglass's *North Star*, described one man by his "strength of limb, the roundness of muscle, mind, tender affection, sympathy" in efforts to combat slavery; such details served to underscore the moral injustice of enslaving these men.[5] In another example, one man was described as "well proportioned" and "muscular" to distinguish him from others.[6]

Strength and power figured as measures of manliness also within slave communities, especially among enslaved men. Competitive fighting and wrestling among men served to highlight physical power as a marker of dominant manliness.[7] Formerly enslaved men commented on power, strength, height, and musculature, often noting exceptional height in their recollections: "There was on one plantation, a slave about thirty years of age and six feet high, named Adam."[8] Frederick Douglass's 1852 novel, *The Heroic Slave,* included an arresting description of the hero, Madison. "Madison was of manly form," wrote Douglass, "tall, symmetrical, round, and strong." He continued: "In his movements he seemed to combine, with the strength of the lion, a lion's elasticity. His torn sleeves disclosed arms like polished iron."[9] Josiah Henson, for example, was proud of his ability to run, wrestle, and jump better than his peers and viewed his own body with admiration, calling himself a "robust and vigorous lad." Others spoke about the impressive bodies of fathers and kin. William Smith, for example, boasted that his father was "very strong" and that he was "all muscle." Lussana analyzes these bodies as "'reclaimed'" and argues that they bonded men within the community and reinforced their sense of masculinity.[10]

Muscular physiques were prized for labor. They were also seen as an indicator that a man could ably fulfill the masculine ideals of competitiveness and serve as the protector of his loved ones. Some enslaved men protected their own honor as they bested other men who pursued their loved ones. One formerly enslaved man recalled how his father was able to successfully beat another who he believed had been too friendly with his wife. The son's own masculine pride was evident as he described his father as a "big and strong" man and the man he attacked as "small."[11] Recall that *The Hunted Slaves* (1861), by Richard Ansdell, illustrates how a man's physical build could symbolize not only his abilities but also his masculine commitment to protect and defend his loved ones (see fig. 1). The painting depicts a muscular man stripped to his waist, defending his wife from dogs set upon them by enslavers as they flee through a field.[12] Half of the painting is taken up by the bodies of the three large dogs as they snarl at the couple. The man shields the woman with his body. Broken manacles indicate his strength and physical resistance to slavery. His bright red sash stands out among tones of brown in the painting. Encircling his waist and dangling between his legs, it highlights his masculinized and sexualized strength and power. His feet are planted firmly in a wide stance, and his gaze is directed fearlessly at the open mouth of one of the mastiffs. He wields an ax above his head. One of the dogs lies in the foreground on his back, apparently incapacitated by the man.

As the culture saw erotic possibilities and beauty in black bodies, skin tone was also noted in addition to musculature. The presence of antebellum "fetish" markets of light-skinned enslaved women, in particular, has been documented by scholars. Edward Baptist, for example, argues that the antebellum domestic slave trade might be reconsidered as a "complex of inseparable fetishisms," given the slave traders' "frequent discussions of the rape of light-skinned enslaved women, or 'fancy maids,'" and "their own relentlessly sexualized vision of the trade."[13]

Although we have little evidence for a formalized sexual fetish market in black male flesh, historical scholarship shows us that light-skinned black men were eroticized and appear with regularity in documented examples of intimacy with white women. Baptist's conclusion that "light-skinned and mulatto women symbolized for traders and planters the claimed right to coerce all women of African descent" can be applied in some measure to light-skinned enslaved men.[14] The evidence leads us to speculate that an unusual interest in light-skinned men may have paralleled the more formalized and documented "fetish" market in "fancy maids." In the antebellum divorce case of one white Virginia couple, Dorothea and Lewis Bourne, Dorothea's chosen lover, an enslaved man named Edmond, is described in the records by more than one neighbor as "so bright in his colour, a stranger would take him for a white man."[15] Similarly, Eliza Potter's description of life in New Orleans included a "series of anecdotes that include descriptions of consensual relationships between white women and mixed-race men across state lines."[16] Similar descriptions can also be found in testimony presented to the American Freedmen's Inquiry Commission (AFIC), which was established by the secretary of war in 1863 to document the conditions of those freed by the Emancipation Proclamation. White abolitionist Richard J. Hinton, for example, testified that "I have never yet found a bright looking colored man . . . who has not told me of instances where he has been compelled, either by his mistress, or by white women of the same class, to have connection with them."[17] In another case, a man testified that a man who had been "brought up in the family" was coerced into sex by his mistress, his family connection suggesting that he also was light-skinned.[18]

We have some evidence of more explicit discourse that points to special sexualization of light-skinned black men. One testimony to the AFIC included a reference to light-skinned men as "fine looking."[19] One man told the AFIC: "It was an extremely common thing among all the handsome mulattoes at the South to have connection with the white women."[20] The association of being light-skinned with being attractive, "fine," "bright," and "handsome" suggests a unique assessment for these men. And while light skin may have been viewed as more attractive than dark skin on men, it could not protect them from sexual violations; indeed, it may have only added another dimension to their exploitation. In patriarchal society, the sexual abuse of "nearly white" men could enable white women to enact radical fantasies of domination over a man with the knowledge that their victim's body was legally black and enslaved, subject to the women's control.

The disjunction between the images of sexualized vigor that circulated especially among abolitionists and the realities of enslaved men's physical health underscores how enslaved men's bodies served important cultural as well as social aims. Because we are still living with a legacy of slavery that established black men's bodies as uniquely powerful and sexually potent, it is important not to overlay twenty-first-century images of muscular athleticism on enslaved men. First, we should keep in mind that standards change over time. The idealized body of today is not the ideal of previous generations (including recent ones), even for athletic bodies. Second, the diet of enslaved men was such that many men's musculature would have been retarded or disproportionate from repetitive work. Bones would have been weakened from calcium deficiencies. One man who had been enslaved in South Carolina explained how little they received to eat: "The time of killing hogs is the negroes' feast, as it is the only time that the negroes can get meat, for they are then allowed the chitterlings and feet; then they do not see any more till next hog-killing time. Their food is a dry peck of corn that they have to grind at the hand-mill after a hard day's work, and a pint of salt, which they receive every week. They are only allowed to eat twice a-day."[21] Similarly, another man discussed his experiences in Georgia and how much work was required on very little food: "[The owner] would make his slaves work on one meal a day, until quite night, and after supper, set them to burn brush or to spin cotton." He continued: "Our allowance of food was one peck of corn a week to each full-grown slave. We never had meat of any kind, and our usual drink was water."[22] The classically developed muscular bodies depicted in many abolitionist accounts would not have been possible on many an enslaved man's diet and workload.

In addition to being malnourished, many enslaved men were also vulnerable to disease. As Larry E. Hudson notes, some enslaved people would have been "frequent visitors to the sick house and generally unable to function at best."[23] One man, for example, a field hand named Frederick, was "covered with ulcers" and "rotten." He died before he was fifty.[24] Runaway notices include descriptors such as "bowlegged" and "bandy-legged," a condition that was probably caused by poor diet.[25] Those enslaved by James Henry Hammond were "extraordinarily unhealthy" because of the diet and treatment that were part of life on his plantation.[26] Masters, Faust explains, provided only what was "minimally necessary for [slaves'] maintenance as effective laborers." The standard diet supplied "inadequate amounts of calcium, magnesium, protein, iron, and vitamins." Venereal disease was not uncommon. In addition to disease, men's bodies were more often subjected to debilitating injuries. Three times as many men as women also suffered from fatal accidents.[27]

While the objectification of enslaved men's bodies could appear to some as a harmless appreciation for the beauty of some enslaved men, overall the same impulses that gave rise to eroticizing enslaved men's bodies fueled the forces of enslavement that were held in place by physical abuses and exploitations. Returning to Belley's portrait (fig. 3), we can also see an interpretation that drew upon and reinforced the culture's lurking negative associations between black manhood, hypersexuality, and hypermasculinity. Belley's portrait was initially displayed under a different title, one that carried a more general connotation, as it stereotyped black manhood. When the painting was first exhibited in 1797 the title did not include his name; instead, the painting was titled *Portrait de Nègre*. The title was no doubt designed to capture the novelty of the subject and catch the attention of those perusing the exhibit catalog. Previously, the Paris salon culture had exhibited only one portrait of a black man. Belley's status was also slightly lessened by his sharing his portrait with the figure of a lauded white abolitionist, who garnered authority by being represented as a marble bust. Perhaps the artist chose to do this strategically to remind his audience of white French abolition, as it figured in making Belley's status as a statesman possible. Together, the naming and the sharing of the portrait had the effect of negating Belley's individuality, an irony of significant measure, given his extraordinary accomplishments.[28]

Perhaps the most striking feature of the image is the way that it undercuts Belley's stature because of the way the artist sexualizes him. The pronounced genital outline is unavoidably centered in the image. The protrusion is also further highlighted by the position of his hand and fingers. For many, the effect would have been to contrast the image of the uncivilized body with his refined and honorable dress and classical pose, ultimately drawing a conclusion about the inherent nature of black men. Belley apparently did not commission the portrait, and we have no record of his response to it. Girodet is known for eroticized and sexualized subjects in some of his works. Other portraits by Girodet follow the form of portraits of masculine leaders, such as Washington and Napoleon, and do not highlight pronounced genital outlines, as this was a mark of incivility.[29]

Undercutting the honor of a man as distinguished as Belley by sexualizing his image was possible because it fed off a long history of sexualized bodies under slavery. Sexualized denigration of enslaved boys and men rested foundationally on the regular exposure of their bodies. As Philip Morgan reminds us, "Daily encounters had a sexual dimension" in part because slaves "wore little or no clothing."[30] Exposure of enslaved men's bodies was one way that the institution of slavery relied upon and reinforced a system of subjugation. Enslaved men and boys were allowed little to no privacy, and their bodies were frequently exposed to masters, mistresses, and others on the plantation. William Seals Brown told an interviewer from Southern University that at the age of sixteen he was still only given a long shirt and no underwear.[31] Clothing was meager. As one formerly enslaved man, John Brown, explained, "The children of both sexes usually run about quite naked, until they are from ten to twelve years of age. I have seen them as old as twelve, going about in this state, or with only an old shirt, which they would put on when they had to go anywhere very particular for their mistress, or up to the great house." Clothing, Brown added, offered little privacy to grown men and women.[32] Historian Stephanie Camp argues that "planters imprinted slave status on black bodies by vesting bondpeople in clothing of the poorest quality, made of fabric reserved for those of their station."[33] One traveler in eighteenth-century Virginia recorded seeing "young negroes from sixteen to twenty years old, with not an article of clothing, but a loose shirt, descending half way down their thighs, waiting at table."[34]

As Brown noted, the clothing enslaved people were given to wear meant that men's and women's genitals were often barely covered. Anglo-American culture projected both desire and jealousy upon an objectified and disembodied black phallus.[35] Colonial accounts contain instances of masters and others commenting on enslaved men's bodies in a sexualized manner. In 1681 in Virginia, for example, several men testified to witnessing one Katherine Watkins's interactions with enslaved men. The comments come to us in depositions taken as part of a rape case that she brought against one of the men and detailed her activities one evening drinking with servants and enslaved men. In one man's recollections, she raised the shirttails of one man and remarked to him that he had "a good long thing" and a "good pricke." Another stated that she approached another enslaved man and "putt her hand into his Codpiece."[36] Watkins's actions and comments focused on anatomy, not personality or overall appearance. One hundred years later, we can see the culture still placing special emphasis on black men's genitals. William Feltman, an officer in the First Pennsylvania Regiment, traveling in Virginia in 1781, noted in his military journal that "young boys of about Fourteen and Fifteen years Old" waited tables with their "whole nakedness Expos'd." Feltman quipped: "I can Assure you It would Surprize a person to see these d——d [damned] black boys how well they are hung."[37] At the end of the eighteenth century, Charles White, an English physician, was among those who argued that black men had larger genitalia than Europeans. "I have examined several living negroes, and found it invariably to be the case," he unabashedly stated.[38] As Amber Jamilla Musser reminds us, "The myth of the large black penis only serves to emasculate the black man," as it dehumanizes him and fuels the "fear and desire" of "Negrophobia."[39]

The nakedness of and interest in sexualized men's bodies could be a source of humiliation for enslaved men. Some enslaved men expressed resentment at this lack of respect for their dignity. Brown complained in his account that the clothing allowed was "not enough." "They are made of the lowest quality of material," he stated, "and get torn in the bush, so that the garments soon become useless, even for purposes of the barest decency." His emphasis on "decency" was underscored as he continued more emphatically: "We slaves feel that this is not right, and we grow up with very little sense of shame; but immorality amongst ourselves is not common, for all that."[40] Here Brown highlighted that despite the conditions of exposure, enslaved people maintained a personal dignity and pride and, in remarks that spoke to abolitionist values, maintained morality. He mobilized these arguments to underscore the violation of enforced exposure.

Although daily interactions resulted in general exposure for black men and boys, particular moments, such as sales and auctions, could bring extreme forms of degradation. Western artists circulated images that captured the invasive physical inspections of enslaved men by prospective buyers. An eighteenth-century French engraving depicts an English man "licking a Negro's chin to ascertain his age, & to determine from the taste of his sweat if he is sick" (fig. 4). An 1854 engraving, *Inspection and Sale of a Negro*, shows a white man scrutinizing an enslaved man's body.[41] Similarly, English artist G. H. Andrews portrayed male slaves being examined nearly naked.[42] *Dealers Inspecting a Negro at a Slave Auction in Virginia* captures the physical touching and examining that occurred at auction houses.[43]

FIGURE 4. *Marché d'esclaves*, from M. Chambon, *Le Commerce de l'Amérique par Marseille*... (Avignon, 1764), vol. 2, plate 11, facing p. 400. Intimate violations of enslaved men occurred regularly at the point of sale. Here a prospective enslaver licks an enslaved man to see if his skin is salty (a test for dehydration). Bibliothèque nationale de France.

Reports from a wide range of locales include reference to the invasive scrutiny of men's bodies when on the auction block or being considered for purchase. Abolitionist newspapers, such as the *National Era*, detailed the ways that buyers would poke and prod: "The negroes were examined with as little consideration as if they had been brutes indeed; the buyers pulling their mouths open to see their teeth, pinching their limbs to see how muscular they were, walking them up and down to detect any signs of lameness, making them stoop and bend in different ways that they might be certain there was no concealed rupture or wound."[44] Images circulated by abolitionists did not regularly explicitly depict the sexual violation of men (and only occasionally suggested it for women), but it was known that men in the slave trade were scrutinized and physically groped and prodded—violated as part of the assessment of their commercial value as workers and, for some, of their reproductive capabilities. Thus, even images that did not include graphic depictions carried a resonance, and an ever-present understanding, that bodies being sold were being violated not only in their absence of freedom or in their forced labors but also sexually. Similarly, one Brazilian slaveholder, "in his advice to the purchase of slaves, makes a point of this: the necessity of paying attention to the Negro's sexual organ in order to avoid acquiring individuals in whom it was undeveloped or ill-shaped; for it was feared that they would prove bad procreators."[45] In his study of the antebellum slave market, Walter Johnson writes, "Buyers inspected their naked bodies minutely." Slaveholders quoted by Johnson described their own actions: "Examined the boy very particularly . . . stripped the boy and examined him . . . stripped all the boys . . . and this boy appeared to be the finest of the lot." Such buyers were looking for signs of illness but also rebelliousness, which was believed to be revealed by deep scars from being whipped and punished.[46] In Barbados white women could be seen "dispassionately fondling the genitalia of semi-naked black male slaves in order to assess their health and future breeding potential."[47] Thus, although visitors may have been surprised to see this spectacle of white women fondling black men, the slave culture of the locality allowed for it, as it served economic interests.

Enslaved men wrote about the dehumanization of being stripped and scrutinized as part of sales. Thomas Johns, enslaved in Alabama in 1847, recalled: "When a man went to buy a slave he would make him strip naked and look him over for whip marks and other blemish, jus' like dey would a horse. But even if it done damage to de sale to whip him, dey done it, 'cause dey figgered, kill a nigger, breed another—kill a mule, buy another."[48] Isaac Williams similarly recalled: "About breakfast time, Dr. —— came and stripped us stark naked to examine us. They frequently do, whether buying women or men."[49] Williams also commented on being stripped naked when his master decided to sell him and described it as part of a potentially sexually violative experience. "He took me to his bedroom, and chained me by one leg to his bedpost, and kept me there, handcuffs on, all night. He slept in the bed. Next morning, he took me in a wagon and carried me to Fredericksburg, and sold me into a slave-pen to George Ayler, for ten hundred and fifty dollars." Williams's description of being chained to his master's bedpost bears a striking similarity to the depiction of Luke in Harriet Jacobs's account, published just four years before Williams's. Luke was also chained to his master's bed, and Jacobs intimated that he was sexually violated. The presence of the master's bed adds a layer of intimacy to this account that raises the specter of sexualized violence, especially in light of the popularity of Jacobs's account, which would have already cemented in many readers' minds the particular sexualized abuses being referenced with this imagery. In one final example, one Pennsylvanian recorded what he witnessed in Richmond in 1861. His words were reprinted in abolitionist accounts in London and in the United States, accompanied by images. The account described men being taken to separate rooms or behind screens, where they were physically examined, including examining their genitals. He described one such scene where an enslaved man was forced to drop his trousers to his ankles and raise his shirt. Andrews remarked that they clearly valued the "*private parts*," "behind & spine," and "thighs and legs."[50] The men around him laughed at his degraded status.

Humiliation from being exposed during sales was more regularly experienced during punishments, especially whippings. Whipping was a common component of life for some enslaved people, but we have not generally viewed it as a kind of sexualized torture. The image of whipping exposed male flesh could carry an erotic charge, one that mirrored the nearly obscene fixation on whipping nude enslaved women.[51] In published accounts, the "treatment of scenarios of suffering, if not narrowly pornographic in nature, assumed that the spectacle of pain was a source of illicit excitement, prurience, and obscenity—the power to evoke revulsion and disgust."[52] Beyond the sadism of victimizers, other aspects make whipping especially sexually charged, including exposure, bodily positioning, and torture of genitals and genital areas.

Although images of the barely clothed enslaved man and the stripped enslaved man being beaten are familiar to many today, those images are understood to reflect the humiliating conditions of enslavement but do not necessarily carry the same resonance that various states of undress carried for many African American men by the late eighteenth and early nineteenth centuries. Consider, however, the powerful symbolism of the enslaved man, barely clothed and in chains, used by early abolitionists. Contrast this image with the portraits of successful, formerly enslaved men that emphasize, as did the portraits of elite whites, the importance of clothing to underscore status.[53] We may have come to accept that removal of clothing was a common element of whipping, with our attention focused most closely on the severity of being whipped. But enslaved men routinely commented not only on being whipped but on the fact that they were whipped without clothing on, underscoring that it deeply troubled their sense of masculine dignity.

Formerly enslaved men shared stories about their experiences being whipped nude. Any removal of clothing served as a marker of humiliation and punishment: "I was stripped of my shirt, and the waistband of my trousers was drawn closely round me, below my hips, so as to expose the whole of my back, in its entire length," Charles Ball recounted.[54] Henry Banks explained how he ran away from his master after being beaten by an overseer: "They took me to the barn, stripped me stark naked, and then he tied my hands together and my feet together, and swung me up so I could move neither way."[55] Solomon Northrop, in his account *Twelve Years a Slave*, mentions being whipped nude shortly after his kidnapping: "I was seized by both of them, and roughly divested of my clothing. My feet, as has been stated, were fastened to the floor. Drawing me over the bench, face downwards, Radburn placed his heavy foot upon the fetters, between my wrists, holding them painfully to the floor. With the paddle, Burch commenced beating me. Blow after blow was inflicted upon my naked body."[56] Henry Bibb's narrative also noted the physical exposure as a component of the degradation of whipping: "I have been dragged down to the lowest depths of human degradation and wretchedness, by Slaveholders. . . . I was a wretched slave, compelled to work under the lash without wages and often, without clothes enough to hide my nakedness."[57] Another man shared: "After dinner he took me to a log-house, stripped me quite naked, fastened a rail up very high, tied my hands to the rail, fastened my feet together, put a rail between my feet, and stood on one end of it to hold it down; the two sons then gave me fifty lashes each, the eldest another fifty, and Mr. Gooch himself fifty more."[58] Other men similarly recalled being "stripped naked, tied up by both hands, and unmercifully flogged."[59] One man described that after being stripped naked he was "compelled to lie down on the ground with my face to the earth. Four stakes were driven in the ground, to which my hands and feet were tied."[60] Abolitionist newspapers carried accounts regarding the nudity of whipping. The lack of clothing added to the inhumanity of the scenes of torture.

The low status and humiliation of being whipped nude were heightened when the punishment was public. After securing their freedom, formerly enslaved men commented on these aspects when they recollected their experiences. One man who had been enslaved in Georgia shared the story of a man being beaten nude in front of others: "Next day he got all the people together, and had Jack stripped and tied up to a rough red oak tree, his hands being made fast round the tree, so that he embraced it."[61] Another man described his punishment: "At the sound of the overseer's horn, all the slaves came forward and witnessed my punishment. My clothing was stripped off and I was compelled to lie down on the ground with my face to the earth."[62] Similarly, an account by Aaron explained: "A bricklayer, a neighbor of ours, owned a very smart young negro man, who ran away, but was caught. When his master got him home, he stripped him naked, tied him up by his hands, in plain sight and hearing of the academy and the public green."[63] In his 1862 account of life as a slave in South Carolina, John Andrew Jackson explained: "On one occasion I saw my brother Ephraim tied up and blindfolded with his own shirt, and beaten with fifty lashes before his own wife and children, by a wretch named Sam Cooper, because he was falsely accused of having stolen a yard of bagging." That his brother was unjustly punished in front of "his own" dependents underscored his emasculation. Jackson continued this passage by emphasizing this point dramatically: "Fathers! think of being tied up and stripped before your wife and children, and beaten severely for nothing at all; and then think that it is a daily, nay, hourly, occurrence in the Slave States of America, and you will begin to have some idea of what American slavery is."[64] For Jackson and others, the exposure of their bodies was one component of the degradation of punishment. But this humiliation was compounded when their nakedness was displayed often in front of loved ones, the enslaved community, and masters and overseers.

Enslavers also forced enslaved men and women into especially vulnerable positions for whipping, often using various apparatuses to secure their bodies. In 1815 one North Carolina paper detailed the punishment of an enslaved man as he was "hung up to the horse-rack, and whipped." As part of his punishment he was taken to a "rack," where they "pulled down his breeches and rolled up his shirt" before continuing to beat him.[65] Jamaican planter Thomas Thistlewood used bilboes on both men and women. With their legs shackled to an iron bar, their bodies would be hoisted up for punishment and for flogging in that position. Nude, their genitals would have been especially exposed.[66] Henry Bibb explained: "The persons who are thus flogged, are always stripped naked, and their hands tied together. They are then bent over double, their knees are forced between their elbows, and a stick is put through between the elbows and the bend of the legs in order to hold the victim in that position, while the paddle is applied to those parts of the body which would not be so likely to be seen by those who wanted to buy slaves."[67]

The brutality of whipping and flogging would almost certainly have meant injury and damage, sometimes permanent, to some enslaved men's genitals. One account detailed the physical wounds a man suffered after being tied naked to a tree and then running around the tree because of the pain of being repeatedly branded on his buttocks: "The poor fellow screamed awfully, and . . . tore round the rough tree, the smoke from his burning flesh rising high and white above the top; he all the time screaming, and master swearing. At last the branding was done, and Jack was loosed, when we saw that in going round the tree, he had torn all the flesh from his chest, which was bleeding dreadfully."[68] Although the account only detailed flesh being torn from his chest, it is difficult to imagine that he did not also suffer cuts on other parts of his body that were exposed to the tree, including his genitals. In Easton, Maryland, in 1862 one African American apprentice sued his master due to cruel treatment that included severe beating with a hickory paddle. He complained to the court that after he had been whipped on his bare backside he fainted. When he regained consciousness he discovered that his "privates were very much injured and swollen very large."[69]

The degrading moments of being whipped while naked did not end once the punishment was over. Sometimes men were left unclothed to suffer further after the whipping. As one man explained, "This was in the evening, and though it was late in the fall, and cold, frosty, icy weather, my master left me thus naked, and tied up, till the morning."[70] After punishments, other men often could not put their clothing back on because of the wounds. One account published in a South Carolina newspaper in 1812 explained: "Whipping has been so severely inflicted, that for days the slave could not wear his clothes."[71] Henry Banks explained that after he was beaten he was so badly injured that he was "unable to do any work." He continued: "I could not even stand," so the overseer "then had me carried by the hands into the shade of a tree, where I laid just as I could,—I could not lie any way long."[72]

In light of this analysis, we should consider reevaluating the well-known image of one man's deep scars on his back from whipping.[73] The photos of Gordon were published in 1863 in *Harper's Weekly* and famously depict the heavy scarring on his back from years of brutal whipping. For many viewers familiar with whipping practices, the photo that showed his scars would have conjured up not only his physical pain but also the sexualized abuses, the degradation of being stripped (often publicly), the particular positioning of the body for abuses, the direct assaults on personal areas of the body, and the continued humiliation of exposure after whipping. Today the photo largely conjures up for viewers the horrific pain of punishment under slavery; the additional layers of sexualized assault have largely been forgotten.

Enslaved men's bodies were also marked in other ways as part of punishment.

Some masters used brands to inflict pain and to signal the punishment in an enduring manner. One newspaper account reported that after one man was beaten "a heated brand was applied to various parts of his lacerated body with more than savage cruelty!"[74] Sometimes branding could be in personal areas of the body. Sharon Block writes about one man enslaved in North Carolina named Ned who had his chest and both inner thighs branded with IL and B, respectively, perhaps to signify his owners' names.[75] An account from Georgia recorded that after tying a slave nude to a tree the overseer "then took a branding-iron, marked T.S., which he heated red hot at the kitchen fire, and applied to the fleshy part of Jack's loins."[76]

At its most extreme, violence against personal areas of enslaved men's bodies took the form of mutilations and castration. The *Boston News-Letter* reported in 1718 the assault of a white woman, but with a focus on black male genitalia that warned off "all Negroes meddling with any White Woman": "A Negro Man met abroad an English woman, which he accosted to lye with, stooping down, fearing none behind him, a Man observing his Design, took out his Knife, before the Negro was aware, cut off all his unruly parts Smack and Smooth, the Negro Jumpt up roaring and run for his Life, the Black is now an Eunuch and like to recover of his wounds & doubtless cured from any more such Wicked Attempts."[77] In 1743 a North Carolina enslaved black man convicted of raping a white woman had his "private parts cut off and thrown in his face" after execution by hanging.[78] Similarly, one account from Brazil argued that enslaved men who had sexual relations with white women "who yielded themselves" would suffer great punishments: they were castrated with a "dull knife" and then suffered the horrors of having the "wound sprinkled with salt" before being "buried alive" and executed.[79] While these articles recall the depiction of black men as agents of sexual assault, still then a notion in formation but one that would long remain in the American tradition, they also underscore how punishments for perceived or actual sexual infractions in the hands of whites focused on black male bodies and in particular on maiming the genitalia of enslaved men. Marisa Fuentes quotes a Doctor Jackson, who lived in Jamaica during the late eighteenth century, as reporting that he was aware of "Negroes having been castrated for trespass on the Black Mistress of the overseer."[80]

A runaway ad placed in a Boston newspaper in 1744 illustrates the total exposure of enslaved men's bodies. Cuff, who had been enslaved in Newport, had escaped. Included in the details designed to secure his identification was that he had "but one Testicle." Cuff had previously been embroiled in accusations of sexual assault against a white woman, charges that he survived. Elaine Forman Crane speculates that Cuff could have been the victim of vigilantes, who partially castrated him because of the accusation. Although Crane also suggested that he was born with an undescended testicle, we might consider that he may have suffered an injury either at the hands of an enslaver or while working. The enslavers' knowledge of his single testicle underscores his enslaved status. In print the advertisement also served to reinforce the association of intimate violations with enslaved men's bodies, a collective voyeuristic violation of Cuff's manhood at precisely the moment that he sought to assert his independence by stealing his body from his enslaver. He took this action on the heels of a public accusation, his sale, and his subsequent demotion from ferry operator to ordinary laborer.[81]

Castration and other genital mutilations served as punishment in the hands of overseers and owners continuing into the nineteenth century. In 1853 one Louisiana overseer nailed an enslaved man's penis to a bedpost as part of his punishment. The enslaved man, Ginger Pop, had his privates nailed to the bed and was whipped until he "pulled loose." He later died from his wounds. As Judith Schafer notes, the Supreme Court of Louisiana "had an unspoken policy of under reporting or omitting entirely from its reports cases involving cruelty of a sexual nature to slaves."[82] The establishment of castration during the era of slavery led to its continued use as a weapon of sexualized terror even after emancipation. Archie Vaughn, enslaved in Tennessee, testified about his experience being caught by local men who castrated him and cut off his ear after forcing him to care for their horses. As he described, the men "tied my hands" and put a rope around his neck.[83]

Some masters violated bodies in particularly vile ways that involved intimate bodily functions. Eighteenth-century Virginian William Byrd occasionally used common medical treatments that were known to be uncomfortable as punishment. He wrote in his diary that he "gave" three enslaved men "a vomit" because they went off the plantation for the night. Indicating that he probably returned to this punishment more than once and that it was traumatic, he recorded that it "did more good than whipping." He also forced one enslaved boy to "drink a pint of piss" as punishment for bed-wetting.[84]

As the comments of men who experienced enslavement testify, mental anguish, humiliation, and emotional suffering rivaled the physical pain inflicted on their bodies, and in no other way would this have been more acutely true than when enslaved men's bodies were used to inflict harm on others. Thistlewood boasted in his diary of using what he called "Derby's dose," which involved forcing one enslaved man to defecate in another's mouth. In at least one instance, a man had his mouth shut for hours, unable to remove the excrement. In such instances, both individuals were violated. Thistlewood noted in his diary several different times that he used this punishment: "Had Derby well whipped, and made Egypt shit in his mouth." Derby "catched by Port Royal eating canes. Had him well flogged and pickled, then made Hector shit in his mouth." Two months later, Port Royal ran away and after being caught was punished in this manner. "Gave him a moderate whipping, pickled him well, made Hector shit in his mouth, immediately put in a gag whilst his mouth was full & made him wear it 4 or 5 hours." In another entry from the same time period, Thistlewood describes the punishment of two men who were caught after running away: "Punch catched at Salt River and brought home. Flogged him and Quacoo well, and then washed and rubbed in salt pickle, lime juice & bird pepper; also whipped Hector for losing his hoe, made New Negro Joe piss in his eyes & mouth &c."[85]

Thistlewood's accounts of torture of enslaved people raise yet another way that men's bodies were violated in intimate ways under slavery: enslaved men were at times psychologically tortured by being forced to assist in sexualized punishments. Attackers understood the anguish this would cause and the divisiveness it could engender within a victim's community. Recall Archie Vaughn, the Tennessee freedman who was castrated by a group of men. Those men had forced a "field hand" to hold him as they tied him up and assaulted him. The use of enslaved men to participate in these acts of sexualized torture further violated those men who had no power to resist and who viewed firsthand the punishment that awaited them if they took action.[86]

Enslaved men were sometimes dangerously caught up in intimate conflicts between masters and mistresses. In her divorce case, North Carolinian Mary Jane Stewart testified that her husband had violently sexually assaulted her and noted that he "ordered" her "to go and lie with negro men."[87] There is nothing else in the record to shed light on this comment. The abuses that enslaved men were coerced to participate in were part of the multilayered abuses and violence of the slave household. Such assaults dehumanized the enslaved man, who became a tool for someone else's abuse. Testimony from an Alabama divorce case in 1839 included a wife's complaint that her husband beat her and also "directed the negroes to whip her" and "told one to get into her lap and kiss her."[88]

In some cases, enslaved men were forced to sexually violate others. Sharon Block first wrote about one eighteenth-century Maryland case in which an enslaved man was forced at gunpoint by two white men to rape a free black woman. One of the white perpetrators of the assault, William Holland, was convicted of assault and battery on the free black woman, Elizabeth Amwood. Holland petitioned the governor of Maryland for a pardon. Included in the pardon file was a memorandum from Amwood detailing the assault.[89] Both the enslaved man and the free black woman were victimized. As the men forced the enslaved man upon Amwood, they taunted them both, mocking them. One later referred to them as horses that he had been breeding. As Block argues, the case illustrates the vulnerability of free black women in this time and place. We can also imagine the psychological toll that such an event would have taken on the enslaved man, who was unnamed. Were they friendly in the neighborhood? Forced to rape Amwood at the point of a gun, he might have also had to deal with any consequences of assaulting a free black woman. Was there retribution from her family or the community?

Other accounts of forced sex reveal that enslaved men could suffer punishment for a forced attack, despite apparently being ordered to do it. An abolitionist newspaper, the *National Era*, reported in 1853 on the case of another unnamed man, described only as a "negro man, belonging to H. France." The man had been "burned at the stake" for having "attempted to commit rape" and for murder. What makes this case unusual, however, is that after the execution the "citizens of Pettis county" requested that the France family leave the community, "having some suspicion that the negro was instigated to the perpetration of the deed by his master." In addition to "aiding and abetting" the murder, the master was criticized for his "bad examples set before slaves, by conversing with them in relation to the virtue and chastity of white women, and in defamation of their character; thereby influencing them to commit deeds of crime and rapine."[90] We must consider that France may well have forced his slaves to assault white women, since to take the story at face value is to accept the rhetoric of an ignorant, animalistic, and docile slave who, excited by France, was set loose upon women.

At a minimum, these examples raise questions about how often enslavers used enslaved men to inflict sexual punishments on others, whether free black, enslaved, or white, and about the toll that these forced rapes would have taken on those men, who could rarely resist the will of their masters and assailants. For the man enslaved by H. France, the incident resulted in him being burned alive. It is important to note again that the man was unnamed. His designation as only a "negro" man dehumanizes him, rendering him in his assault on the woman a symbol perhaps of all black men, another type of victim in a multilayered sexual assault perpetrated by white men on both black men and white and black women.

The above examples can help us as we try to imagine the situation of Rufus and Rose. In her interview, Rose described Rufus as a "bully." Might he have been selected because they both had reputations as strong-willed fighters? Might pairing them up be about more than just reproducing strong children but also about managing and controlling Rose with an enslaved man who could do so? Although the intent was not to punish Rose, forcing Rufus upon her had a similar effect of subjugation, one that she resented deeply and that surely must have played itself out in their interpersonal dynamic. We can piece together some telling clues that indicate that their relationship was probably one of long-term resentment and pain. Rose apparently gave birth to only two children during their relationship, raising questions about their intimacy. This is further supported by the fact that they did not stay together after being freed and by Rose's declaration that she never again had relations with men after emancipation.

Rufus lived in a social and cultural context that fixated on black male bodies with both desire and horror. Sexual assault took a wide variety of forms, but the common factor in all was the legal ownership that enabled control of the enslaved body. Winthrop Jordan notes the conflicting messages embraced by Anglo-American culture as it sought to control and circumscribe the bodies of enslaved men and women, on the one hand, voicing repulsion for Africans, framing them as beastly, ugly, and unappealing, while on the other hand, viewing them as hypersexual. Anglo-American culture had a long-standing view of black men as "particularly virile, promiscuous, and lusty."[91]

Objectification of black men affected bodies and minds. Depictions of sexual prowess and the nascent myth of the black rapist constituted one form of sexual abuse. This general depiction of enslaved men contributed to the legal and political disenfranchisement of black men from the earliest days of the nation.[92] Yet the psychic toll was also high. Being told that one is hypersexual and uncontrollable could have inflicted great emotional pain, informed identities, shaped interpersonal and intimate interactions.

The bodies of enslaved men were sites of contestation over the definition of black manhood recognized by white men and women, as well as by enslaved people. Masters and overseers punished those bodies in sexualized ways, violating private dignity and emasculating men through public exposure. Physical tortures also damaged men's bodies and rendered them less physically able to enact manly norms of capability. But bodies also enabled enslaved men to celebrate physical power, prowess, and endurance. Enslaved men's bodies were sexually violated, exploited, and abused, but that would only deepen the physical ways in which manhood could be enacted. Bodies were sources of intimate pain, but, as we will see in the next chapter, they could also continue to be associated with pleasure and power.

CHAPTER 2

"No Man Can Be Prevented from Visiting His Wife"

Manly Autonomy and Intimacy

> He looks at me steady for a minute and you's could tell he thinkin' hard. Den he go and set on de bench and say, "Jus wait. You thinks it am smart, but you's am foolish in de head. Dey's gwine larn you somethin.'"
>
> —ROSE WILLIAMS

Rose Williams and Rufus ended up in a physical altercation because their master saw fit to put them together for his own financial gain. From Rose's account, it does not appear that he consulted Rufus, nor did he approve of a choice that Rufus made. From Rose's telling of how they came together, the master told Rose to go set up a household with Rufus. Rufus apparently was told by the master to go live in the cabin with Rose. He followed those orders and found himself in conflict with Rose, who did not like him and did not wish to be married to him. When Rose resisted, Rufus did not refer to his own authority over her as head of household or husband. Indeed, according to Rose, he referred only to their master's power and authority, having placed them together. Even in Rose's telling, in which she calls Rufus a "bully" and offers him no sympathy, she never implies that Rufus had any power in that situation.

For enslaved men such as Rufus, the command to set up a household probably was complicated. Although it enabled him to begin assuming the role of head of household, the meaning would have had strong resonance beyond the veneer of traditional patriarchy, given that it was largely a fiction for enslaved men. This chapter uses a range of sources to examine enslaved black men's ideas about manhood that emphasized the importance of autonomy in affairs of love and family and the role of protector and guardian of family dependents. In the words of John Lewis: "Slavery deprives him of the enjoyment of wife, children, parents, brothers, sisters, the social enjoyments of life. Despotism aims a well directed, legalized blow on his manhood."[1] Enslaved men developed their own models of masculinity in the area of intimate relationships, highlighting the importance of personal intention and desires, strength and endurance in the face of penalties, and resistance against obstacles to realizing those relationships.[2] By the nineteenth century, for enslaved men, notions of inherited traditions of West African manhood that emphasized roles of father, husband, and warrior were at direct odds with the conditions of enslavement.[3] Tera Hunter offers an important reminder as we discuss patriarchal ideals and the importance of family for enslaved men: "Slave families were much more complex in structure than the normative patriarchal, nuclear family ideal can capture."[4] For all men, the ability to develop family relations and to persist in maintaining marriage and family, in all their forms and despite physical and psychological barriers erected by enslavement, was a key component of manliness.[5]

Given that there are no reflections from Rufus, this chapter contextualizes Rose's description of his experiences by listening to the voices of other enslaved men as they shared their thoughts and feelings about intimate relationships and trying to protect chosen spouses. These aspects of manhood were widely shared in white nineteenth-century culture as well, but for enslaved men they took on special meaning, given that masters so regularly denied enslaved men autonomy in these decisions, and, as has been well documented, enslaved men were unable to protect loved ones from the conditions of enslavement.

The master's decision to pair up Rufus and Rose could have held particular resonance for Rufus because of norms of manliness that emphasized family and patriarchy and because enslaved men often experienced interference in their interpersonal relationships. Masters denied them privacy and full autonomy by monitoring their intimate relations with women, from courtship through marriage.[6] Some masters took full control over these aspects of an enslaved man's life. Others simply controlled or manipulated enslaved men at key moments. For all enslaved men, masters had the power and authority to intervene regardless of whether they did so or not. Enslaved men expressed their own thoughts and feelings regarding the importance of being able to choose romantic partners, marry and establish a family with whom they wanted, and structure their sexual and romantic lives in their own manner. When these desires were in direct conflict with a master's intentions, enslaved men paid a price.[7]

Enslaved men had long espoused the importance of choosing their own romantic partners, even in the face of harsh restrictions on their autonomy. In Virginia in 1681 one Mary Williamson was fined for fornication with an enslaved man named William. In sentencing William to be whipped thirty lashes on his "bare back," the court took into consideration what it referred to as his having "very arrogantly behaved himself in Linhaven Church in the face of the Congregation." He had rejected the congregation's interference with his relationship, the meddling from the minister, who then brought the case to the court.[8] Similarly, in Massachusetts in 1705 one Cesar, who was enslaved in Boston, was convicted of having a child with Mary Goslin, a white woman. Cesar was sentenced to be whipped, but he protested loudly and "behaved himself impudently" toward the court. He defiantly and publicly "swore that he would be again guilty of the same crime." Cesar specified in his declaration that this was not simply about his general right to be intimate with whomever he chose but about his claimed right to be intimate with his choice of romantic partner, Mary Goslin. He told the court that he would commit this "same crime" again "with the sd Goslin." His defiance resulted in a harsher punishment, and he was publicly whipped for it.[9]

Providing for one's family was an important aspect of early modern manliness, broadly shared among cultures in Europe, the Americas, and West Africa. In the example above, Cesar had also taken steps to ensure the maintenance of his family, steps that brought him into conflict with the legal system in Boston. Cesar provided what he could to one Abigail Trott for allowing his child to be born at her house and for taking care of it. Limited in what he could earn, he made use of the colonial barter economy, providing Trott with "other things" as well as money. Support for his family would also lead him to steal and then attempt to sell items to raise money for his family. One woman, a widow, was hauled into court for purchasing cheese from Cesar that she admitted she knew was stolen.[10]

Courtship among enslaved people was one important means of resisting the dehumanization of slavery. Autonomy in matters of courtship and intimacy was of great importance to many enslaved men. The ideal also permeated the culture. As Rebecca Griffin has argued, in folklore the "male character occupied the active, assertive role" in "courtship contests." Reflecting dominant ideals among enslaved communities, in such vernacular stories, "male characters were generally cast as the active participants."[11] Stephanie Camp examines sources to understand the importance of examining moments of "pleasure" and autonomy in the sexual and social interactions of men and women. Camp reminds us that "brutality did not constitute the whole of black bodily experience." She importantly positions these actions as resistance in the face of a system that coerced black bodies and minds in an endless variety of ways. "Despite planters' tremendous effort to prevent" socializing that could not be overseen or regulated, "enslaved women and men sporadically 'slip[ped] 'way' to take pleasure in their own bodies."[12]

Men remarked on the importance of courtship at social gatherings and highlighted the risks that they took to participate in them. Hugh Berry described it in the following way: "I'm goin' back over there to see that girl. And then they said and you gonna go too, said they goin' over there to see the girls and the first thing they know say, here come the patterollers!"[13] Such gatherings were important sites for courtship. Historian Rebecca Griffin found that in North Carolina work gatherings and Christmas gatherings were two of the most important sites of social gathering for courtship. Thus, not only nighttime gatherings but also "corn shuckings" and "candy pullings" served to bring together enslaved men and women and give them opportunities to pursue interpersonal romantic relationships.[14]

Enslaved men valued their role as protector of wives, children, and kin even as slavery violated their ability to protect and provide for family dependents. Although this was clearly articulated in abolitionist literature in a manner that appealed to antebellum white middle-class audiences, for generations many enslaved men had embraced this ideal. As early as the seventeenth century, enslaved men spoke of it. In the 1640s, for example, several enslaved men successfully petitioned the New Netherlands Company, apparently requesting their freedom in part on the basis that they could not support their families "as they be accustomed to do, if they continue in the Company's service."[15] Similarly, in 1774 slaves in Massachusetts petitioned for their freedom based on the state's new constitution, and they also argued for their familial independence. They asked: "How can a slave perform the duties of a husband to a wife?"[16]

The violation of fatherhood, with its emphasis on protecting dependent loved ones, became a theme in abolitionist literature written and published by free blacks and formerly enslaved men who had escaped their captivity. In 1827 *Freedom's Journal*, a New York City weekly that was published by free blacks, decried physical punishment but emphasized that it was but one component of the brutality of slavery: "He sees the mother of his children stripped naked before the gang of male negroes, and flogged unmercifully; he sees his children sent to the market to be sold at the best price they will fetch; he sees in himself, not a man, but a *thing*."[17] The inability to prevent such abuses, for some men, could be bound up with a traditional patriarchal ownership of a wife's sexuality. All enslaved marriages "had to endure the third flesh of the master," as Tera Hunter describes the powerlessness to keep loved ones safe under slavery.[18] "Abroad" (off the plantation) marriages may have spared men the emasculating pain of witnessing the abuse of spouse and children on a daily basis even though they also brought stresses and challenges that resulted from being kept apart. Abroad marriages could have served enslaved men's sense of manhood by providing that protection.[19]

In his 1849 account, Henry Bibb, born enslaved in Kentucky in 1815, shared his deep feelings toward his wife and how slavery obstructed and frustrated men in their marriages: "We kept up a regular correspondence during the time, and in June, 1848, we had the happiness to be joined in holy wedlock. Not in slave-holding style, which is a mere farce, without the sanction of law or gospel; but in accordance with the laws of God and our country. My beloved wife is a bosom friend, a help-meet, a loving companion in all the social, moral, and religious relations of life." For Bibb, being unable to protect his wife was one of the ways that enslavement denied both him and his wife their freedom: "She is to me what a poor slave's wife can never be to her husband while in the condition of a slave; for she can not be true to her husband contrary to the will of her master. She can neither be pure nor virtuous, contrary to the will of her master. She dare not refuse to be reduced to a state of adultery at the will of her master; from the fact that the slaveholding law, customs and teachings are all against the poor slaves."[20] Bibb escaped slavery twice. Having made it successfully to freedom in Ohio, he risked capture by returning to rescue his wife. His attempt failed, however, and he was taken to New Orleans, where he was eventually able to free himself again. His account contains a vivid description of him physically defending his wife and child from a pack of wolves while in the woods. His description and the accompanying image (fig. 5) bear a striking resemblance to Richard Ansdell's later

FIGURE 5. Henry Bibb's autobiographical account included this engraving, which demonstrates that black men can protect their dependents unless the conditions of enslavement render them unable to enact that prized characteristic of black manhood. From *Narrative of the Life and Adventures of Henry Bibb, an American Slave, Written by Himself* (New York, 1849), p. 125, courtesy J. Y. Joyner Library, East Carolina University, Greenville, N.C.

painting, *The Hunted Slaves* (fig. 1), a painting that some speculate was inspired by the description of a runaway found in *Uncle Tom's Cabin*.[21] Both images capture the compelling power and commitment of men who protected their dependents and thereby secured their dignity in the face of a system of enslavement that rendered that role untenable.

Henry Brown, born enslaved in Virginia in 1816, also echoed these views and explained how enslavement made marriage an impossibility. "Talk of marriage under such a system," Brown exclaimed. "Why, the owner of a Turkish harem, or the keeper of a house of ill-fame, might as well allow the inmates of their establishments to marry as for a Southern slaveholder to do the same. Marriage, as is well known, is the voluntary and perfect union of one man with one woman, without depending upon the will of a third party. This never can take place under slavery, for the moment a slave is allowed to form such a connection as he chooses, the spell of slavery is dissolved." For Brown, not being able to protect his wife was paramount. "The slave's wife is his, only at the will of her master, who may violate her chastity with impunity: It is my candid opinion that one of the strongest motives which operate upon the slaveholders, and induce them to retain their iron grasp upon the unfortunate slave, is because it gives them such unlimited control in this respect over the female slaves." Brown's account noted that this inability to govern one's marriage came with emotional costs: "Suffice it to say, that no slave has the least certainty of being able to retain his wife or her husband a single hour; so that the slave is placed under strong inducements not to form a union of love, for he knows not how soon the chords wound around his heart would be snapped asunder, by the hand of the brutal slave-dealer."[22]

Family connections sustained many enslaved men, even though those connections also put men in the vulnerable position of suffering loss, something that so frequently occurred. One enslaved man, according to his mistress, "died for want of proper attention" after his wife and children were sold away from him.[23] Berry notes the pain that this could cause, pointing to another example: Stephen Jordan, enslaved in Louisiana, explained how he was forced to leave his wife and children and then was put with another woman, herself forced to leave her husband. The woman had no children, and presumably the pairing was because the husband was deemed to be the problem. For Jordan and the woman, it was painful. "We were put in the same cabin, both of us cried, me for my old wife and she for her old husband."[24] In another example, Josie Jordan recalled tenderness between her parents when her mother grieved for her children who had been sold away: "Pappy tried to ease her mind but she jest kept a'crying for her babies."[25] Masters denied men the ability to provide necessities, taking the role of supplying food and shelter, but enslaved men were able to provide emotional comfort to wives and children.

Formerly enslaved men recalled the family disruptions and lack of autonomy when speaking about their family histories. Masters closely watched the interpersonal relationships of enslaved people and interrupted, controlled, and inserted themselves whenever they desired to do so. Jamaican planter Thomas Thistlewood monitored the relationships of men and women whom he enslaved: "Jimmy wants to throw away Abba, he having long kept Phoebe slyly; Phoebe has also thrown away Neptune (or wants much to do it) upon Jimmy's account. A hopeful chap!" In another diary entry he recorded twice the intimate interests and pursuits of one of his enslaved men named Cudjoe: "Cudjoe has made it up with an old woman named Chloe, belonging to Mr Beckford." A couple of months later, after purchasing "Mary" from the Lucea jail, he had a special collar with "two prongs" attached to her neck, "marked her on each cheek," and "sent her into the field to work." Cudjoe, he noted, "took her for his wife."[26] Rosa Starke explained how masters and mistresses would determine pairings regardless of individual feelings, "'specially de young misses, who liked de business of match makin' and matin' of de young slaves."[27] An 1859 account by a man enslaved for fifty years before his escape shared the thoughts he had after being sold or kidnapped and his new master grabbed him and told him that he would be going away with him:

> At the sound of these words, the thoughts of my wife and children rushed across my mind, and my heart beat away within me. I saw and knew that my case was hopeless, and that resistance was vain, as there were near twenty persons present, all of whom were ready to assist the man by whom I was kidnapped. I felt incapable of weeping or speaking, and in my despair I laughed loudly. My purchaser ordered me to cross my hands behind, which were quickly bound with a strong cord; and he then told me that we must set out that very day for the South. I asked if I could not be allowed to go to see my wife and children, or if this could not be permitted, if they might not have leave to come to see me; but was told that I would be able to get another wife in Georgia.[28]

Unable to even say parting words to his wife and children, Charles Ball—the man here who recalled so bitterly this painful and callous separation from his family—years later would share this pain with the world in a published account of his life.

Enslavers did more than just study the various relationships that formed on their plantations. They also whipped and punished men and women for behaviors they wanted to discourage. Thistlewood wrote about whipping a couple for being intimate: "Flogged Jimmy and Phoebe for Crim[inal] Con[gress] &c." Thistlewood also wrote about punishments that resulted from quarrels among slaves: "Flogged Franke & Strap for disturbing me last night between 10 and 11 o'clock quarrelling about Caesar being catched by Strap in her room. They made a terrible uproar."[29] John Brown, enslaved in Georgia, wrote about a fellow slave, Jack, who suffered brutal punishments in defiance of his owner's intention. Jack had been sold to Brown's plantation from one nearby and was forced to leave his wife behind. Although he was forbidden from visiting her, "Jack used to manage to creep out of a night and visit her, always taking care to be back betimes." But he was eventually caught by his new master and punished. As Brown explained, the punishment was so severe that "he was afterwards compelled to take a young woman named Hannah, as a wife, and to abandon his former one." For Jack, this would not be the end. His master would again control his relationships, as "after he had been with her about eight years, he was sold away from her and their children, to one Robert Ware, of De Cator Town, in De Calb County, Georgia, about ten miles from Stevens' place."[30]

As has already been shown, through incentives, punishments, and sales, masters interfered in the internal dynamics of partnered slave couples. The relationships were never fully private, and many masters punished what they saw as inappropriate behaviors in an effort to control and determine the stability of the unions. Eighteenth-century Virginia planter William Byrd recorded in his diary a quarrel with his wife over their conflicting interference in a slave couple's intimacy.[31] Thistlewood wrote about interfering in the relationships of enslaved people: "Sancho found Morris sleeping with Quasheba his wife; complain to me; I advise them to part, which they accordingly did."[32] James Henry Hammond, like most masters, interfered in the marital relations of enslaved men and women. This ranged from encouragement and support for those who selected each other to punishments for adultery and preventing certain relationships at all. Hammond recorded in his diary in 1840 that he had beaten one man and "ordered him to go back to his wife," as he had with another couple. A third couple he separated, and he personally flogged one man for having a relationship with another's wife.[33]

Some men who escaped slavery described a sense of liberty that encompassed individual choice and freedom in marriage and love. Henry Bibb, born enslaved in Kentucky in 1815, espoused that his own autonomy was central to his understanding of marriage and manhood. He wrote: "Agreement on those two cardinal questions I made my test for marriage. I said, 'I never will give my heart nor hand to any girl in marriage, until I first know her sentiments upon all important subjects of Religion and Liberty. No matter how well I might love her, nor how great the sacrifice in carrying out these God-given principles. And I here pledge myself, from this course never to be shaken while a single pulsation of my heart shall continue to throb for Liberty.'"[34] Enslaved men such as Bibb partly formed their sense of masculine self in relation to their independence in marriage. Many, like Bibb, resented the control that masters had over this aspect of their lives. Historian Heather Andrea Williams argues that "it must have humiliated some enslaved men and women to request permission to marry."[35] James Green, enslaved in Virginia and Texas, recalled that his master "chooses de wife for every man on de place. No one had no say as to who he was golin' to get for a wife. All de weddin' ceremony we had was with Moster's finger pointin' out who was whose wife."[36] Focusing on the master's "finger" captures the humiliating power imbalance that was inherent in enslavement.

Once relationships were established, if they took place across plantations, visitations and time together would require approval from both sets of owners, and some men suffered punishments for visiting their loved ones without permission. Ambrose Douglass, born free in Detroit in 1845, was kidnapped and enslaved in North Carolina with his parents when they went to visit enslaved relatives. He recalled that at the age of sixteen he "was given a sound beating by his North Carolina master because he attempted to refuse the mate that had been given to him."[37] John Andrew Jackson, enslaved in South Carolina, wrote about his experiences after falling in love and marrying a woman who was enslaved at a nearby plantation: "About this time, I fell in love with a slave girl named Louisa, who belonged to a Mrs. Wells, whose plantation was about a mile off. Mrs. Wells was a comparatively kind mistress. Shortly after, I married Louisa." Jackson's master, however, did not agree with the arrangement and doled out savage punishments whenever Jackson went to visit his wife: "My master was exceedingly angry when he heard of my marriage, because my children would not belong to him, and whenever he discovered that I had visited my wife's plantation during the night, I was tied up and received fifty lashes." Jackson defiantly received those punishments, declaring that they were tied to his sense of manhood. "But no man can be prevented from visiting his wife," he declared, "and the consequence was, that I was beaten on the average, at least every week for that offence." But even the ability to endure beatings could not ensure his manly prerogative of staying married to the woman he loved: "My wife had two children, one of whom died. But we were soon separated, as her owner removed to Georgia, and we were parted for ever."[38]

Jackson's narrative spoke not only of his own experiences but of what he witnessed as other men endured punishments and other abuses from masters who sought to control their intimate lives. For some, the threat of punishment was enough to cause action. Jackson's own brother was "compelled to leave his wife and marry the house girl."[39] Jackson explained that for others, physical abuses occurred: "There was on one plantation, a slave about thirty years of age and six feet high, named Adam. He had a wife on a neighbouring plantation belonging to Mr. Hancock. My master bought a young slave girl about fourteen years old, named Jenny Wilson, and he then ordered Adam to leave his present wife and take Jenny." Adam and Jenny resisted this forced arrangement, however, but as with Jackson's own experience, it resulted in physical punishment: "Adam, after having some hundreds of lashes for obstinately persisting in loving his wife, at last consented, but not so Jenny, who was in love with me and I with her. But she was at last compelled to obey her master by the bloody cowhide. My master served nearly all his male slaves in the similar manner."[40]

The narrative of John Brown, enslaved in Georgia, includes his reflections on the experience of a free man named John Glasgow who had been illegally enslaved and who was tortured for pursuing a relationship against his master's intentions. While enslaved, Glasgow met and fell in love with a young woman named Nancy after seeing her frequently while running errands. They established their own marriage, which enraged his master because, as Brown explained, "Nancy being Ward's property, her children would be Ward's also: so John was flogged for marrying Nancy" instead of someone selected for him on his own plantation. He was also "forbidden to visit her."[41]

Glasgow continued to visit his wife and for some time succeeded before being punished again: "Still he contrived to do so without his master's discovering it." The account continued: "One Christmas-day—a holiday for all—he thought he would slip away from the other slaves who were having a feast before Stevens' house, and go see Nancy. Accordingly, watching his opportunity, he soon succeeded in getting away, unobserved as he fancied." But his master saw him leaving, and he was captured and brought back to quarters, "and the other slaves were called together to witness the infliction upon him of a punishment called bucking."[42] For his infraction, he was brutally and savagely beaten and tortured:

> The poor fellow having been stripped stark naked, his hands were fast tied and brought down over his knees, he being compelled, for this purpose, to assume a sitting posture, with his knees doubled up under his chin. A stout stake was then thrust under his hams, so that he was rendered completely powerless. In this position he was turned first on one side then on the other, and flogged with willow switches and the cowhide, until the blood ran down in streams and settled under him in puddles. For three mortal hours he endured this in-

> human punishment, groaning piteously all the time, whilst his master looked on and chuckled. At last he was taken out of the buck, and his lacerated body washed down with salt, red pepper, and water. It was two weeks before he went to work again.[43]

Brown poignantly underscored that this beating did not break Glasgow. As the account explained, "It did not smother John Glasgow's affection for the poor mulatto girl who shared his sorrows, and who was, perhaps, the only human being to whom he durst unburden his whole soul." It continued: "As soon as he felt able to go so far, that is, in about three months, he made another attempt to see her, was missed, pursued and caught. Then Thomas Stevens swore a fearful oath that he would cure him of 'wife-hunting. If he must have a wife, there was a plenty of likely yallow gals on the plantation for such as he to choose from. He might have the pick of 'em. But he (Stevens) wasn't going to let his niggers breed for another man's benefit, not he: so if John couldn't get a wife off the plantation he shouldn't have one at all. But he'd cure him of Nancy any how.'"[44] The punishment was again brutal:

> The unfortunate fellow was taken to the whipping-post, which on Stevens' estate consisted of two solid uprights, some ten feet high, with a cross-beam at the top, forming a kind of gallows. Along the cross-beam were three or four massive iron cleets, to which pulleys were fixed, having a fine but closely-twisted cord passing over them. John Glasgow having been stripped, as on the previous occasion, the end of one of these cords was tightly fastened round his wrists. His left foot was then drawn up and tied, toes downwards, to his right knee, so that his left knee formed an angle by means of which, when swung up, his body could conveniently be turned. An oaken stake, about two feet long, was now driven into the ground beneath the cross-beam of the whipping-post, and made sharp at the top with a draw-knife. He was then hoisted up by his hands, by means of the pulley and rope, in such wise that his body swung by its own weight, his hands being high over his head and his right foot level with the pointed end of the oaken "stob" or stake.[45]

By the end of the beating "he could not stand, much less walk, so they carried him to his quarters, where the usual application of salt and water, and red pepper, was made to his wounds, and he was left to die or to recover, as might be." His recovery took over a month and was incomplete. Unable to walk for another five months, he eventually suffered from a limp for the rest of his life.[46]

Some resented the control over their personal lives so strongly or so feared for their lives that they ran away. In 1783, for example, an enslaved Massachusetts man named Luke ran away after being denied permission to marry by his master, William Taylor. Taylor recorded the details and explanation in a letter to his son in which he wrote that Luke had requested his "consent" to marry a woman he loved, but Taylor denied it because he believed there would be too many costs involved, as she had children.[47] Abolitionist accounts and narratives from enslaved men who escaped to freedom offer numerous examples of men espousing similar resistance to this violation: "The man to whom I belonged was opposed, because he feared my taking off from his farm some of the fruits of my own labor for Malinda to eat, in the shape of pigs, chickens, or turkeys, and would count it not robbery. So we formed a resolution, that if we were prevented from joining in wedlock, that we would run away, and strike for Canada, let the consequences be what they might."[48] Thistlewood recorded in his diary the unsuccessful attempt at running away made by an enslaved man named Lincoln: "Lincoln went out yesterday, and did not come till today noon, and then brought a note from Mr Hughes begging I would forgive him, he having been at the Prospect Estate to see his wife, and overslept himself." He was punished with extra work, but when he did not perform that work, his coat was taken from him and sold "before his face" to another slave "for 2 bitts, to mortify him." He promptly ran away, was caught, and was whipped.[49] Henry "Box" Brown, who famously escaped by successfully mailing himself in 1849 from Richmond to Philadelphia, did so, as Tera Hunter reminds us, because he was "motivated by the disruption of marital bonds and family life suffered by so many slaves in antebellum America."[50]

As Daniel P. Black has argued, for enslaved men by the nineteenth century, the "concept of manhood became inextricably bound to the ability to secure freedom via escape."[51] Although more men than women ran away, as Stephanie Camp reminds us, "enslaved fathers were important to their families, as their families were to them." Some men would not run away because of ties to their families, but some men ran away to be with family and loved ones. During the Civil War, some enslaved men who had escaped to federal camps would risk capture to gather their families and loved ones and bring them together out of slavery. These men would learn routes, testing the way to freedom before then returning and risking everything to bring out their wives, children, and kin.[52] Men who escaped slavery sometimes shared their experiences in publications, providing for us some of their views of courtship, marriage, manhood, and slavery.

Physical beatings and being sold away were not the only tactics in a master's arsenal of intimate coercion. As all enslaved men knew, life and limb were risked when countering a master's will, and in some cases enslaved men paid with their lives. Jackson explained that in one particular case an enslaved man was beaten to death for refusing to stop seeing his wife. The murdered man, Abraham, was described as "unusually obstinate, and would not give up his wife." Jackson's master, unable to break him and "in despair, sent him to his son-in-law's plantation, Gamble M'Farden, who was an inveterate drunkard, and who murdered my sister Bella, as related elsewhere." Abraham's new master commanded that he was "not to go up to see his wife any more; but Abraham loved his wife too much to be parted from her in that manner, so he went fifteen long miles once every fortnight, on the Saturday night, for the pleasure of seeing his wife for a short time. He was found out, and whipped to death by that drunkard Mr. M'Farden."[53]

Some men may have taken their own lives as a result of the conditions of enslavement, which denied them their freedom to form relationships of their own choosing. *The Dying Negro,* which was reprinted in eighteenth-century American newspapers, told the story of an enslaved man who killed himself when he was unable to secure his freedom and find a wife.[54] The published version included this synopsis for readers:

> THE *following* POEM *was occasioned by a fact which had recently happened at the time of its first publication in 1773. A Negro, belonging to the Captain of a West-Indiaman, having agreed to marry a white woman, his fellow-servant, in order to effect his purpose, had left his master's house, and procured himself to be baptized; but being detected and taken, he was sent on board the Captain's vessel then lying in the River; where, finding no chance of escaping, and preferring death to another voyage to America, he took an opportunity of shooting himself. As soon as his determination is fixed, he is supposed to write this Epistle to his intended Wife.*[55]

Some commented at the time that men, more often than women, took their own lives when faced with enslavement. In one case in 1712 an overseer recorded that an enslaved man named Roger had killed himself, hanging himself in the tobacco barn, because he had been "hind[e]red from keeping other negroe men's wifes."[56]

Given the direct conflict between masculine ideals of autonomy and the financial incentives that masters had for interfering in relationships, enslaved men had to carefully negotiate the will of masters and mistresses in the area of intimacy. Much is therefore hidden in the simple statement provided by Rose Williams that her master told her to go set up a household for Rufus. Rufus would have likely had to fear resisting his master's decision regardless of his own feelings for Rose. Consider the account of William Wells Brown, born in Kentucky, who wrote at length about the situation he found himself in, his mistress's interference in his personal and romantic affairs, and how he managed to survive the dangerous situation that interference presented for him:

> One of the female servants was a girl some eighteen or twenty years of age, named Maria. Mrs. Price was very soon determined to have us united, if she could so arrange matters. She would often urge upon me the necessity of having a wife, saying that it would be so pleasant for me to take one in the same family! But getting married, while in slavery, was the last of my thoughts; and had I been ever so inclined, I should not have married Maria, as my love had already gone in another quarter. Mrs. Price soon found out that her efforts at this match-making between Maria and myself would not prove successful. She also discovered (or thought she had) that I was rather partial to a girl named Eliza, who was owned by Dr. Mills. This induced her at once to endeavor the purchase of Eliza, so great was her desire to get me a wife![57]

Brown found himself in a difficult and dangerous conversation with his mistress. "Before making the attempt, however, she deemed it best to talk to me a little upon the subject of love, courtship, and marriage. Accordingly one afternoon she called me into her room—telling me to take a chair and sit down. I did so, thinking it rather strange, for servants are not very often asked thus to sit down in the same room with the master or mistress." During the conversation, his mistress proceeded to interfere with him and question him: "She said that she had found out that I did not care enough about Maria to marry her. I told her that was true. She then asked me if there was not a girl in the city that I loved." For Brown, this was too personal. "Well, now," he wrote, "this was coming into too close quarters with me!" "People, generally, don't like to tell their love stories to everybody that may think fit to ask about them, and it was so with me," he explained. "But, after blushing awhile and recovering myself, I told her that I did not want a wife. She then asked me, if I did not think something of Eliza. I told her that I did. She then said that if I wished to marry Eliza, she would purchase her if she could."[58]

Brown indicated that he did not wish this for reasons that he could not share with his mistress and that certainly had nothing to do with personal privacy. He intended to run away and explained that "I knew that if I should have a wife, I should not be willing to leave her behind; and if I should attempt to bring her with me, the chances would be difficult for success." Regardless of his lukewarm reaction, "Eliza was purchased, and brought into the family."[59]

Brown was well aware that this was not simply indulging his desires as his mistress presented it, and indeed referred to it as a threatening situation and a "trap." He wrote, "BUT the more I thought of the trap laid by Mrs. Price to make me satisfied with my new home, by getting me a wife, the more I determined never to marry any woman on earth until I should get my liberty." For Brown, his autonomy as a man was key to having a real and successful marriage. His response was to maintain an outward appearance of compliance to ensure his safety and possible plan for freedom. He referred to his feelings as his own, a "secret" to be kept. "But this secret I was compelled to keep to myself, which placed me in a very critical position. I must keep upon good terms with Mrs. Price and Eliza. I therefore promised Mrs. Price that I would marry Eliza; but said that I was not then ready. And I had to keep upon good terms with Eliza, for fear that Mrs. Price would find out that I did not intend to get married."[60]

In Brown's account he was careful to explain that his views of marriage and of manhood were at direct odds with what enslavement allowed: "I have here spoken of marriage, and it is very common among slaves themselves to talk of it. And it is common for slaves to be married; or at least have the marriage ceremony performed. But there is no such thing as slaves being lawfully married."[61] For Brown, his freedom and security rested upon his ability to appease his mistress in her interference with his interpersonal relations. Eventually, he was able to escape to freedom and become an abolitionist and writer.

Men expressed resentment of and resistance to the confinement placed upon their abilities to choose loved ones and form families they could protect. Did Rufus chafe at the thought of being told to live with Rose? Masculine norms emphasized independence even in the face of enslavement, and while some masters allowed men to select their own partners, all involved knew that those relationships had no legal standing: they were formed only with permission, either explicit or tacit. Also known was that the relationships could be, and often were, ended without ceremony, without regard for bonds of tenderness or support, which also served to erode the ties that could give men and women strength. The norms and ideals of enslaved manhood in the area of intimacy and romantic life were both challenged by enslavement and forged and reinforced within its confines. The tighter the binds of those restrictions, the more they ensured that independence, autonomy, and the ability to endure physical and emotional pain would remain masculine ideals in the realm of family and intimacy.

CHAPTER 3

"Just Like Raising Stock and Mating It"

Coerced Reproduction

> She say, "Yous am de portly gal and Rufus am de portly man. De massa wants you-uns for to bring forth portly chillen."
>
> De nex' day de massa call me and tell me, Woman, I's pay big money for you and I's done dat for de cause I wants yous to raise me chillens. I's put yous to live with Rufus for dat purpose. Now, if you doesn't want whippin' at de stake, yous do what I wants.
>
> —ROSE WILLIAMS

Like most enslaved men and women, Rose and Rufus were expected to reproduce. Some enslaved men and women were beaten for resisting forced coupling and reproduction. Ambrose Douglass recalled that at the age of sixteen he "was given a sound beating by his North Carolina master because he attempted to refuse the mate that had been given to him—with the instructions to produce a healthy boy-child by her—and a long argument on the value of having good, strong, healthy children."[1] Rufus's warning to Rose after her initial refusals—"Dey's gwine larn you somethin'"—has an ominous tone and underscores that he understood the power of master and mistress to enforce their decision.

Forced reproduction divided men along lines of fertility and virility, isolated men who were prolific, and fractured families and communities. Forcing men to father children was but one way that slavery affected gender and sexuality for enslaved men. The practice itself is still debated among scholars on slavery, and those scholars who do take it seriously focus on women and their experiences. This chapter pushes beyond those debates about the existence of forced reproduction and builds on scholarship on women by examining existing evidence, including what former slaves have told us about the experiences of men and their communities.

This chapter draws upon the reflections of those who were enslaved as they recounted their own remembered experiences and the oral histories passed down by others. Many of the recollections of former slaves about the practice of forced reproduction of men mention fathers, kin, and community members. The exploitation of men's reproductive capabilities affected many more people than simply the individuals coupling; it affected entire communities in which these men lived. The control of masters and the wider threat of forced reproduction impacted an even broader range of enslaved people, touching even those who did experience it in their own community.

In the 1970s scholars used quantitative analysis to try to answer the question of whether forced reproduction had occurred. Richard Sutch concluded that demographic information confirmed that slave breeding was widespread in the border states and southern states on the Atlantic coast.[2] He argued that demographic data supported the conclusion for "systematic and widespread interference with the sexual life of the slaves."[3] Robert William Fogel and Stanley L. Engerman's 1974 work, *Time on the Cross*, however, examined quantitative data and determined that slave "breeding" was a "myth." Like other works, *Time on the Cross* set the bar quite high—at the level of "systematic" breeding for a "market" and a "major share" of economic profit—and argued that it was not a "systematic" and hugely profitable enterprise.[4]

Subsequent scholars continued to echo the conclusions in *Time on the Cross* about the lack of systematic breeding.[5] David Lowenthal and Colin G. Clarke, for example, decried in 1977 the "myth" of "slave-breeding" in Barbuda. They argued against what they saw as a widespread belief that Barbuda served as a "stud farm" for other islands in the West Indies.[6] Richard Dunn argues in his 2014 study of Mount Airy plantation in Virginia that there is "absolutely no reason to suppose that William Tayloe ever engaged in such a practice." Dunn continues: "He had no need to. His slaves were young and vigorous, and—like most people—they enjoyed sex." Although Dunn is comfortable asserting that sex was pleasurable, he is unwilling to imagine that reproduction could have been coerced. He employs a similarly high bar as those who study reproduction only in terms of mass production. That reproduction continued after the move from Virginia to Alabama is, for Dunn, evidence of the "vigor" and normal sexual disposition of the enslaved people.[7] In sum, both sides of the debate generally share one thing in common: they both use a standard of proof that recognizes forced reproduction only if it was widespread *and* successful.[8] These studies thus operate at the level of the institution of slavery, discounting the palpable possibilities of lived experience.[9] Yet, at the same time, *Time on the Cross* argues that the family was the "main instrument for promoting the increase of the slave population."[10] And in that formulation there is much room for coercion and forced reproduction.

This chapter builds on what Jacqueline Jones concluded in 1985: "The suggestion that masters failed to engage in systematic or widespread breeding (as evidenced by the relatively late age at which slave women bore their first child, for example) does not negate the obvious conclusions to be drawn from the slave narratives—that white men and women at time seized the opportunity to manipulate slave marital choices, for economic reasons on the one hand, out of seemingly sheer highhandedness on the other."[11] This chapter goes further in arguing not only that marital choices were manipulated but also that reproduction itself was affected by the actions of slave owners.

Those scholars who do accept the significance of forced reproduction to the enslaved experience focus the brunt of their attention on the experiences of enslaved women. Most recently, Marie Jenkins Schwartz has noted that slave owners' exploitation of "the reproductive lives of women" has been "all too often ignored."[12] Paul D. Escott's examination of the Works Progress Administration interviews with former slaves only tersely observed the incidence of enslaved men being forced to reproduce. Escott concludes that "interference" in the coupling of enslaved men and women was "rare" and that the numbers "cannot suggest the suffering and degradation [it] caused."[13] Existing scholarship on forced reproduction has offered little sustained examination of the men's experiences. One recent excellent book on "slave breeding" included a portion of a chapter on men but maintained throughout an overall focus on women. (Indeed, the introduction mentioned only women's experiences.)[14] It echoed the traditional focus on "violence against black men" and "sexual exploitation of enslaved women."[15]

The lack of attention paid to the significance of forcing men to reproduce has resulted from a variety of factors. First and foremost is that while the quintessential slave has traditionally been a male subject, that subject had not been a gendered one until recent scholars began to concern themselves with constructions of masculinity and manhood. The literature has for a longer period focused on women's experiences as sexual assault survivors under slavery in part because abolitionists highlighted the situation of enslaved women early and relatively often. The experiences of men have been less well analyzed in part also because of the vexed nature of recognizing the sexual assault of men at all, given that patriarchal systems have long defined rape as the violation of one man's female subordinates by another rival male. Patriarchal notions of manhood and masculine power have also contributed to a general cultural avoidance of topics that highlight the vulnerability of men, especially in ways that could feminize otherwise masculine male subjects. Finally, the richest source of testimony about the forced reproduction of men is the collection of interviews conducted in the early twentieth century by the U.S. government. The sources for too long have been viewed with skepticism for a host of reasons, ultimately adding to the other concerns and leading to a relative silencing of male victims of sexual abuse and exploitation under slavery.

This chapter finds that some men were valued not only for their ability to work but also for their ability to reproduce. This conclusion has generally been applied to women alone, but it must be drawn about men as well. Forced coupling affected men's hearts and minds and was a type of sexual assault. It created family bonds and offspring. It could even bolster a man's sense of masculinity and prowess in some situations.

FORCED COUPLING

As Emily West argues for enslaved people in South Carolina, "slaves married for love," and such bonds were "of immense value to them."[16] Given this emphasis on love and choosing one's spouse, as discussed in chapter 2, the violation of this process would have been almost unbearable to many. One formerly enslaved man spoke of his own experiences: "The marriage ceremony was very often omitted with us, and the overseer would simply bring some female slave and say, 'you live with this woman,' and that was about all there was to it. At a later date on another plantation that is just the way I was married myself."[17] The pain inflicted by such unions would have been compounded when enslaved individuals were denied the ability to create a family unit based on love with which to shield themselves from the traumas of enslavement.

Not all men and women were forced to reproduce, although virtually all were expected to do so. Enslavers mandated that bondspeople would reproduce. Jennifer Morgan's research in wills showed that other sources provide evidence that reproduction was assumed to be one way that slave owners were to benefit from slavery. Bequeathing not only living slaves but also their "increase," "a planter could imagine that a handful of fertile African women might turn his modest holdings into a substantial legacy."[18] Many masters allowed men and women to find their own relationships and establish their own families. Natural increase of the population then occurred, and allowing enslaved people to form their own relationships was in some cases the path of least resistance for some masters. Others did not engage in forced reproduction because of their religious views.[19] Many slave owners allowed enslaved men and women to develop personal ties and to form relationships and families of their own choosing. Some masters clearly took a more active role in selecting for the qualities they wanted in slaves, forcing some to have children or to live as husband and wife. Controlled reproduction of specific individuals ensured greater profits and increased slave owners' control over enslaved people. The conclusions that historian Thelma Jennings draws about the power that slave owners held over enslaved women should be applied as well to enslaved men: "The white patriarch had the *power* to force them to mate with whomever he chose, to reproduce or suffer the consequences, to limit the time spent with their children, and even to sell them and their children."[20]

Some formerly enslaved people recalled extreme instances of coerced sex. Some masters could and did force couples to have sexual intercourse, and if "either one showed any reluctance, the master would make the couple consummate the relation in his presence."[21] Some also encouraged reproduction by forcing groups rather than specific individuals together. Ida Blackshear Hutchinson, enslaved in Alabama, spoke about this occurrence on her plantation: "They used to strip them naked and put them in a big barn every Sunday and leave them there until Monday morning. Out of that came sixty babies."[22] Restricted to the barn for the night and stripped of their clothing, these young people would have known that they were expected to reproduce. The pressure to impregnate and to become pregnant as a result of being forced into this closed space together would have been palpable.

Although much more scholarly attention has been paid to the antebellum era, the practice of forcing slaves to reproduce had colonial roots. Most scholars identify the early nineteenth century as the period of greatest expansion of this practice, coinciding with the growth of slavery in the United States and the maturation of the domestic slave trade. But as other scholars have shown, evidence of interference and expectation of profiting from forced copulation has long been part of the institution. Even as early as the seventeenth century—and in New England—some slave owners were forcing men and women together. One English traveler published in his account what he observed while visiting one Mr. Mavericks. While there he observed an enslaved woman who through her "countenance and deportment" clearly "expressed her grief." When he asked his host the reason for her sorrow, he learned from this man who owned her that he "was desirous to have a breed of Negroes" and that "she would not yield by perswasions to company with a Negro young man he had in his house." In response to her resistance, the master had "commanded" the enslaved man to force her to accept him, but she "kickt him out." "She took [her predicament] in high disdain beyond her slavery, and this was the cause of her grief."[23] That this occurred in the seventeenth century and in New England, with its relatively small enslaved population at the time, tells us that the practice and public discussion of forced reproduction were endemic to slavery and not restricted to the particular conditions of the antebellum era. It was a predictable element of enslavement. Slavery, after all, was hereditary and followed the status of the mother.

Other sources, some unpublished, provide further evidence that in the colonial era, forced coupling occurred. Jennifer Morgan's research in wills found that even in the earliest decades, individuals were essentially forcing couples together. Even from beyond the grave, planters did so by including in their wills named male and female pairings that were to be placed together and willed as property to various heirs, with a specific understanding of both present and future values. Some 13 percent of wills in 1730s South Carolina "brought specific men and women together in their bequests."[24] Thus, even after death, masters interfered with the reproduction of enslaved people. Enslavers were well aware of the profit to be had from reproduction.[25]

In the antebellum era, abolitionists drew attention to the practice of forced reproduction to highlight the sexual assault of enslaved women as symbolic of the inhumanity of slavery. But even before abolitionists were a political force, politicians and others were pointing to the practice.[26] *American Slavery as It Was*, written by Sarah Grimké, Angelina Grimké Weld, and Theodore Dwight Weld, included firsthand accounts from freedmen and detailed descriptions of slave life. It also included proslavery arguments made by politicians and legislators as a way of exposing their corruption and flawed logic. Some of these arguments contained specific references to forced reproduction, called "slave breeding" at the time. The book quoted a number of speeches before the 1832 Virginia Legislature. Mr. Gholson, for example, was quoted as stating: "It has always (perhaps erroneously) been considered by steady and old-fashioned people, that the owner of land had a reasonable right to its annual profits; the owner of orchards, to their annual fruits; the owner of *brood mares*, to their product; and the owner of *female slaves, to their increase*. . . . I do not hesitate to say, that in its *increase consists much of our wealth*." The book also quoted Thomas Mann Randolph: "It is a practice and an increasing practice, in parts of Virginia, to rear slaves for market. How can an honorable mind, a patriot and a lover of his country, bear to see this ancient dominion converted into one grand menagerie, where men are to be reared for market, like oxen for the shambles." The book argued that so widespread was recognition of this practice that the president of William and Mary concluded that the situation in fact "ENCOURAGE[S] BREEDING, and to cause the *greatest number possible to be raised*. &c." "*Virginia*," he concluded, "*is, in fact, a negro-raising state for other states*." For proslavery legislators, the practice of forced reproduction could besmirch an institution they wished to protect, making it appear to be a corruption of economic enterprise and of the depiction of slavery as a benevolent institution.[27]

In addition to these proslavery individuals, the book also quoted from meetings of the American Colonization Society: "In Virginia and other grain-growing slave states, the blacks do not support themselves, and the only profit their masters derive from them is, repulsive as the idea may justly seem, in breeding them, like other live stock for the more southern states."[28] For antislavery legislators, forced reproduction symbolized much of what was wrong with slavery, in particular, its inherent violations of Christian family structure and values in the name of financial gain. Eddie Donoghue analyzes the debates around ending the slave trade in London as a time when breeding was openly discussed, given concerns about potential population declines if the slave trade stopped. Donoghue looked at one London publication in particular, *Practical Rules for the Management and Medical Treatment of Negro Slaves in the Sugar Colonies*, for concrete evidence of breeding approaches among slave owners. Donoghue argues that the 1788 debates and eventual vote to end the slave trade led to changes in the law in the British West Indies that contained elements "designed to facilitate the breeding of slaves already in the West Indies and thus provide an assured source of labor for the plantocracy." These incentives included encouraging monogamous unions, financial payments for children, and relief from hard labor.[29]

Nineteenth-century published slave narratives also noted the practice. In his 1857 account of his experiences as a slave, William J. Anderson described what he knew about one master's attempts at forcing couples together: "I have known him to make four men leave their wives for nothing, and would not let them come and see them any more on the peril of being shot down like dogs; he then made the women marry other men against their will. Oh, see what it is to be a slave? A man, like the brute, is driven, whipped, sold, comes and goes at his master's bidding."[30] Henry Bibb shared his experience of being told that he and his wife would have to reproduce and wrote of it as unspeakable: "*Malinda's master was very much in favor of the match, but entirely upon selfish principles. When I went to ask his permission to marry Malinda, his answer was in the affirmative with but one condition, which I consider to be too vulgar to be written in this book.*"[31] Frederick Douglass described what he had witnessed on the Maryland plantation where he grew up. His overseer, Covey, had purchased just one slave that he could afford, a woman "breeder." "After buying her, he hired a married man of Mr. Samuel Harrison, to live with him one year; and him he used to fasten up with her every night!" "The result was, that, at the end of the year, the miserable woman gave birth to twins." Covey, he explains, was "highly pleased, both with the man and the wretched woman."[32] Individuals who had survived enslavement and told of their experiences testified to the practice and its effects on those still enslaved.

After emancipation, forced reproduction became part of the shared memory of the violations of enslavement. Fiction and nonfiction books referred to it. Some have contended that individual plantations devoted themselves to the practice of reproducing slaves for sale. Scholars have noted, for example, the Covingtons, who consciously established a plantation for the express purpose of "raising young negroes."[33] The account of Stephen Jordon, recorded in the 1890s, similarly noted that his master in New Orleans would "never allow the men to be single after they were eighteen, nor the women after they were fifteen."[34]

Thus, long before the WPA interviews of the early twentieth century, slaves and freedmen discussed the violations of forced reproduction. But it would not be until the early twentieth century that a significant number of individuals would record the various experiences and their meaning for those individuals and their communities. By the early twentieth century, the surviving generation who had experienced slavery firsthand and who were most familiar with the stories told to them by parents and kin shared their experiences and memories with interviewers. The WPA interviews and those conducted by John Cade at Southern University corroborate what we see in other types of records from other times produced for other reasons. Tom Douglas, born enslaved in Louisiana, remarked that "in slavery white folks put you together. Just tell you to go on and go to bed with her or him. You had to stay with them whether you wanted them or not."[35] Others similarly recalled that "the master mated his hands."[36] Across the centuries, individuals echoed the comments made by John Josselyn in the seventeenth century, that masters sought wealth by exploiting not only the labor but also the reproductive capabilities of their slaves. As one interviewee recalled, "Some not 'lowed to git married, 'cause de marster anxious to raise good, big niggers, de kind what am able to do lots of work and sell for a heap of money."[37]

Not all masters engaged in forced reproduction, but few slaves and masters would have been unaware of the practice. Some slaves acknowledged that their masters did not do this but that they were aware of the practice. J. M. Parker, who was enslaved in South Carolina, recalled that his master "didn't force men and women to marry" and that "*he didn't* put 'em together just to get more slaves." The interviewer's underlining of "he didn't" could indicate emphasis in speech or the emphasis of the interviewer. Regardless, it highlights that stories about forced coupling were not unusual. Parker noted that "some times other people would have women and men just for that purpose. But there wasn't much of it in my country."[38] Similarly, Amsy O. Alexander, who was born enslaved in 1854, stated that his parents' masters "never forced any breeding." "I have heard of that happening in other places," he noted, "but I never heard them speak of it in connection with our master."[39] Even slaves whose masters did not engage in this practice would have been aware that they could one day be victimized by it either by their master if he changed his mind or by a new master if they were sold.

Many used the analogy of animal husbandry to refer to forced reproduction.

Ida Blackshear Hutchinson, enslaved in Alabama, recalled that her grandfather "was bought and given to his young mistress in the same way you would give a mule or colt to a child."[40] According to Barney Stone, his father "was used much as a male cow is used on the stock farm."[41] Sarah Ford, enslaved in Texas and around fifteen years old by the time of emancipation, recalled being told by her mother that "de white folks . . . puts a man and breedin' woman together like mules."[42] As Daina Berry and others have shown, masters (and slaves) were engaged in the practice of breeding animals for labor and sale. The similarities to their predicament would not be lost on enslaved people.

As a practice designed to maximize agricultural production, forced reproduction was also about selection of certain individuals in order to create children with similar desirable physical traits to their parents. Recall that Rose and Rufus were forced together because both were "portly." According to one interviewer's notes, masters "bred" slaves "like live stock . . . just like horses, cattle, dogs and other animals are managed today in order to improve stock."[43] One man remarked that the control over marriages was "just like raising stock and mating it."[44] Will Ann Rogers, enslaved in Mississippi, similarly remembered that her mother, who had been enslaved in Virginia, told her that her owner "mated" slaves "like stock."[45] Masters forced slaves into couples because they wanted slaves to "breed like livestock."[46] In nineteenth-century Brazil, cultural associations of animal mating and breeding with slaves circulated and illustrate dehumanization.[47]

Enslaved people knew that forced reproduction occurred in order to maximize profits for masters. Thomas Hall, born enslaved in North Carolina in 1856, commented that masters allowed relationships "to raise more slaves in the same sense and for the same purpose as stock raisers raise horses and mules, that is for work."[48] Indeed, many used the very term "stock" to describe the men who were forced to reproduce. James Green recalled that his master "breeds de niggers as quick as he can—like cattle—'cause dat means money for him."[49] According to one interviewer's notes, masters "bred" slaves "like live stock . . . in order to get a good price."[50]

Some enslaved people recognized the value in performing for masters. Katie Darling, born enslaved in Texas in 1849, recalled that "what he want am the stock."[51] Frances Anne Kemble, an antislavery actress who married into a large slaveholding family, noted this in her diary, kept in the early nineteenth century. On the Sea Coast Islands in Georgia she recorded that "the more frequently [the enslaved woman] adds to the number of her master's livestock by bringing new slaves into the world, the more claims she will have upon his consideration and good will." "This," she quipped disdainfully, "was perfectly evident to me from the meritorious air with which the women always made haste to inform me of the number of children they had borne."[52] Eliza Jones illustrates this by calling herself a "good breeder," referring to the fact that she had fifteen children.[53]

Forced reproduction was not simply analogous to how animals were bred; it also signaled the inhumanity of the practice. Thomas Johns, born enslaved in Alabama in 1847, recalled: "Dey figgered, kill a nigger, breed another—kill a mule, buy another."[54] Willie McCullough recalled that his "grandmother said that several different men were put to her just about the same as if she had been a cow or sow."[55] Forced reproduction was not only about profit but also about control over enslaved bodies, male and female. Sam Everett, enslaved in Virginia, recalled that "if there seemed to be any slight reluctance on the part of either of the unfortunate ones 'Big Jim' [the owner] would make them consummate this relationship in his presence." He also noted that for his master this was pleasurable, beyond the profits to be gained: "He enjoyed these orgies very much and often entertained his friends in this manner; quite often he and his guests would engage in these debaucheries, choosing for themselves the prettiest of the young women. Sometimes they forced the unhappy husbands and lovers of their victims to look on."[56]

DIVIDED MEN

Forced reproduction zeroed in on certain individuals, scrutinized and assessed their bodies and reproductive capacities, and left others to suffer the residual trauma of witnessing this intimate brutality. Ultimately, the practice created categories of men who were in a way isolated from their communities and from other men. Men who were used for their reproductive abilities were singled out from other men, dividing the community of men. Dora Jerman, enslaved in Arkansas, recalled that "they had a regular stock man."[57] Cornelia Andrews, born enslaved in 1850, didn't know who her father was but speculated that this might have been because he was the "stock nigger on de plantation."[58] According to one interviewer's notes, he was a "male negro who was kept for that purpose because of his strong physique."[59] Such men were "kept," according to G. W. Hawkins, who was born in slavery in Alabama in 1865.[60] Julia Cole, enslaved in Georgia, explained that masters observed the strength and power of offspring—what a man could produce. If a man was credited with "raising up strong black bucks," then he was expected to produce more. Cole underscored such a man's singular status by referring to such men as a "species."[61] The men who were singled out for this particular type of exploitation were labeled individually, distinguishing them from other men. This would have the effect of marking them, as well as those men who were not used in this manner. John R. Cox, who had been born enslaved in Kentucky in 1852, told the interviewer that "the species was propogated by selected male negroes, who were kept for that purpose."[62] Bill Cecil-Fronsman argues that folktale humor from eastern North Carolina illustrates how "common" whites viewed black men as hypersexual. It is also worth noting that they also apparently understood that some enslaved men served as "studs." In the tale, when approached about borrowing an enslaved man to impregnate women on his plantation, an owner left it up to his slave but pressured him by saying that there were "nice black gals waiting there." When the enslaved man learned that there were "five or six," he decided not to go, claiming that it was too far to travel for "jes' a half-day's work."[63]

In addition to assessing the offspring of certain men, masters evaluated enslaved men's bodies for their reproductive potential. Larger men were deemed to be more virile and also more desirable to reproduce laborers. Height was one indicator. West Turner, who had been enslaved in Virginia, recalled that on his plantation was Joe, "de breedinges' nigger in Virginia," whom he described as being unusually tall, "'bout seven feet tall."[64] Willie McCullough recalled that his mother had told him that when she turned sixteen the owner went to a nearby plantation and "got a six-foot" man to impregnate a woman.[65] Another woman, Ida Blackshear Hutchinson, enslaved in Alabama, recalled that her grandfather "was a 'stock' Negro." She recalled his son's stories about her grandfather, that he was "six feet four inches tall and near two hundred fifty pounds in weight" and was "known as the GIANT BREEDER."[66] To be a tall man or a powerful man was to be seen by masters as an individual who could create not only by his labor but also by his fertility.

General assessments of health and vigor also could have led to a man being singled out. Jeptha Choice, born enslaved in Texas in 1835, remembered that his master "was might careful about raisin' healthy nigger families and used us strong, healthy young bucks to stand the healthy nigger gals."[67] Here we have a firsthand recollection from a man who recalled being used for "breeding." Mary Ingram recalled that her master would "select de po'tly and p'lific women, and de po'tly man, and use sich for de breeder an' de father ob de women's chillums."[68] Henry Nelson, born enslaved in Arkansas, recalled that his mother had been "made to marry" her first husband because both of them were "fine and stout," and "they wanted more from that stock."[69] According to G. W. Hawkins, "big fine men" who "masters wanted the women to have children by" were "kept" and forced to reproduce.[70] Fred Brown, born enslaved in Louisiana in 1853, recalled that the overlooker "used fer to father de chillum" because he was a "portly man" and would pick women who were "portly" and "healthy" to produce "portly chillen."[71] Katie Darling, born enslaved in Texas in 1849, recalled that "massa pick out a po'tly man and a po'tly gal and jist put 'em together."[72]

Forced coupling thus created a lesser status for men who were beyond the years thought suitable for reproduction. Former slave Lulu Wilson noted that her father was forced off her plantation once the slave owner considered him to be "too old for breeding."

> My paw warn't no slave. He was a free man, 'cause his mammy was a full blood Creek Indian. But my maw was born in slavery, down on Nash Hodges' paw's place, and he give her to Wash when he married. That was the only woman slave what he had and one man slave, a young buck. My maw say she took with my paw and I's born, but a long time passed and didn't no more young'uns come, so they say my paw am too old and wore out for breedin' and wants her to take with this here young buck. So the Hodges got the nigger hounds on my paw and run him away from the place and maw allus say he went to the free state.[73]

As this example indicates, free men could suffer from this system as much as enslaved men did, with broad repercussions for families. Masters also sometimes sold older men away, as Mary Reynolds recalled that her master only sold those who were too old to work and "past their breedin' times."[74]

Other men who might be young enough to reproduce but were deemed undesirable were prevented from fathering children. Benjamin Russell shared how certain men would be deemed undesirable because of their perceived inferiority for reproduction: "The master and mistress were very particular about the slave girls. For instance, they would be driving along and pass a girl walking with a boy. When she came to the house she would be sent for and questioned something like this: 'Who was that young man? How come you with him? Don't you ever let me see you with that ape again. If you cannot pick a mate better than that I'll do the picking for you.' The explanation: The girl must breed good strong serviceable children."[75] Smaller men could be devalued by the community as well as by masters. Bill Simms, who was born in slavery in Missouri in 1839, recalled that "if a Negro was a small man he was not cared for as a husband, as they valued their slaves as only for what they could do, just like they would horses."[76] One Tennessee slave woman remarked that a "scrubby man" would not be permitted to father children. Another slave woman, Polly Cancer, noted that her suitor was forced by her master to discontinue seeing her and told "to git coz he didn't want no runts on his place."[77] Thomas Johns, enslaved in Alabama in 1847, recalled: "If a owner had a big woman slave and she had a little man for her husban' and de owner had a big man slave, dey would make de little husban' leave, and make de woman let de big man be her husban', so's dere be big chillen, which dey could sell well."[78] Similarly, William Matthews explained that "if a unhealthy buck take up with a portly gal, de white folks sep'rate 'em."[79]

The bodies of men were thus examined for their reproductive capabilities and were sometimes medically assessed and treated accordingly. Cornelia Andrews, born enslaved in 1850, recalled that "dey ain't let on little runty nigger have no chilluns. Naw sir, dey ain't, dey operate on dem lak dey does de male hog so's dat dey can't have no little runty chilluns."[80] One recalled that doctors sometimes scrutinized bodies: "De marster picks out de big nigger and de doctor 'xamine him, too."[81] Irene Robertson, enslaved in South Carolina, recalled that "durin' slavery there was stockmen. They was weighed and tested."[82] Recall that chapter 1 noted that at slave auctions in Barbados white women could be seen "dispassionately fondling the genitalia of semi-naked black male slaves in order to assess their health and future breeding potential" and that in his account of slavery in Brazil one man remarked that "the necessity of paying attention to the Negro's sexual organ in order to avoid acquiring individuals in whom it was undeveloped or ill-shaped [was known]; for it was feared that they would prove bad procreators."[83] Henery Hickmon, enslaved in Missouri, shared with an interviewer from Southern University that at his plantation the "overseer would sometimes announce... a big black breeding stallion for sale." As he explained, "A large, strong, portly, well-built negro was placed upon the block, stripped of his clothing and his fine qualities enumerated they dubbed him as 'Daddy.'" If buyers couldn't afford the sale or did not want to make a purchase, they could rent him to impregnate women whom they enslaved: "Those who did not care to buy would bring girls from New Orleans and sometimes it seemed from everywhere just for breeding purposes."[84]

The distinctions drawn between certain males began at an early age, affecting not just adult men and women but children, fathers, mothers, and their wider communities when masters employed forced reproduction.[85] Children and young men were also scrutinized for their size and potential reproductive capability. Jordan Smith recalled that buyers selected men and women in their late teens with an eye toward reproduction.[86] George Austin explained that his father was purchased specifically for reproduction: "Marster Morris buys him fo' de stud nigger w'en him gits old 'nough to wo'k."[87] Fred Brown, born enslaved in Louisiana in 1853, recalled that when the children were "half-grown" some would be sold away as "fine, portly chillen."[88] Similarly, J. W. Whitfield recalled that marriages were broken up if masters decided to put together others, and "when a boy-child was born out of this marriage they would reserve him for breeding purposes if he was healthy and robust. But if he was puny and sickly they were not bothered about him."[89] Recall also Ida Blackshear Hutchinson, enslaved in Alabama, who spoke about group-forced intimacy. Her recollection was that the individuals forced into the barn naked for the night were "boys and girls" who were "thirteen years old or older."[90]

Forced coupling thus created a number of distinctions among men along lines of height, musculature, number of healthy children, and general strength. In designating some men as a "species" to be "kept" for reproduction, forced coupling had implications for labeling other men as lesser men. Singling out certain men as bucks and others as less than worthy affected the community of men and could be an additional factor dividing it.

DIVIDED FROM THE COMMUNITY

Dividing men along lines of reproductive capabilities had significant implications for the community as a whole. As William Mathews's comment about men singled out for reproduction being given "four, five women" indicates, often these men were denied the opportunity to develop monogamous relationships and family ties and were used with multiple women. As scholarship has shown, the family unit was a building block of the slave community, and the two-parent family was the norm.[91]

Since the appearance in 1972 of the work of John W. Blassingame and continuing into the 1980s and 1990s, there has been great debate among antebellum historians regarding the structure of slave families. Some have argued that there was a "natural tendency" for enslaved people to develop "stable" families whenever possible. In her study of nineteenth-century Louisiana, Ann Patton Malone found that most families contained two parents.[92] Emily West, in her study of antebellum South Carolina, found that most enslaved people desired to live in "stable, nuclear partnerships" even when that was not always possible.[93] Alternatively, Brenda E. Stevenson argues that the families were largely matrifocal. This does not mean that a significant number of slaves did not grow up with fathers. Indeed, many did. Stevenson uses George Washington's slaves as an example. Of 183 men and women enslaved by Washington in 1799, 40 lived together as husband and wife. More than 70 percent of those who were identified as married had spouses at another plantation.[94] As others have pointed out, abroad marriages did not necessarily mean the lack of a bond between husband and wife and between father and children.

Although most slave families did not and could not follow the nineteenth-century idealized patriarchal model, scholars have shown that we would be remiss to conclude from this fact that fatherhood and family meant little to men or to their families. As Blassingame argued, the family served as a "survival mechanism" for the enslaved.[95] And yet as Heather Andrea Williams points out, the "relationship of father and child was not protected at all." Williams concludes, "While many enslaved children lived in homes with both mother and father, or had a father who lived nearby, for others, fathers were only vague memories."[96] She also argues that the assault on family for enslaved people may have only heightened its meaning and value. Such meaning included marriage as an "expression of love," "an antidote for loneliness and emotional pain," "what made the hard labor and abuse of slavery bearable," and an "act of soul preservation." She also notes that marriage could be a "costly compromise," as family ties and bonds of emotional attachment could threaten a slave's hope of running away and could leave him or her vulnerable to the pain of separation.[97]

Not knowing one's father has traditionally been interpreted as harmful because of the presumed inferiority of woman-headed households. The low prevalence of male-headed households has often been misread as the absence of fathers and fatherhood. Fathers, even those from other plantations, played key roles in their children's lives. But some children did not know their fathers at all, and the significance of African lineage for enslaved people suggests that not knowing one's father denied those children and adults the ability to trace ties to Africa through their fathers. As Michael Gomez has argued, knowing one's African lineage could serve as one of the "psychological weapons of resistance" available to enslaved people. Gomez gives the examples of one Samuel Ringgold Ward, who noted in his biography that he descended from "an African prince." Certainly, for an earlier generation such ties to Africa held even greater resonance. An advertisement for a runaway slave in 1780 stated that he "boasts much of his family in his own country, it being a common saying with him, that he is no common negro."[98]

Forcing some enslaved men to reproduce with many different women denied them a fatherly role even while it prevented their children from bonding with them. A Texas woman who had been enslaved attested to this result when she noted that "half of us young negroes didn't know who our fathers were." Similarly, one enslaved woman named Mary Young remarked: "We never hardly knew who our father was." Another enslaved woman, Millie Williams, also commented: "Shuck's nobody knows who der father waz."[99] It is possible that African and African American men would have viewed this violation differently from Anglo-Americans, given Anglo-American norms of monogamy and traditional West African matrilineal kinship practices, although these differences would have become lessened within long-enslaved populations. Nonetheless, men from both cultures shared the values of male independence and mastery in a broad sense.[100]

Many men singled out for reproduction were not allowed to get married. Jacob Manson, enslaved in North Carolina, recalled that "a lot of de slave owners had certain strong healthy slave men to serve de slave women." Such men were restricted and controlled: "Ginerally dey give one man four women an' dat man better not have nuthin' to do wid de udder women."[101] Another former slave similarly noted how his master had prevented him from engaging in sexual relations with only one woman, forcing him to reproduce with about fifteen women and to father dozens of children.[102] One man recalled that such men "have 'bout ten wenches him not 'low to git married."[103] George Austin recalled that "Pappy am used wid de diffe'nt womens on de place."[104] Ida Blackshear Hutchinson, enslaved in Alabama, recalled that her grandfather "Luke was the father of fifty-six children."[105] Lewis Jones, born enslaved in Texas in 1851, recalled that his father had "close to 50" children with seven or eight different women. His mother explained to him that his father was "de breedin' nigger."[106] What other men would this practice have affected? The women's other lovers and family members would have also had both a connection and a sense of separation from this man.

Slave life revolved around work, and in this most important, and defining, area, men singled out for reproduction would have been further demarcated in contrast to their communities. Men who were forced to reproduce could be treated differently in terms of workload. Many recalled that men who were used for reproduction did not have the same workload as other men. Jeptha Choice, born enslaved in Texas in 1835, remembered, "When I was young they took care not to strain me and I was . . . in demand for breedin'."[107] West Turner's recollections suggest that the man he identified as a breeder had a separate status from other slaves. He "didn't have no work to do, jus' stay 'round de quarters sunnin' hisself 'till a call come fo' him."[108] Oscar Junell, enslaved in Arkansas, stated that he was told by his father that enslaved men taken by an owner for "breeding" were treated differently: "They wouldn't let them strain themselves up nor nothin like that. They wouldn't make them do much hard work."[109] Ida Blackshear Hutchinson, enslaved in Alabama, explained that although her father was not a field hand he suffered punishment not expected for a man forced to reproduce: "Although he was a stock Negro, he was whipped and drove just like the other Negroes. . . . He had to labor but he didn't have to work with the other slaves on the farm unless there was no mechanical work to do."[110] Another man recalled that workload was limited to reproduction: "Dat nigger do no work but watch dem womens and he am de husban' for dem all. De marster sho' was a-raisin' some fine niggers dat way."[111] George Austin, whose owner was slave dealer Ab Morris in Texas, explained that his father performed energetically when he was on the block because his owner told him that it would result in a higher price and better treatment. His father was well aware of the different workload for men who were selected for reproduction and didn't intend to work hard: "Him makes up hims mind not to be no good at tudder kind of wo'k."[112] Austin in effect tried to play the system by signaling to buyers the markers they sought to evaluate a man's reproductive capabilities, including his energy level and physique. In the end, when he failed to produce what masters wanted he was resold, and feuds between slave traders erupted with charges of false representation. Irene Robertson recalled that masters treated "stockmen" differently—"didn't let them work in the field and they kept them fed up good."[113]

The significance of this different workload was not lost on many—it could engender ill will, and it also inhibited the kind of community building and networking that slave work could foster. Working socials and gendered work were both important for developing a sense of community.[114] The workload distinction may well have nurtured resentments among men: "Dr. Ware had a fine man he bred his colored house women to. They didn't plough and do heavy work. He was hostler, looked after the stock and got in wood. The women hated him, and the men on the place done as well. They hated him too."[115]

Some men who were selected to reproduce were not only separated from family and community because of the work that they performed on the plantation but also physically removed from their own plantations. Men were taken from the community by being rented out to owners of other plantations. George Austin recalled that his father was "hired out to be diffe'nt plantations 'roundabout 'cause him am such a fine big nigger an' bound to build up a Marster's slave stock of niggers."[116] Irene Robertson recalled that "a man would rent the stockman" to other masters.[117] Julia Cole, enslaved in Georgia, told her interviewer: "If a hand were noted for raising up strong black bucks . . . he would be sent out as a species of circuit-rider to the other plantations. . . . There he would be 'married off' again—time and again."[118] Willie Blackwell, who had been enslaved in North Carolina, recalled that his father was the Blackwell plantation "stud" and "was used on de Glover place [plantation]" nearby because the owners wanted to "breed" him.[119] Barney Stone discussed how his father was "hired out to other plantation owners for that purpose."[120] Others noted that the men were rented out to others: "The owners of this privileged negro, charged a fee of one of every four of his offspring for his services."[121] Cross-plantation families were not unusual and did not mean weaker family ties for those who formed such families. But for a man who crossed plantations as a "species" of "breeder," his status as an outsider could have significantly affected his interpersonal ties to that community.

A man who was rented out may well have missed out on the vitally important day of Sunday for visiting and socializing. He may have taken part in Sunday activities, but as a man brought in, what were his relations with the men and women on that other plantation, and what would he have missed on his own plantation? These questions would be especially important if a man's visits were infrequent or if it was known that he was there for this special task. West Turner's recollections about a man named Joe included the fact that Joe was not at his home plantation on Sundays and that it was known that he was rented out to "a white man what lived down in Suffolk." "Dey come an' got him on a Friday," Turner explained. "Dey brung him back Monday mo'nin'. Dey say dat de next year dere was sebenteen little black babies bo'n at dat place in Suffolk, all on de same day."[122] The ripple effect of being singled out as a man selected to impregnate women and sometimes travel between communities to do so must have been quite large. Workload, sex-segregated work, and shared experiences were all key to building slave communities. For those men who found themselves unable to access these networks, as the final section explores, ties of the utmost importance were challenged.

DIVIDING MEN AND WOMEN

Men selected for forced reproduction were in fact being driven apart from enslaved women even as men and women were being paired together. Although sex-segregated work nurtured gendered ties, a primary relationship for enslaved people was that of husband and wife. Forced reproduction complicated these relationships. Men who were forced to reproduce bore the responsibility of ensuring women's compliance and had to negotiate this dynamic with their own personal skills. For some men, this meant the use of force and the threat of violence. For others, it could involve reasoning or even tenderness. In all cases, men's actions were supported in the background by the threat of punishment against the women if they resisted—and in the back of men's minds was their own punishment for disobeying a master's directive to reproduce.

Many men lived under the threat of punishment. Forced reproduction, as we have seen, meant not only money but also control. Some enslaved people offered no comment about what happened to men who resisted but focused instead on women's experiences: "Iffen the women don't like the man it don't make no diff'rence, she better go or dey gives her a hidin'."[123] But others did note that both the men and the women had only the choice of reproducing or being whipped. Thomas Johns, born enslaved in Alabama in 1847, similarly stated: "If de man and woman refused, dey'd get whipped."[124] G. W. Hawkins, who was born in slavery in Alabama in 1865, said that if the "slave woman didn't do it, the masters of the overseers whipped them till they did."[125] Ponder the situations that could arise for enslaved men under this system. Did they have full freedom to refuse? They were selected for their size, another uncontrollable attribute, and then put in situations that, if they didn't go well, could result in the women being whipped. No doubt the women would likely be known to these men. They might be friends or even kin. The men were violated, as their bodies were used to violate the bodies of others. Willie McCullough recalled a man who was "almost an entire stranger to her," and she was told that "she must marry him." "Her marster read a paper to them, told them they were man and wife and told this negro he could take her to a certain cabin and go to bed. This was done without getting her consent or even asking her about it."[126] John Henry Kemp, enslaved in Mississippi, remarked that his master employed overseers who were known for "brutality" and who threatened the slaves if they did not "behave," which he defined as including "mating only at his command and for purposes purely of breeding more and stronger slaves on his plantation for sale." Kemp explained that severe punishment awaited those women who might resist: "In some cases with women—subjecting to his every demand if they would escape hanging by the wrists for half a day or being beaten with a cowhide whip."[127]

Some masters concocted elaborate scenarios perhaps to shore up their own sense of benevolence to slaves, and some thus created a tainted veneer of autonomy for men and women who were forced to be together. Louisa Everett, enslaved in Virginia, recalled that her master forced her and her husband, Sam, together:

> Marse Jim called me and Sam ter him and ordered Sam to pull off his shirt—that was all the McClain niggers wore—and he said to me: Nor [her name before she changed it], "do you think you can stand this big nigger?" He had that old bull whip flung acrost his shoulder, and Lawd, that man could hit so hard! So I jes said "yassur, I guess so," and tried to hide my face so I couldn't see Sam's nakedness, but he made me look at him anyhow. Well, he told us what we must git busy and do in his presence, and we had to do it. After that we were considered man and wife.[128]

Louisa's passage suggests that her master believed women, too, evaluated men based in part on their bodies. But what informed her decisions, as she explained, was the master's cruelty and the threat of whipping. She knew perfectly well that there was but one answer to his question, even if he pretended otherwise.

Some masters used enslaved men to enforce their will. Some testimony suggests that enslaved men in this situation could use force to sexually assault women in a multilayered instance of sexual exploitation. Some enslaved men used tenderness. Some men employed reason. Louisa Everett explained that because they produced "fine, big babies," she was spared ever having "another man forced" on her, to which she added, "Thank God." Despite that final comment that it was by the grace of God that she only experienced forced pairing once, she also observed that her partner, Sam, "was kind to me and I learnt to love him."[129] Similarly, for children of forced couples, kindness was not taken for granted, as evidenced by some accounts. For example, Jacob Branch, born enslaved in Louisiana and sold to a plantation in Texas when a baby, recalled that his father and mother were put together by his mother's owner. "Old massa go buy a cullud man name Uncle Charley Fenner. He a good old cullud man. Massa brung him to de quarters and say, 'Renee, here you husband,' and den he turn to Uncle and say, 'Charley, dis you woman.' Den dey consider marry. Dat de way dey marry den, by de massa's word. Uncle Charley, he good step-pa to us."[130]

The forcing of couples together not only affected those individuals and their offspring but also often resulted in other couples being broken apart. Louisa's partner, Sam, recalled that slaves on their plantation were "mated indiscriminately and without any regard for family unions. If their master thought that a certain man and woman might have strong, healthy offspring, he forced them to have sexual relation, even though they were married to other slaves."[131]

In addition to being forced into sexual situations with women they did not choose, enslaved men could also face the emotional withdrawal and resentment of these women. Rufus, for example, faced the physical resistance of Rose Williams: "After I's in, dat nigger come and crawl in de bunk with me 'fore I knows it. I says, 'What you means, you fool nigger?' He say fer me to hush de mouth. 'Dis am my bunk, too,' he say." But Rose persisted: "You's teched in de head. Git out, I's told him, and I puts de feet 'gainst him and give him a shove and out he go on de floor 'fore he know what I's doin.'" When Rufus started to proceed to the bunk, Rose recalled that she "jumps quick for de poker. It am 'bout three foot long and when he comes at me I lets him have it over de head. Did dat nigger stop in he tracks? I's say he did. He looks at me steady for a minute and you's could tell he thinkin' hard. Den he go and set on de bench and say, 'Jus wait. You thinks it am smart, but you's am foolish in de head. Dey's gwine larn you somethin.'" A second night "I grabs de poker and sits on de bench and says, 'Git 'way from me, nigger, 'fore I busts yous brains out and stomp on dem.' He say nothin' and git out." After emancipation she was able to leave Rufus, with whom she bore only two children, which some have taken to suggest a resistance to him throughout their marriage.[132] As Wilma King points out, the account "raises questions" about such pairings: "Did they learn to love each other and build mutual respect and trust?"[133] Thelma Jennings's observations on the psychic trauma of forced marriage for women should also be applied to men. Forced marriage, she argues, caused both "physical and mental anguish" and "may have even caused greater humiliation than concubinage . . . since marriage was long term."[134] A level of resentment and even hatred could more easily be aimed at the enslaved male husband than at the slave master or white overseer. One woman, Mary Gaffney, told her interviewer: "I just hated the man I married . . . but it was what Mas[t]er said do."[135] In forced coupling, the levels of victimhood were multilayered. Irene Robertson recalled that a "stockman" would be put "in a room with some young women he wanted to raise children from. Next morning when they come to let him out the man ask him what he done and he was so glad to get out. Them women nearly kill him. If he said nothin' they wouldn't have to pay for him. Them women nearly kill him."[136]

Men such as Joe in Virginia who were forced to have children with many women might also have found themselves unwanted within the slave community. These unions might have led to children who would have been desired by the white planter class but certainly not always by enslaved women. Some slave women, for example, rejected husbands and lovers because of their promiscuity, as did one woman "on account of his having so Many Children."[137] Deborah Gray White notes in one example that after a slave named Molly lost her husband because he ran away, she was "given" a new husband—meaning forced into another arrangement to produce children. Despite having nine children with this man, however, Molly would later reject him and exclaim that he was not her "real" husband, despite their years of cohabitation. "In Molly's heart her *real* husband was the man sold away by their master."[138] For such men, the rejection and resentment of their forced wives would have further compounded their dehumanized situation. Women they were placed with could also resent them. Silvia King, born in Morocco and enslaved in Texas, recalled rejecting, as best she could, the man whom she was forced to be with by not acknowledging his name and physically resisting him until she was forced to concede under penalty of whipping. She told her interviewer: "I don't bother with dat nigger's name much, he jes' Bob to me. But I fit him good and plenty till de overseer shakes a blacksnake whip over me."[139]

Pressures for couples did not end after they were forced to be together. As Jennifer Morgan points out, some observers in early eighteenth-century North Carolina understood the importance of planters' interference with slave coupling and that this meant that couples who did not reproduce were often separated from one another and paired with others. In his history of North Carolina, physician John Brickell declared that women who did not reproduce were to take "second, third, fourth, and fifth and more Husbands or Bedfellows" if children were not born after a "year or two."[140] According to Morgan, women "bore the burden and pain" of these "manipulations and scrutiny."[141] The evidence here suggests that weakly or small men similarly experienced these repercussions. Many enslavers carefully scrutinized enslaved women, and this had significant implications for men: "If a woman weren't a good breeder, she had to do work with de men." Thus there were incentives for reproduction. Husbands would be aware of this pressure to protect their wives and to reproduce. They were also well aware that if they did not sire children, their wife could be sold away.[142] Frances Anne Kemble, an antislavery actress who married into a large slaveholding family, noted this practice in her diary and also observed that masters not only put men and women together to produce children but also broke up quarreling couples so that the "estate lost nothing by any prolongation of celibacy on either side." This practice, she lamented, was "arbitrary destruction of voluntary and imposition of involuntary ties" and the cause of "misery."[143] A ripple effect occurred when weak or infertile men were deemed unfit by their masters. Daina Berry notes the pain that this could cause. Stephen Jordan, enslaved in Louisiana, explained how he was forced to leave his wife and children and put with another woman, herself forced to leave her husband. The woman had no children, and presumably the pairing was because the husband was deemed to be the problem. For Jordan and the woman, it was painful: "We were put in the same cabin, both of us cried, me for my old wife and she for her old husband."[144] Sam Everett explained that his master forced him and Louisa to copulate in front of him and that "he used the same procedure if he thought a certain couple was not producing children fast enough."[145]

Although it is difficult to determine the number of men who found themselves singled out for their reproductive capabilities, the evidence presented here suggests that the impact of the practice was widespread and not only changed those individual men but also altered their relationships in countless ways.

For the generations of African Americans in the early twentieth century who only heard about slavery and had not experienced it firsthand, the sexual use and abuse of enslaved men figured in the larger narrative of trauma and pain. The WPA interviews and other evidence presented here capture the recollections of many who were born enslaved. The men and women who recalled the status of their fathers lived with their own particular memories of that abuse and how it informed their sense of manhood and family.[146] The practice of forcing enslaved men to reproduce thus influenced black manhood during slavery and beyond.

CHAPTER 4

"Frequently Heard Her Threaten to Sell Him"

Relations between White Women and Enslaved Black Men

> De nex day I goes to de missy and tells her what Rufus wants and missy say dat am de massa's wishes.
>
> —ROSE WILLIAMS

When Rose's mistress coerced her to establish a household with Rufus, she asserted her authority. In Rose's account, her mistress did not weigh Rufus's or Rose's concerns and instead reminded her of her supposed indebtedness to her master and of the physical punishment that awaited Rose if she did not obey his orders. The mistress in this situation ensured that Rufus would also be coerced into sexual intimacy with Rose.

Scholarship on the power that white women held in slave societies has generally emphasized the overwhelming subordination of white women to white patriarchs and their "domestic confinement."[1] Their husbands' infidelities with white and black women, spousal abuse, restrictive divorce laws, and the legal and economic restraints placed on white women all underscore their degraded status. But this characterization of their position is possible only in relation to white men. When we widen our field of view to include enslaved people, we can see some of the forms of power that white women held.

Scholars have shown that mistresses were often as sadistic and abusive as masters and overseers.[2] Cecily Jones argues that white women in Barbadian plantation society, for example, were "pivotal actors in the reproduction of ideologies and practices that secured white identity."[3] Gilberto Freyre argued that in Brazil, women as well as men operated in a climate of power and privilege that nurtured "sadism" and abuse. A jealous white mistress who knew of or feared sexual liaisons between enslaved women and the mistress's husband often physically punished enslaved women, making them victims of both husband and wife.[4] Likewise, Stephanie Jones Rogers reminds us that "white slaveholding women exercised life and death power over enslaved women and men" and did so as enforcers of the slave system.[5] Others note that white women participated in sexualized violations of enslaved people in a variety of ways, including exploiting enslaved women as wet nurses and the forced and coerced prostitution of enslaved women in ports.[6] This chapter contributes to that revised image of the role that white women, slave-owning and not, played in enforcing slavery and racial hierarchies.

The prevalence of sexual contact between white women and enslaved black men has been noted by numerous scholars, but few have explained the occurrence using the lens of sexual exploitation of enslaved men. The widespread presence of persons of mixed racial ancestry across the American South in the era of slavery has long stood as firm evidence, in the face of denials, that white men regularly sexually assaulted black women. Madison Hemings, for example, who was enslaved in Virginia by Thomas Jefferson, argued in 1841 that "the proof" of the rape of enslaved black women by white men was that "a very considerable portion of the slaves are of the mixed race."[7] But the converse situation, the regular instances of intimacy between white women and enslaved men, has not similarly been recognized as stemming from the sexual vulnerability of enslaved men and white women's expression of power and dominance. The shards of evidence that we have about white women's sexual actions toward enslaved men would indicate that the occurrences were produced by the very conditions of slavery that also fostered sexual contact between white men and enslaved women—the sexual availability of enslaved people and the use of sexual contact to maintain hierarchies conducive to the slave system. The absence of any explanation for sex between white women and enslaved men enables a naturalized assumption of consensual sexual contact, at best—and a traditional view of passive white women and the sexually aggressive black men who desire them, at worst. Characterizations of the men in sexual relationships with white women as "lovers" and "husbands" capture the general view of the relations as consensual.[8]

Sexual relations between white women and enslaved black men have not generally been viewed with the same concern about power imbalances as have relations between enslaved women and white men partly because we are still influenced by the legacy of slavery, a legacy that characterizes enslaved men as hypersexual. We are also still confronting legacies of patriarchy that denied white women sexual agency. Those powerful views of enslaved men and white women have long informed how we could see and understand relationships between white women and black men. Legacies of slavery also influenced the histories we have told and remembered. Initially, many of these histories espoused the vantage point of white patriarchs, denying white women virtually all agency and experiences and nurturing views of enslaved men that emphasized hypersexuality and dangerous manhood. Generations of scholars have worked to examine the evidence of enslavement and have redressed many of these historical fictions—but much remains to be (un)done.

Many of the sources that allow us to recognize the troubled nature of intimate relations between white women and enslaved black men are problematic. Some of these sources come to us from white men who had personal motives for characterizing white women as having engaged in aggressive sexual behavior with enslaved men: divorce cases filed by angry husbands and sexual assault cases provide commentary about white women's sexual agency in a manner that was designed to attack their character in order to skew the outcome against the women. Taken individually, few of these cases would stand the scrutiny and weight placed on them as strong and unbiased evidence of women's behaviors. However, these sources echo what we find in other types of sources and cases: the testimony of neighbors who appear to be without strong bias relating their knowledge of actions, the testimony of formerly enslaved men recalling their experiences, and the recollections of formerly enslaved women about what they witnessed. These sources all corroborate the evidence from white men regarding white women's sexual actions. Collectively, the preponderance of evidence from a wide range of periods and geographic locations makes the case for white women's sexual violations of enslaved men.

PREVALENCE AND OPPORTUNITY

Despite legal, social, and cultural prohibitions, sexual contact between white women and black men has been documented in virtually all colonies and states throughout the time of slavery. As Eugene Genovese argued over a generation ago, "White women of all classes had black lovers and sometimes husbands in all parts of the South, especially in the towns and cities."[9] Court and church records and newspaper accounts evidence that sexual intimacy between white women and enslaved men was not uncommon. As Richard Dunn has noted, in the early years of colonization in the West Indies it was "not unknown . . . for white women in the islands to cohabit with black men."[10] In 1681 one white woman married an enslaved black man in Maryland, apparently with impunity.[11] In 1785 a woman in Virginia was punished by her church for "committing fornication by cohabiting with a negro."[12] As Bill Cecil-Fronsman concludes, in the antebellum era common whites believed that "their own place in society depended on the maintenance of a degraded black place." However, some lower-status whites broke social and cultural barriers and "forged alliances with slaves."[13]

In the era of slavery, white patriarchal society recognized white women's sexual agency, resulting in social and cultural conditions in which white women were punished more often than white men for their sexual interactions with enslaved men. This has been correctly explained by a double standard that served white men's positions in society, but it is also the product of a recognition of white women's threats to white male patriarchy by troubling racial definitions and patriarchal bloodlines as well as standards of white male patriarchy. The courts punished nonelite white women disproportionately as a way to police the color line and in recognition of white women's violations of it. Elite women generally escaped punishments and had greater opportunity and advantages to establish contacts with enslaved men that have escaped documentation.

We probably have more robust data on relations between white women and black men than those between enslaved women and white men because the former were more readily punished. This occurred in a wide variety of locations. In Virginia, Kathleen Brown found that the practice only increased from the late seventeenth century to early eighteenth century.[14] In eighteenth-century North Carolina, for example, Kirsten Fischer reminds us that although interracial marriages were outlawed, only white women seem to have paid the price for forming them.[15] Trevor Burnard and others have also observed this double standard whereby white women were punished for interracial relations while white men's relations were kept as an open secret, especially in the Caribbean.[16]

Records of mixed-race children born to unmarried white women also evidence these sexual relations. One sixteenth-century traveler to the Portuguese settlements on São Tomé recorded that "few of the women bore children of the whitemen; very many more bore children of the negros."[17] Ira Berlin argued that roughly one-quarter to one-third of bastard children born to white women during the seventeenth century in Virginia were mulatto.[18] Kathleen Brown found that in Norfolk County, Virginia, between 1681 and 1691, four of the seventeen white women punished for bastardy had children with enslaved black men. In the wake of that law, the number of white servant women punished by the courts for having "mulatto" children out of wedlock grew: in the 1690s they were 17 percent of cases, and by the 1700s, nearly 30 percent.[19] In 1689 in Charles City, a servant named Rebecca Corney was convicted of giving birth to a "Mulatto bastard." She was ordered to serve her master additional time as reimbursement for his payment of her fine.[20] Mechal Sobel points out that Virginia records of "mulatto children, born to white women, appear in virtually all the church and county court records, although their number declines in the eighteenth century."[21] In eighteenth-century Maryland in the 1740s and 1750s, ten women were charged with having bastard mulatto children.[22] In early eighteenth-century Maryland, for example, one white woman who lived with an enslaved man had seven children.[23] In the 1720s and 1730s sixteen white women were convicted of having children with enslaved black men.[24] Mary Skinner in 1769 had a child by a man she enslaved.[25] Glenda Riley notes that in 1790 the first divorce granted in the postrevolutionary South was in Maryland—a case brought by one John Sewall, who sued for divorce after his wife gave birth to a "mulatto child."[26] The same was true for Virginia in 1802.[27]

Antebellum divorce records also evidence white women's actions. Loren Schweninger's examination of divorce in the antebellum South concluded that sexual relationships between black men and white women were "not uncommon in the southern states."[28] Bill Cecil-Fronsman noted that 7.5 percent of North Carolina divorces from 1800 to 1835 were for cohabitation with "black lovers."[29] As Thomas E. Buckley found, in Virginia roughly 9 percent of divorce petitions from 1786 to 1851 were for interracial adultery, with twenty-three of those petitions coming from white men who complained about their wives' relationships with black men.[30] Between 1800 and 1835 almost 8 percent of divorce petitions were for interracial adultery.[31]

As the above findings demonstrate, sexual contact between enslaved men and white women appears in virtually all slave-holding regions during the era of enslavement and has long been recognized by scholars as a feature of those disparate societies. What has escaped scholars, however, is an explanation for this contact that takes into account what we know about sex and slavery: power is always present in such occurrences.

WHITE WOMEN'S AGENCY

Given what we know about white women's active participation in enslavement as well as the sexualized cultural view of enslaved men, the regular occurrence of sexual contact between enslaved men and white women must be viewed accordingly. The actions that white women take in this context help us to better understand the sheer numbers of enslaved men who were exploited by white women.

Examples of white women portrayed as the instigators of intimate relations with enslaved men appear in virtually all types of available sources. One traveler recorded that in Virginia he had learned about a "planter's daughter having fallen in love with one of her father's slaves, had actually seduced him."[32] In addition to sexual contact, some enslaved men suffered intimate contact in a broad sense at the hands of mistresses. One formerly enslaved man described a degree of physical intimacy that occurred with his enslaver, whom he described as a "tyrant." "While I was at home she kept me all the time rubbing furniture, washing, scrubbing the floors; and when I was not doing this, she would often seat herself in a large rocking chair, with two pillows about her, and would make me rock her, and keep off the flies." He shared that his enslaver would require him to attend to her body and that some of the interactions occurred in her bedroom: "She was too lazy to scratch her own head, and would often make me scratch and comb it for her. She would at other times lie on her bed, in warm weather, and make me fan her while she slept, scratch and rub her feet." As if to emphasize that such intimacy was tenuous and resulted in no better treatment, he added: "But after awhile she got sick of me, and preferred a maiden servant to do such business."[33]

Sexual overtures toward enslaved men added to the aspects of enslavement that black men endured and, in some cases, navigated. Court records include instances of white women allegedly approaching enslaved men. Recall from chapter 1 that one Virginia woman, Katherine Watkins, had been accused of aggressively commenting on and groping enslaved men's bodies and genitals. In 1681 Watkins found herself the subject of communal talk as part of the criminal investigation surrounding her own accusation of sexual assault. Testimony gathered in the course of investigating that sexual assault included several individuals who witnessed the victim drinking and making sexual advances toward enslaved men sometime during the week before the sexual assault. Twenty-six-year-old Lambert Tye similarly testified. He was there working with other servants when he saw Katherine with what he described as "very high Colour in her face," which was explained to him as being the result of drinking cider with those present. He saw her tell Jack that "she loved him for his father's sake."[34]

One man, thirty-two-year-old John Aust, observed Watkins making sexually suggestive comments and physical advances toward enslaved men. He testified that while "Negroe dirke" walked by her she "tooke up the taile of his shirt (saying) Dirke thouh wilt have a good long thing, and soe did several tymes as he past by her." The testimony did not mention how he responded but stated that she also approached a second enslaved man and "putt her hand on his codpiece, at which he smil'd, and went on his way." Shortly thereafter, she went to a third enslaved man, named Mingoe, "tooke" him "about the Necke and fling on the bed and Kissed him and putt her hand into his Codpiece." Shortly before he left he saw her go into a room with Jack but could not say what might have transpired. According to the records, it "being near night this deponent left her and the Negroes together, (He thinking her to be mich in drinke)." Aust's decision to leave her there indicates no concern for her safety among the men, suggesting that he believed that she was in a position of power.

Other testimony corroborated Aust's version and added additional details. Thirty-five-year-old William Harding witnessed her "turne up the tale of Negroe Dirks shirt, and said that he would have a good pricke." A twenty-two-year-old woman, Mary Winter, who was present testified that she saw Katherine drinking with the men and "tooke Mulatto Jack by the hand in the outward roome and ledd him into the inward roome doore and then thrust him in before her and told him she loved him for his Fathers sake for his Father was a very handsome young Man." In response he "went out from her," but she "fetched him into the roome againe and hugged and kist him." The language of having "thrust" him, of being the one who "tooke" him and "fetched" him, and of having "ledd" him all indicates agency on Watkins's part. His response suggests a certain amount of measured resistance in trying to handle a situation that could perhaps have been difficult.

Taken at face value, the testimony describes a variety of tactics used by Watkins, as well as responses by the enslaved men that seem well rehearsed through past experience. None of them expressed any surprise at her behavior. If we are more skeptical of the testimony of the men present, it is worth considering that they believed such comments would be plausible, suggesting that this kind of behavior was not out of the ordinary between white women and enslaved men.

The practice of forcing enslaved boys and young men to wear long shirts without pants left them vulnerable to such assaults. Women were well familiar with this, as we have already seen in the recollections of one eighteenth-century traveler in Virginia who recorded seeing "young negroes from sixteen to twenty years old, with not an article of clothing, but a loose shirt, descending half way down their thighs" as they waited on "ladies" as well as men. He noted that the women were well accustomed to this exposure, with a hint of a suggestion of impropriety on their part for not having "any apparent embarrassment," and he underscored the unsavory nature of the scene by highlighting that in the course of their work, enslaved men were exposed.[35]

Recall from chapter 1 that white women had access to men's bodies. Cecily Jones argues that all white women in Barbados had some "access" to "the bodies and labour power of enslaved women and men." The practice of hiring out allowed poorer white women access to enslaved men even if only for short periods of time.[36] Jones notes that Hilary Beckles correctly pointed out that what was expected of white women in terms of sexual restraint allowed for seemingly contradictory moments, such as when at slave auctions in Barbados white women could be seen "dispassionately fondling the genitalia of semi-naked black male slaves in order to assess their health and future breeding potential."[37]

White women's sexual intimacy with enslaved black men was noted by more than one early American observer, often as derisive attacks against the women. Thomas Thistlewood's eighteenth-century diary denounced a white woman in Jamaica who was "making free" with male slaves.[38] His comment, although brief, indicated her agency in the matter. Such behaviors were echoed in negative depictions of white women that appeared in the culture. For example, in 1731 one white woman declared about another woman that she "would have Jumpt over nine hedges to have had a Negroe."[39] One Maryland planter commented in 1739 that a white woman who had heard about a slave rebellion from one of her slaves did nothing because, he quipped, "perhaps She had a mind for a black husband."[40]

In the eighteenth and early nineteenth centuries, white women's actions were targeted for legal punishments and cultural derision. Newspaper accounts, for example, criticized white women beyond the local orbit of church and court gossip. In 1769 a Maryland man declared that he would not honor his wife's debts because she had "polluted" his "Bed" by having a child by "her own Negro Slave."[41] Similarly, in New Orleans in 1852 an article about the arrest of a black man and white woman for "cohabitation" reported that "Snowy White" was "sent to the workhouse for a quarter of a year," and "Sooty" was flogged. It quipped: "The frail female woman ought to be also flogged."[42]

Divorcing husbands and wives occasionally documented white women's sexual agency in relations with enslaved men. In Nancy Graves's case for divorce from her husband, testimony included mention of her alleged involvement with enslaved men. The justice of the peace visited neighbor Mary Leatheram at her home and took testimony about what she knew. She had heard Mr. Graves stating that his wife "kept a negro lodge and a negro hoardom at my house." He also "said his wife caught the Clap of Spencer's negro—Hard—and said she was a negro hoar." In her petition, Nancy complained that her husband "frequently charged" her "with having connexion with Negroes." For his part, the husband denied many of her accusations of physical abuse, but about sex with enslaved men he explained that he did not make this charge until she made it about him. According to the case records, it was "the neighbourhood report that petitioner had been having illicit intercourse with John Spencer's negro man 'Hard.'"[43]

The accusation that she "kept a negro lodge and a negro hoardom" should be considered in the context of research that has shown that some white women did prostitute enslaved women. The same man enslaved by Spencer figured in another divorce case from the region, suggesting perhaps that Mr. Graves's claim might have been correct. In Mr. Williams's petition for divorce, he contended that his wife had a reputation for having "sexual intercourse" with numerous men in the neighborhood and that she left him to live with one of those men, Samuel Spencer. While there, he argued, she gave birth to a child that he heard was fathered by a "negro man by the name of Hand belonging to Samuel Spencer." According to Williams, Hand had also "been caught several times in carnal intercourse with her." Mary Williams denied the relationships with other men and complained that her husband turned her out, that she was forced to reside at

Spencer's house and "work for a living," and that any appearance of adultery was false. According to the records, "any appearance of impropriety of conduct on her part has been the result of his own harsh and cruel treatment and exposure to the temptations of the world deprived of that arm of protection which had been pledged to protect and support & sustain her through life."[44] Her explanation that she was forced into "exposure to the temptations of the world" suggests perhaps that sexual contact may indeed have occurred.

If sexual contact did take place, Mary Williams would certainly not have been alone, as records include other instances of women who stood accused of intimate relations with neighboring enslaved people. In his petition for divorce, Rhodias Riley stated that his wife, Nancy, had separated herself from him, that they had had nothing to do with each other for the last six years, and that she had "kept up promiscuous adulterous intercourse with divers other men particularly with Dave, a negro slave belonging to Hugh McCain."[45] Henry Shouse complained to the courts that he became suspicious of his wife after he could no longer deny that the baby she gave birth to was "mulatto." For some time after the birth, he tried to believe that the child's skin color was due to "disease" or some other "cause unknown." He continued to refuse her betrayal for over a year, until he became "neighbourhood talk," and so he had a "medical gentleman of high reputation" examine the child, and he "pronounced it to be of negro blood." Shouse believed that she had the child with one of his own slaves, perhaps from observing previous interactions.[46]

As the enslaved man, Dave, was within the household we can speculate about that dynamic and the danger that the situation would have posed for him. Might he have kept this relationship silent if it had not become town talk? Did some white husbands, seeking harmony in their homes, allow women to have intercourse with enslaved men and look the other way? This scenario is raised by another divorce case, that of the Hickmans. William Hickman similarly waited to file for divorce and only did so once he could no longer avoid community knowledge of the slave paternity of his wife, Nancy's child. He was "unwilling to publish his own shame," but eventually she left him. Their marriage had been childless from 1805 until about 1820. She then had a child, and William did not suspect anything until three years later, when she had another, and "rumors" in the neighborhood gave him great concerns. By 1827 she had moved out. He accused her of relations with more than one man, but "especially with a mulatto slave living in the neighbourhood" whom he "believes is the father of the children."[47]

The divorce case of Dorothea and Lewis Bourne reveals another instance that tells us that women took the initiative with enslaved men. In this 1825 divorce, testimony from neighbors and friends revealed that Dorothea had enjoyed a long-term relationship with Edmond, a man enslaved by her neighbor and with whom she had probably had several children. Neighbors revealed themselves to be well aware of her conduct and, perhaps more surprisingly, did not frame it as wholly unusual. Martha Hodes argues that this case is yet more evidence that black men were not necessarily assumed to be the initiators in such relationships and that the figure of the aggressive black man or that of the sexually passive white woman had not yet emerged as cultural stereotypes. Indeed, Judith Richardson, who owned Edmond, testified that Dorothea was often seen "lurking about her negroes houses."[48]

Abolitionist literature also occasionally drew attention to white women's agency in depictions of interracial intimacy. Harriet Jacobs noted in her account that sex between white women and black men was not all that unusual, as did another former slave named J. W. Lindsay, who said, "There are cases where white women fall in love with their servants."[49] Martha Hodes explains that one African American man told the AFIC that when he had worked as a steward on the Mississippi River it was common for black men who worked on the river to exchange information about "the desires of certain white women to 'sleep with them.'"[50] Another told the AFIC that during his time in Tennessee he observed that "planters here in Tennessee have sometimes to watch their daughters to keep them from intercourse with the negroes. This though of course exceptional, is yet common enough to be a source of uneasiness to parents."[51]

White abolitionist Richard J. Hinton's testimony with the AFIC included several examples that illustrated what he had learned about women's coercive practices during his time with freedmen during the Civil War. Hinton told the AFIC that one enslaved man recounted to him a story of being "ordered" "to sleep with" his mistress within a year of her husband's death, something that he said had happened "regularly." In another example, he told of hearing that "colored men on that river knew that the women of the Ward family of Louisville, Kentucky, were in the habit of having the [black] stewards, or other fine looking fellows, sleep with them when they were on the boats."[52] Recall from chapter 1 that he also testified that "I have never yet found a bright looking colored man . . . who has not told me of instances where he has been compelled, either by his mistress, or by white women of the same class, to have connection with them." In all three examples, we see that his language supports the conclusion of coercion and force. Women in these instances "compel," "order," and "have" men engage in sexual contact with them.

Divorce records similarly include instances that underscore women's agency in pursuing sexual contact with enslaved men. Katherine Jones of Virginia, for example, was accused by Samuel Smith of "consorting and keeping company" with the men and women that he enslaved, and he added that this occurred often in her kitchen.[53] Similarly, in North Carolina James Larrimore accused his wife of the following with a man that he enslaved named Peter: "At various times before said Catherine left his house, she has at late hours of the night long after all the family had gone to bed and after she herself had gone to bed, has got up went to the kitchen where the fellow staid, has remained with him for hours together no person being present except her and the negro."[54] Stephen Cole alleged that his wife, Mary, had a child with "a Negro man slave by the name of Richmond belonging to the estate of Daniel McDonald, deceased, or with some other Negro man to your Petitioner unknown." A physician told Cole that the baby's color was dark due to the mother's health during "procreation," but Cole then came to believe that the child's real father was a black man. In her testimony, Mary accused her husband of extreme physical cruelty. She also interestingly stated that she was "frequently compelled to seek protection and sleep in the kitchen among the negroes, and is not conscious of what may have taken place with her in that condition, but she admits that the child which she has is a mulatto child." Here the white woman portrayed herself as a victim and used her position to claim no culpability for what "may have taken place with her in that condition." Mary Cole further contended that Stephen regularly "was in the habit of keeping a negro girl of his" in the bedroom and that she had woken up to find them in bed.[55] As scholars have shown, the conflicts of husbands and wives could add dimensions of danger to the lives of enslaved people in the household. This case raises the question of the bodies of the enslaved being used in jealous moments of revenge between husbands and wives, a danger for the men as well as the women.

METHODS OF COERCION

The fact that white women at times took the initiative in interracial sex is not, of course, in itself evidence of the sexual abuse of enslaved men, although it is worth repeating that the enslaved status of black men in such interactions made them necessarily vulnerable. Other evidence more clearly points to instances of coercion and sexual exploitation.

White women derived power from a variety of social and culture mechanisms, including the courts. Although the view of white women as passive victims of black male sexual aggressions would not become culturally dominant until after slavery ended, we must keep in mind that even in the colonial era, rape accusations against black men by white women were generally successful in prosecution, standing in contrast to rape accusations against white peers. As Betty Wood concludes in her study of white servant women in seventeenth-century Virginia, for example, enslaved men "had to be extremely wary of those women who made advances to them lest they allege rape."[56] Kathleen Brown found the same for the eighteenth century, arguing that white women had a better chance than others of securing convictions against black men. Twelve of the nineteen black men accused of rape between 1670 and 1767 were executed.[57] As Sharon Block has shown, overall convictions of black men were disproportionately harsher and more easily obtained than those of white men.[58]

White women of the planter class were certainly able to wield power over black men—although all white women could coerce enslaved black men, given the legal and social settings in which they lived. Planter-class women might more easily and more believably have persuaded the community to view them as innocent victims of their sexual contact with black men. One black man who recruited black Union soldiers told the AFIC that another black man had told him how white women could assume the mantle of white female purity to facilitate the sexual assault of black men. Even women who may have been physically smaller and weaker than their victims may have wielded a powerful threat. The recruiter testified about "a young girl" who "got him out in the woods and told him she would declare he attempted to force her, if he didn't have connection with her." Others testified that this sort of coercion was not unusual; one Patrick Minor, for example, told Hinton that he knew of "several cases of the same kind."[59]

One Tennessee man's claim in 1822, that his wife had a six-month relationship with an enslaved man formerly owned by her husband, suggests that the woman was able to secure silence not only from the enslaved man but also from a large number of enslaved people in her household. The man complained to the courts that the relationship was well known among the men and women he enslaved. As Loren Schweninger argues, enslaved people "were wise to remain silent" when they observed marital discord, as choosing one spouse over another could frequently backfire.[60] Although women risked a great deal in such relationships, cases like this hint that women would have been able to secure silence from enslaved people and go undetected in the records.

In nineteenth-century Louisiana, relationships between black men and white women tended to involve servant women more than planter-class women, given the "powerful stigma" of interracial sexual relations. Ann Patton Malone notes, however, that because of that stigma the relationships would have been "more carefully concealed."[61] The high stakes for women, especially planter-class women, would have encouraged those who sought to exploit enslaved men to do so using intensely manipulative methods to conceal their actions. The following newspaper notice underscored the punishments and public humiliation that awaited any black man who risked such intimacy and suggests the power that white women held: "Eliza Saucier, or *Liz*, for short, and Mary Darey, a pair of fallen angels—dwellers in *Sanctity* Row, on *Elysian* Fields street, were arrested for cohabiting with two snow balls one of them Spencer, owned by the Cotton Press Co.; the other Ambrose, the property of Mr Cucullu. The frail fair ones were sent to the parish prison—the darkies received a half hundred of lashes between them."[62]

Even in cases where white women's reputations were impugned by stories of sexual assault by enslaved men, enslaved men faced the greatest threat to their well-being. In 1825, for example, one North Carolina woman, Polly, who accused an enslaved man named Jim of rape found her own reputation being scrutinized, with many neighbors testifying to her socializing with black men, including Jim, while others testified that the couple had a long-term relationship as common-law husband and wife.[63] However, as Hodes notes about the case, Polly wielded power in the relationship, and Jim was the one who "truly lacked choices" and who "spent months in the county jail, probably chained to a filthy, cold floor, thinking about mounting the gallows."[64]

As an alternative to or in conjunction with threats of retribution, some white women may have wielded the purse as a means of coercing enslaved men to have sex with them. That is to say, following the custom of occasionally tipping enslaved men for services provided to individuals, some men may have been paid for their sexual services to white women. One black steward reported that a white woman from Louisville, Kentucky, "offered him five dollars to arrive at her house in Louisville at a particular time."[65] The words suggest that she might have been negotiating a way to discreetly engage in sex with him. Enslaved men, like enslaved women, may well have turned opportunities that sex under slavery presented them to their advantage. For men, this would have posed a paradox: the wages could provide a measure of manly independence while also potentially emasculating them as sexually subservient. One black man testified to the AFIC precisely how such encounters might have begun: "I will tell you how it is here. I will go up with the towels, and when I go into the room the woman will keep following me with her eyes, until I take notice of it, and one thing leads to another. Others will take hold of me and pull me on to the sofa, and others will stick out their foot and ask one to tie their boot, and I will take hold of their foot and say 'what a pretty foot!'"[66]

The promise of freedom may also have been used to entice enslaved men into sexual contact with white women. In eighteenth-century Pennsylvania, one court record of punishment meted out to a white woman and an enslaved man for having a child together sentenced her to be whipped and ordered him to "never more" "meddle with white women uppon paine of his life." When the man was examined by the court he defended himself by complaining that she had "intised him and promised him to marry him." His version was corroborated by the woman, who "confest the same." Was this a promise to free him? Did she entice him *and* promise to marry him, or was the promise of marriage part of the enticement?[67]

A similar case suggests that a promise of freedom may have figured as a method of enticement. In 1813 an enslaved man named David was convicted of rape in Virginia. In a petition to the governor in David's defense, one neighbor testified that the woman Dolly Getts had in fact engaged in "improper intimacy" with David for three years prior to the rape accusation. Dolly and David were known by her father to "bed together" in the father's house. He contended that Dolly had "admitted" that David's "improper conduct arose from her persuasions, that she frequently made use of great importunities to the said David for the purpose of prevailing on him to run off with her which he for some time refused to accede to." Several times she apparently convinced David to spend time together miles away from the house. On one such occasion, she "earnestly solicited David to go to her father and tell him they were married and perhaps they might be permitted to remain together." Unwilling to take these risks, "David refused and charged her with having brought him into his then unpleasant situation."[68] In another related example, in 1826 a white woman was captured after having stolen a horse and an enslaved man. She had disguised herself as a man, and according to the account, "she persuaded him off and that she was the whole and sole cause of his stealing his master's horse." The enslaved man was punished for the theft of the horse.[69]

The promise of freedom was probably less common than the threat of selling an enslaved man away. Court testimony from an 1841 Kentucky case involved an enslaved man and a white woman who lived together as husband and wife and whose case had come to court over the woman's ability to sell her own land. The court declared that their relationship was not marriage but was instead one of "concubinage." Moreover, the case included testimony that revealed the power dynamic within the relationship, since it was reported that the white woman "sometimes threatend to sell" the man, James, "when vexed with him." Another neighbor testified that he "frequently heard her threaten to sell him if he did not behave himself."[70] In a related example, William Thomas complained that his wife, Sarah Jane, knew that he was going to sell an enslaved man, "for previously on two occasions defendant had found said negro too near Petitioner's Bed in the night time and slipping away from her Bed privately."[71] The threat of being sold was a constant fear for enslaved people; it included the terror of being sold to southern states and the West Indies, known for brutal conditions and higher mortality rates, and the pain of being wrenched away from loved ones, kin, and community.

Violations of privacy included punishments that involved nakedness; the threat of such physical punishment could also be wielded by some women. One former slave described his mistress as whipping him: "Mr. Hammans was a very severe and cruel master, and his wife still worse; she used to tie me up and flog me while naked."[72] Another man described his mistress in similar terms, emphasizing physical contact that occurred after being "stripped naked":

> His wife was a harsh, cruel, hardhearted, tyrannical woman, her whole being was filled with hatred of the blackest and bitterest kind against the poor down-trodden, crushed, despised and trampled slave; she seemed possessed with some Satanic influence, and never was in her glory unless she could have her slaves tied up to the whipping post, stripped naked, with a pair of flat irons fastened to their feet, then she would stand by, drawing the lash like an infuriated demon, all the nicer sensibilities of her womanly nature seemed to be crushed out of existence. She would ply the lash until the poor victim would faint dead away.[73]

Hinton's testimony also revealed something about the variety of tactics that women employed toward men in such circumstances, many of them strikingly similar to the strategies employed by white owners against black women: "I have generally found that, unless the woman has treated them kindly, and won their confidence, they have to be threatened, or have their passions aroused by actual contact."[74] Here we see that direct threats accompanied some of these relationships, or indirect manipulation, with a subtler threat of violence. Once physical contact and arousal had been achieved, a man might have little ability to resist.

Regardless of the circumstances that prompted these varied arrangements, many of them clearly took place in the context of servitude and highlighted the power of the enslaving woman over the enslaved man. Harriet Jacobs, in her mention of a white woman who preyed on an enslaved man, wrote that she had picked a man who was "the most brutalized, over whom her authority could be exercised with less fear of exposure."[75] Anecdotes such as these suggest that some white women initiated sexual encounters and made clear what they wanted, knowing that their cultural role, the sexual innocence expected of them, helped to hide their actions. Jacobs's account noted that she was personally familiar with this household. Her account also suggested that the woman preyed on more than one man. She "did not make advances . . . to her father's more intelligent servants" but singled out for sexual assault instead a man "over whom her authority could be exercised with less fear of exposure" because he was so traumatized. Such a man, it is suggested, had been terrorized into submission on the plantation, and she took advantage of his state of mind to force herself upon him—with the threat of additional punishment if he did not accept her assault and if he did not keep it clandestine.

Wives and daughters of planters who formed these sexual relationships took advantage of their position within the slave system. Having sex with their white counterparts in the insular world of the white planter class, if exposed, would certainly have risked opprobrium, and even gossip about the women's actions might have marred their reputations. Daughters of planters could use enslaved men in domestic settings, however, retain their virtue, and maintain the appearance of passionlessness and virginity while seeking sexual experimentation. In other words, one of the ways that some southern women may have protected their public virtue was by clandestine relations with black men. Hinton also told the AFIC that a white doctor reported to him that in Virginia and Missouri "white women, especially the daughters of the smaller planters, who were brought into more direct relations with the negro, had compelled some one of the men to have something to do with them."[76]

Sons of planters also engaged in such conduct, as Hinton also noted, even suggesting that young women imitated the behavior of their brothers. Hinton explained that some daughters of wealthy individuals on the American frontier, where interactions with male suitors were also relatively limited, as they were for planters' daughters, given social constraints, "knew that their brothers were sleeping with the chambermaids, or other servants, and I don't see how it could be otherwise than they too should give loose to their passions."[77] Another man reported that the conditions of slavery not only brought about the "promiscuous intercourse among blacks, and between black women and white men" but also created a context that encouraged white women to be "involved" in the "general depravity."[78] Harriet Jacobs wrote that daughters "know that the women slaves are subject to their father's authority over men slaves" and therefore "selected" and coerced certain enslaved men to be sexual partners. Although Hinton and Jacobs perhaps could not conceive of women taking the initiative on their own and understood them as following the example set by their fathers and brothers, we should note that daughters seem to have engaged in the same behavior as fathers and sons, if not perhaps as many. Although clearly from Jacobs's testimony, field hands were abused, we should also note that house slaves, given their closer proximity to white women, would have fallen under special control.

White women's sexual exploitation of enslaved men may well have led to marital tensions among enslaved couples. In antebellum Alabama, one white man petitioned for divorce and alleged that his wife had been "delivered of a black child, the fruits of illicit intercourse carried on between the said Matilda [his wife] and a negro slave" owned by her father. Loren Schweninger uses the case as an example of how enslaved people sometimes seized opportunities to run away when husbands and wives, and thus households, were disrupted.[79] In this case, the enslaved man's wife ran away at this time. It might also be worth pondering this case from a different angle. What would have been the experience of this enslaved man? His master's daughter, Matilda, engaged him in sexual relations. His wife ran away. Was love lost? Was he able to say no to Matilda? Or did she break up this enslaved family, with the man's wife running away to escape an unbearable situation?

From Rose's interview we glean no indications about Rufus's experiences with white women other than that his mistress played a key role in his forced coupling with Rose. Sexual relations between white women and enslaved black men were well known in early America and resulted in court and church pronouncements and punishments, cultural derision, and the dissolution of white marriages. Efforts to police intimate relations between black men and white women stemmed in part from a desire to control women. Such behavior threatened white men and their authority over white women's sexuality. Discussions of these relationships have often taken their cues from late nineteenth-century understandings of white women's passive victimhood and black male sexual aggression, but even a cursory examination of the extant records surrounding these interactions suggests that much more was at work in these deeply fraught interactions. The relative power that white women had over enslaved black men's bodies and their lives and circumstances makes it possible for us to view their sexual relations as defying white patriarchal authority but at the expense of enslaved men and their families, kin, and communities. Whatever white women's actions accomplished in terms of solidifying their own autonomy was not equally shared by the enslaved men with whom they had intimate relations. Those men lived under constant threat of punishment and could only carefully navigate and negotiate the thorny path that white women presented them whenever sexual intimacy occurred. One wonders if the myth of the black rapist that emerged after emancipation, the fiction that black men uncontrollably sought sexual contact with white women, was not partly informed by white women justifying their actions during enslavement—and their fear of revenge.

CHAPTER 5

"Till I Had Mastered Every Part"

Valets, Vulnerability, and Same-Gender Relations under Slavery

> After I been at the place 'bout a year, de massa come to me and say, "You gwine live with Rufus in dat cabin over yonder."
>
> —ROSE WILLIAMS

White men's sexual manipulation and coercion of enslaved men often occurred in indirect ways as a secondary sexual assault, as when Rose's enslaver instructed her to live with Rufus. As we have seen in previous chapters, white men, especially masters and overseers, could and did assert sexualized control over enslaved men's bodies. As we have seen, enslaved men like Rufus were sexually violated by the directions and actions of white men through forced coupling and reproduction. This chapter argues that some white men also sexually violated some enslaved men through fetishized objectification and direct sexual contact. Such violations were conducive to maintaining the degradation of enslavement. Same-gender sexual violations stand in contrast to other relationships that were also nurtured within the conditions of bondage: the positive and affirming same-gender love that was forged between enslaved men in the crucible of enslavement.

This chapter uses an array of sources to understand the range of ways that male enslavers sexually violated enslaved men. It analyzes accounts from formerly enslaved men and women and visual culture, including Western art, as evidence of communal knowledge of the types of exploitative and violent sexual assaults that were inherent in slavery across and within a wide range of contexts. It begins by examining the broader context of same-gender tenderness shared between some enslaved men. It then raises the issue of same-gender abuses between enslaved men before focusing on the various ways that enslavers sexually violated enslaved men, paying special attention to the unique and vulnerable position of enslaved valets or manservants.

Same-sex sexuality is a topic seldom covered in histories of slavery. To date, none of the major studies of slave life take up the topic of same-sex sexuality in any depth, and slavery has been only marginally present in the major scholarship on same-sex sexuality in early America.[1] The double standard that pervades academic history, whereby historical subjects are presumed heterosexual until overwhelming documentary evidence proves otherwise, holds sway in the literature on slavery. Following tradition, the issue need not even be raised in studies of slave life and culture, and it continues to be acceptable for same-gender intimacy to go entirely unremarked upon.

Enslaved people would be surprised to learn that today we do not know about same-gender abuses. They were spoken of in the nineteenth century in appropriate terms so that audiences understood what was being said without being offended by overly explicit language and imagery.[2] Enslaved people would also be surprised to know that love between enslaved men had become a taboo subject. The pathologizing of same-sex sexuality that took root at the turn of the twentieth century forced the abandonment of that knowledge, leaving it aside, uninterpreted for the next generation. The discreet ways in which it was spoken of languished in the archive, and the meaning was largely lost to historians. In a 2002 interview historian Winthrop Jordan told literary scholars Richard Goddard and Noel Polk that although he believed such interactions occurred, he knew of none that had been documented.[3]

While academic histories of slavery have been slow to include same-sex romantic and sexual experiences, stories of white men sexually abusing enslaved men have percolated through modern culture, through oral tradition, and through artistic forms such as novels and film, representing a disjuncture between popular and academic histories. Modern fictional literature has imagined the same-sex sexual violence that occurred during slavery. A 1968 novel by William Styron, *The Confessions of Nat Turner*, used the specter of same-sex sexual abuse to underscore the particular depravity of slavery in America. In Styron's fictional account, Nat Turner is asked by his enslaver, as he grabs Nat's "upper thigh," "'I hear tell a nigger boy's got an unusual big pecker on him. That right, boy?'" Turner also shares that his enslaver tried to "ravish" him.[4] Scholars have also noted Toni Morrison's inclusion of sexual abuses of enslaved men by white men.[5] More recently, the film *Django Unchained* (2012) depicted a scene of sexually charged whipping and torture of the title character by his master. Django, in the striking scene, vulnerably nude and hanging from his wrists, is leered at by his tormentor.

Do such examples use modern concerns and biases projected onto the past—homophobic metaphors for slavery's other unmentionable horrors—or are they something else—vestiges of communal knowledge about actual practices passed down from those once enslaved? The evidence discussed in this chapter would suggest that it is almost certainly a little of both. The fictionalized depictions in modern sources undoubtedly resonate with current homophobia, but they also stem from long histories of oral tradition that originate in actual practices and experiences under slavery. The underlying discomfort with same-gender sexual intimacy in such accounts is evident in the way that only abuses, and not loving bonds between enslaved men, appear in modern fictional accounts.

Enslavement in America spanned centuries and encompassed millions of men of African descent. During the period of American slavery, the dominant culture did not have a concept of modern sexual orientations, neither heterosexual nor homosexual. Those concepts would develop in medical discourses only in the late nineteenth century, after slavery had ended. It is true that many early Americans believed that some individuals were erotically inclined to others of the same sex, but many also believed that same-sex sexual contact did not indicate a permanent or broader sexual orientation or identity. The absence of medical and psychological models of homosexuality that initially conceived of romantic and sexual attraction to the same gender as unhealthy and disordered allowed for a greater freedom in expressions of same-sex intimacy, and such tenderness was idealized for much of the eighteenth and nineteenth centuries. And because affection between two men would not be of concern, it also provided opportunity for those few individuals who indeed sought romantic and sexual love from members of the same sex. One caveat: those experiences undoubtedly had the potential to inform the participants' sexual and relational lives and even their identities, but it would be anachronistic to use modern sexual orientations in assumptions about the sexual identities of any of the men in this chapter—in either close relationships or abusive sexual contact.

AFFECTIONATE TIES BETWEEN ENSLAVED MEN

It is important to understand that white men's intimate violations of enslaved men took place in a context in which enslaved men valued bonds of love and affection among men.[6] Some of these relationships could have been sexually intimate. All took place before our world of modern sexual orientations and identities during a time that allowed for more fluidity in experiences unrelated to identities. In the late 1990s Robert Richmond Ellis concluded that the poetry of Cuban slave Juan Francisco Manzano "expresses what might be called a homoracial bond" and speculated that same-gender love and intimacy developed among enslaved friends and between family members.[7] But since then no scholars have further explored this important aspect of slavery. This section briefly sketches examples of bonds among enslaved men and argues that approaching those relationships with an openness about romantic and sexual intimacy allows us to more fully understand the range of interpersonal experiences for enslaved men and to situate the abusive corruption of same-gender bonds that slavery enabled. This chapter takes seriously the logical supposition that among the millions of enslaved men, loving queer bonds of intimacy were established and that traces of those most private inner feelings can still be found in records, if one listens and hears.

Same-gender intimacy among whites was a facet of mainstream life in the era of slavery and was widely embraced in the culture.[8] Black women also found bonds of love with each other. Karen V. Hansen's examination of correspondence between Addie Brown and Rebecca Primus illustrated that the "fluidity of boundaries in nineteenth-century sexuality" extended beyond the circles of middle-class and elite white women and men in the Northeast. Brown and Primus's "erotic" relationship was partly recorded in letters written while they were separated and Rebecca helped establish and taught at a school for ex-slaves in Maryland.[9] This chapter finds ample evidence that similar bonds of intimacy also existed between enslaved men.

Although the conditions of slavery played a key role in forging connections between enslaved men, bonds and intimacies occurred broadly in Africa before and during the era of slavery. Scholars have argued that a nascent concept of "homosexuality in precolonial Africa" existed. Indeed, it has been argued that "through the institutions of boy-wives, spirit mediumship, and male initiation rituals, homosexuality was indeed a regular part of the sexual patterns of many African ethnic groups."[10] Scholarship on African traditions and practices of same-gender intimacy does not focus on West Africa, from which slaves were generally taken, but the broader literature on Africa generally can provide some clue about practices that appear to be widely held and that would have also circulated in West Africa. Vincent Woodard points out that the account of a Cuban slave, Esteban Montejo, contains numerous examples of "cultural practices" and "plantation values" that underscore the "continuities between Central and West African cultures."[11] The homoerotic bond of African men was illustrated in Auguste-Xavier Leprince's 1826 painting, *Lion Hunt*, for example, which features three nude or seminude men having just conquered a lion, their gaze directed at one another's eyes.[12] This bond was similarly captured in Léon Bonnat's 1876 Orientalist painting *Le Barbier nègre à Suez*, in which a standing, nearly nude barber with a straight-edge razor tenderly holds the head of the man seated beneath him. The seated man's head rests against the barber's crotch. The length of the razor is placed just under his mouth, which is depicted in sensual detail.[13]

While all-male contexts may have been particularly conducive to developing bonds among enslaved men, we also see shards of evidence in other areas that suggest that the broad African traditions were continued and developed under the conditions of slavery. And indeed, as some scholars have argued, the conditions of the Middle Passage itself may have fostered "queer relationships" among men and among women "in the holds of slave ships."[14]

In the context of slavery in the Americas, we do see same-gender bonds among men figuring in important ways in both labor and leisure. Works by Sergio Lussana and David Doddington have helped us to better appreciate the predominantly male worlds that nurtured bonds of cohesion and competition among men. Lussana has focused on the sex-segregated spaces within which so many enslaved men found themselves confined, including mines, forests, factories, and mills and during the building of canals and railroads. Lussana argues that same-gender friendships served to support and bond together communities of enslaved men.[15] Leisure time in these environments and on large plantations also included homosocial spaces and activities, including physical contacts of fighting and wrestling. As Lussana argues, such conditions nurtured a climate of fraternal support.

It would seem that there was enough concern about the radical potential of black male-male intimacy and the disruptive bonds that it could engender for Pennsylvania to outlaw it specifically and to apply harsher penalties than for same-gender intimacy among whites. Quaker laws in Pennsylvania made a distinction between black and white sodomy offenses. In 1700 and 1706 statutes established that blacks convicted of "buggery" would be sentenced to death, although the laws made sodomy for whites a crime that would result in life imprisonment instead of execution.[16]

Cultural awareness of the bonds among enslaved men may have been some cause for concern. For example, intense bonds among men are at the heart of a story reprinted in *The Spectator* in 1711 in which two enslaved men, in love with the same woman, engage in a "long Struggle between Love and Friendship." They were deeply in love with the woman but "at the same time were so true to one another, that neither of them would think of gaining her without his friend's consent." After stabbing the woman in the heart, the men were discovered having taken their own lives, lying on each side of her on the ground kissing her.[17]

Formerly enslaved men reflected on meaningful relationships formed with other men. Some of these included young white men as well as other enslaved men. Olaudah Equiano, for example, wrote of a white man, Richard Baker, whom Equiano met while on board a ship for England soon after being brought to Virginia and sold. Equiano describes Baker as "a young lad" several years older than himself: "He showed me a great deal of partiality and attention, and in return I grew extremely fond of him. We at length became inseparable; and, for the space of two years, he was of very great use to me, and was my constant companion and instructor." The relationship was marked not just by tutelage but also by mutual support, because the two young men had "gone through many sufferings together on shipboard." It was also punctuated by physical intimacy and tenderness: "We many nights lain in each other's bosoms when we were in great distress." Reflecting on Baker's death, Equiano wrote that he "never ceased to regret it" and described him as a "kind interpreter, an agreeable companion, and a faithful friend."[18] In another example, Frederick Douglass described the importance of his relationship with one "Little Tommy," whom he "professed much love for" until he was around fifteen years old and the boys assumed their social hierarchical roles of master and slave.[19] We also see hints of this type of bond in Solomon Northrop's relationships with his rescuer, Bass, described as an "old bachelor," and also with Uncle Abram, whom he described as having a "contempt of matrimony." Northrop describes the sixty-year-old Abram as a man who is no longer interested in sexual intimacy with women, including his wife.[20] Uncle Abram was a "kind-hearted" man and a "patriarch" to those around him, including Northrop.

Formerly enslaved men link these relationships to having endured moments of great difficulty, underscoring the importance of the connection, and some highlighted the intensity of trust between the men, particularly when the relationship occurred in the context of running away. One Isaac Mason, for example, wrote of being "very intimate" with one young man named Joshua with whom he shared his plan to run away. Joshua ended up joining Isaac: "Mr. Mansfield had secured from his father's estate a young fellow by the name of Joshua. He had been with him about two years this Christmas. We were very intimate and I had placed the utmost confidence in him. Feeling he would not betray my secret, I ventured to inform him where I had been and what I had done. He felt much elated over the project and said he would go with me."[21] Similarly, William Parker wrote of one Alexander, to whom he became "greatly attached" after his "comrade" of many years, Levi, was sold. Parker described the pain of separation from slave sales and the effect it had on separating families and husbands and wives, and he used the example of Levi to illustrate his own loss as an adolescent boy.[22] In another example, Louis Hughes described talking about running away and freedom with "fast friends": "Thomas, the coachman, and I were fast friends. We used to get together every time we had a chance and talk about freedom."[23] Such discussions were dangerous and could only occur within bonds of trust. The secret shared could then strengthen that bond. The bonds shared could be revolutionary in this context of running away, but even for those who did not take that step, bonds of mutual respect and love were a form of resisting enslavement, as the work of Stephanie Camp has argued. And as Lussana has argued, "Few men could have survived the brutality of slavery, without the support of friends, without male company."[24]

Two examples from Cuba provide erotically charged descriptions of intimacy among enslaved men. In his depiction of enslaved life in Cuba, Esteban Montejo described his experiences and having witnessed erotic relationships between men.[25] Woodard and others have noted his observations that some men "had sex with each other and didn't want to have anything to do with women." "Sodomy," he recalled boldly, "was their life." The sexual interactions were not isolated or hidden, according to Montejo, and were sometimes part of long-term relationships. Men used the term "husband" to refer to a male partner, and Montejo noted that cooking, economic support, and washing clothes were all part of this type of marriage between enslaved men.[26] A poem by Juan Francisco Manzano includes passages addressed to his brother that Ellis reads as queer, given the physical and emotional affection expressed. The poem includes lines that emphasize intimacy poignantly: "He embraces me, I kiss him / And oh Lord! In his arms / I felt my affection grow. . . . lovingly I clasp him in my arms."[27]

While Manzano's lines contain the most erotically charged of the examples presented here, we must consider the broader context and conditions of slavery when examining the bonds that developed among enslaved men. Scholars such as Lussana have chosen the term "friendship" to capture the depth of emotional connections among enslaved men and the radical potential that it held for survival and resistance while remaining true to what the evidence can support. At the same time, such a characterization runs the risk of closing down queer possibilities. Social acceptance of close relationships among men provided opportunities for physical intimacy to go unrecorded. The sentiments expressed by enslaved men are significant because they are what same-gender love looks like. An expansive rather than narrow understanding of love among enslaved men must allow for erotic, romantic, and physical love. Maintaining an openness to same-gender intimacy within slavery must be part of our histories and future approaches, or we risk destroying the richness and diversity of thoughts, feelings, and experiences that make up our past.

SAME-GENDER ABUSES BETWEEN ENSLAVED MEN

The same-gender sexual violations that enslaved men endured thus stood in contrast to the practices and traditions involving same-gender intimacy. Although slavery forged ties among men, it also nurtured hierarchies and abuses between them. That same-gender abuse occurred between enslaved men should not surprise us. We know that same-sex sexual abuses occurred in other captivity contexts in North America. Some of these abuses were ritualized, and some were violent.[28] One traveler noted that Native American warriors, for example, sodomized "the dead bodies of their enemies, thereby (as they say) degrading them into women."[29] Ramón Gutiérrez has argued that the berdaches were frequently prisoners of war who were sexually exploited and degraded by their captors.[30]

Studies of slavery have tended to emphasize community among enslaved people, but a relatively small body of work also examines various types of conflict. Stephanie Camp and others remind us that enslaved women were at times abused by both enslaved men and white men.[31] Eugene Genovese argued that "some drivers forced the slave women in much the same way as did some masters and overseers" and that it was an "open question which of these powerful white and black males forced the female slaves more often."[32] We know that fights occurred among slaves—sometimes resulting from jealousy, but other times stemming from conflicts and power struggles.[33]

Slavery in Brazil, some have argued, nurtured a "sadistic" relationship in the shape of bonds of intimacy, with some of these acts taking place among enslaved men in addition to masters. One classic study by Gilberto Freyre claimed, "Through the submission of the black boy in the games that they played together, and especially the one known as *leva-pancadas* ('taking a drubbing'), the white lad was often initiated into the mysteries of physical love." It continued: "As for the lad who took the drubbing, it may be said of him that, among the great slave-holding families of Brazil, he fulfilled the same passive functions toward his young master as did the adolescent slave under the Roman Empire who had been chosen to be the companion of a youthful aristocrat: he was a species of victim, as well as comrade in those games in which the '*premiers élans genesiques*' [first reproductive impulses] of the son of the family found outlet."[34] This same author argued that Europeans and Italians in particular had brought the practice of sodomy to Brazil in the sixteenth and seventeenth centuries. Among the Portuguese and Spaniards who colonized Brazil, he argued, "this form of lust was intensely practiced." Additionally, the Portuguese men of the fifteenth and sixteenth centuries, "possibly by reason of their long maritime crossings and their contact with the voluptuous life of Oriental countries," spread these cultural same-sex sexual practices.[35]

The disproportionately male environments of the sugar plantations in Brazil and Cuba nurtured ripe conditions for sexual assault among slaves, as well as between male owners and overseers and enslaved men. Genovese noted that scholars of slavery in Latin America argue that slave owners' sons who did not abuse enslaved women might be suspected of sexual interest in men. "Perhaps," he speculated the logic would go, "his earlier indulgence in *leva-pancadas* with the slave boys, instead of whetting his appetite for richer treasures, had caught his fancy as a way of life. Had he become a 'sissy'?"[36]

A seventeenth-century case from New York suggests that an African tradition of intimacy between an older man and a younger boy may have been practiced in the colonial Americas. In 1646 Jan Creoly, a "Negro slave," tried for a "second offense" of "sodomy," was sentenced to be "strangled" to death and then "his body burned to ashes." Creoly confessed that he had "also committed the said heinous and abominable crime on the island of Curaçao." A ten-year-old black boy, Manuel Congo, was identified as a victim and was spared the death penalty because the courts believed the act was committed "by force and violence." (He was, however, sentenced to be taken to the place of Creoly's execution, tied to a post, with "wood piled around him, and be made to view the execution and be beaten with rods.") The age difference suggests that it followed the African custom of older men and younger boys. However, the court record indicates that the original accusations were brought by black community members, suggesting that the violence of the attack may have violated any existing social norms. Thus, what is most striking is that the language suggests that there may well have existed a scenario that allowed for a certain degree of same-gender intimacy—bonds that did not include assault and that would therefore not have triggered a response from the community.[37]

The all-male environment on ships also presented men with conditions that were conducive to same-gender sexual violations. At the turn of the nineteenth century, American media had sensationalized the specter of sodomy and captivity in coverage of the Barbary pirates. Newspapers and books described North African men as morally corrupt in their sexualized captivity of American and European men. As Jason R. Zeldon argues, such coverage "forced readers to confront the uncomfortable notion that the American hostages were getting raped."[38]

Although we have no documentation for sexual assault during the Middle Passage, the conditions were certainly there. Ships were both sexually charged and physically abusive spaces. Sailors were abused by superiors and degraded those beneath them. We also know of rapes and sexual exploitation of enslaved women.[39] And we know from scholarship on same-sex sexual behavior in this time and place and under seafaring conditions that such abuse would not have been unknown.[40] It is likely that abusive sexual relationships could have also occurred within that context.

Consider also the American and British familiarity with same-sex sex at sea.[41]

After leaving the United States Navy in 1842, Jacob A. Hazen reflected on his experiences onboard:

> I have already hinted that the Columbus was a school-ship. That is, if a den where some two hundred boys are collected together, exposed to every kind of sinful vice—where swearing, gambling, cheating, lying, and stealing, are the continual order of the day; where drunkenness, obscenity, and self-pollution, stalk unrestrained; and where crimes abound of even so deep and black a dye that it fires the cheek with shame to name them, and which yet escape the just punishment their heinousness deserves; if, I say, such a place constitutes a school-ship then was the Columbus, like the North Carolina, emphatically a school-ship.[42]

His description echoes the scholarly literature on life onboard navy ships and at sea for merchant ships in general. Mutual masturbation was not uncommon and could most easily go undetected, but even sodomy occurred and would generally go unpunished unless disruptive. The offenses in 1848–49 included multiple types of infractions that would have covered same-sex sexual conduct, including "scandalous conduct," "filthiness," and "taking indecent liberties with boy in hammock."[43]

Marcel Antoine Verdier's 1849 painting of a naked enslaved man tied to four stakes in the ground captures the sexualized vulnerability of enslaved men to the abuses of other enslaved men (fig. 6). The image draws the eye to the body of the man on his stomach, his legs forced apart by the way he is staked. In the center of the image, witness to the violence, is an enslaved man who is stripped to his waist. He stands with his hands tied behind his back and does not look at the man on the ground; instead, his gaze is cast squarely at the enslaved man who holds the whip over his head. That man looks downward at the fully exposed buttocks and genitals, which are hidden from the viewer.

WHITE MEN AND VIOLATIONS OF ENSLAVED MEN

Sexualized violations of enslaved men also occurred at the hands of white men. As we have seen in chapter 1, fetishized objectification of black men's bodies resulted from a culture of racism and white supremacy. The example of the portrait of Belley dramatically illustrates the social and cultural messages present at the time, some of which appear to be competing—on the one hand, lauding the black male body for its power and potency, while on the other hand, holding up black manhood as inherently uncivilized and animalistic (fig. 3). Some scholars have even speculated that the artist of the portrait must have been personally captivated by Belley, experiencing a sexual attraction to the subject while still

FIGURE 6. Marcel Antoine Verdier, *Beating at Four Stakes in the Colonies* (*Châtiment des quatre piquets dans les colonies*), 1849. Verdier's vivid painting captures the intimate violations of enslaved men during punishments such as whippings. Here the white man in the image leers at the victim, his gaze squarely at his genitals and buttocks. It also illustrated divisions among enslaved men, the man exacting the punishment apparently also enslaved. Oil on canvas, 59¼ × 84½ in. (150.5 × 214.6 cm). Photographer: Paul Hester. The Menil Collection, Houston.

embedding the image with visual clues that contrast Belley with classical references. "Undoubtedly, Belley was an object of Girodet's desire and fantasy," concludes Darcy Grimaldo Grigsby. "The thirty-year-old artist standing before the fifty-year-old black deputy and military officer was fascinated by Belley's hidden virility, his sexual power, his potential erotic domination."[44]

White men's erotic objectification of black men was illustrated in an 1807 satirical watercolor of a nearly nude muscular African man modeling in a way that exposes his buttocks (fig. 7). The subject stands alone in a studio with six white men, all of whom are in various poses of aroused gaze. Two of the men are staring squarely at the man's genital region. A third has the round end of a vertical cane suggestively in his own mouth. Three of the men are holding their hats, symbolically creating open orifices at or near their posteriors. As the model strikes a classical pose (Apollo), the image, like the portrait of Belley, manages to present the body in celebratory ways while still drawing a contrast to civility that ultimately undercuts the subject's manhood.

FIGURE 7. John Boyne, *A Meeting of Connoisseurs*, ca. 1790–1807. This satirical engraving pokes fun at the white artists whose penchant for muscular black models made them suspect as men. Victoria and Albert Museum, London. William Smith Gift.

The English caricature of an African American man as the intense focus of male artists bears a striking similarity to the real-life experiences of a man from Boston named Wilson. Wilson found himself the subject of a great deal of scrutiny and attention in London as an artist's model, with numerous artists professing adoration for his physique.[45] One man, Benjamin Robert Haydon, made drawings and studied Wilson's "exquisite form" for a full month, writing in his diary that he was the "perfect model of beauty and activity" (figs. 8 and 9). What Wilson endured as Haydon's model is not fully clear, but Haydon noted that Wilson was a "beauty in any position." That his artist's eye was viewing his subject in a racialized way comes through in Haydon's reference to Wilson, a man for whom Haydon professed great physical admiration and with whom he spent significant time, as only "the black," instead of by his name.[46]

Haydon's fascination with Wilson's body neatly illustrates the broader culture's objectification of black men, including its concomitant disregard for their well-being. As was popular at the time, Haydon also attempted to make a plaster cast of his subject, in this case, indicating Haydon's wish to possess Wilson entirely, of his full body. The casting was unsuccessful, nearly compressing Wilson to death as the plaster set. "The moment it set," wrote Haydon, "it pressed so equally upon him that his ribs had no room to expand for his lungs to play." Wilson, evidently in desperation, "gasped out, 'I—I—I die.'" After breaking him out of the form, Haydon was pleased that he had succeeded in molding Wilson's "hinder part" and the front of his body, presumably including his genitals. Haydon recalled that when the mold of Wilson's posterior "was joined to the three front pieces there appeared the most beautiful cast ever taken from nature." It was, he gushed, "the most beautiful sight on earth." In his autobiography, Haydon boasted that he had been "pushed to enthusiasm by the beauty of this man's form." In striking parallels to the ways that objectification of black bodies served the institution of slavery so well, he melded his calling as an artist with his total control of Wilson's body, writing, "I cast him, drew him and painted him till I had mastered every part." Haydon's fascination with Wilson's physique was part of his larger view of white supremacy. He noted elsewhere in his diary that his study of "physical construction" led him to conclude that the "Negro was the link between animal and man."[47]

Wilson was a free man, but free men were still subjected to the cultural evaluation of black men's bodies that enslavement produced. We can see similar

FIGURES 8 and 9. Benjamin Robert Haydon's sketches of Wilson, a free black man whose "beautiful" body Haydon found to be "exquisite." MS Eng 1331 5, Houghton Library, Harvard University.

objectification and scrutiny at work—more explicitly and obviously serving a racialized hierarchy—in an example from ethnographic research. In 1850 Swiss naturalist Louis Agassiz commissioned photographs of five enslaved men, Alfred, Fassena, Jack, Jem, and Renty, and two women, Delia and Drana, from South Carolina plantations, in the belief that the photos would assist in his argument for the biological inferiority of Africans (figs. 10 and 11). Some of them, including the women, were photographed without shirts on. Two of the men were photographed completely naked, their buttocks and genitals part of the scientific gaze, their exposure and exploitation preserved by the camera.[48]

Formerly enslaved men described the kind of everyday physical violations and humiliations that they endured. In Solomon Northrop's account of his experiences enslaved in Mississippi, he wrote about two men scrutinizing his body. When Epps and Bass discuss Platt (Northrop), Epps brags that he was offered $1,700 for Platt but refused it. Explaining that Platt is strong and smart, Epps encourages Bass to feel Platt's body. "'Why, just feel of him, no,' Epps rejoined. 'You don't see a boy very often put together any closer than he is. He's a thin-skin'd cuss, and won't bear as much whipping as some; but he's got the muscle in him, and no mistake.' Bass felt of me, turned me round, and made a thorough examination, Epps all the while dwelling on my good points."[49]

As Vincent Woodard has argued, Frederick Douglass viewed himself as metaphorically raped by the slave system and was likely also literally the victim of sexual assault. He "described himself as playing the role of the male concubine and male daughter to the plantation system and to certain white male authority figures." As Woodard argues in his analysis of the public letter that Douglass wrote to his former master, he "speaks vicariously through the voice and body of a young white daughter" and "alludes to a relationship—a very intimate, erotic relationship—between himself and his former master in this female voice." Woodard argues that the letter and positionality make sense when one views this as Douglass writing about "his own rape," his own "ravishing at the hands of white men."[50] Woodard reads this as a silence that suggests perhaps sexual abuses. From Douglass:

> THE foregoing chapter, with all its horrid incidents and shocking features, may be taken as a fair representation of the first six months of my life at Covey's. The reader has but to repeat, in his own mind, once a week, the scene in the woods, where Covey subjected me to his merciless lash, to have a true idea of my bitter experience there, during the first period of the breaking process through which Mr. Covey carried me. I have no heart to repeat each separate transaction, in which I was a victim of his violence and brutality. Such a

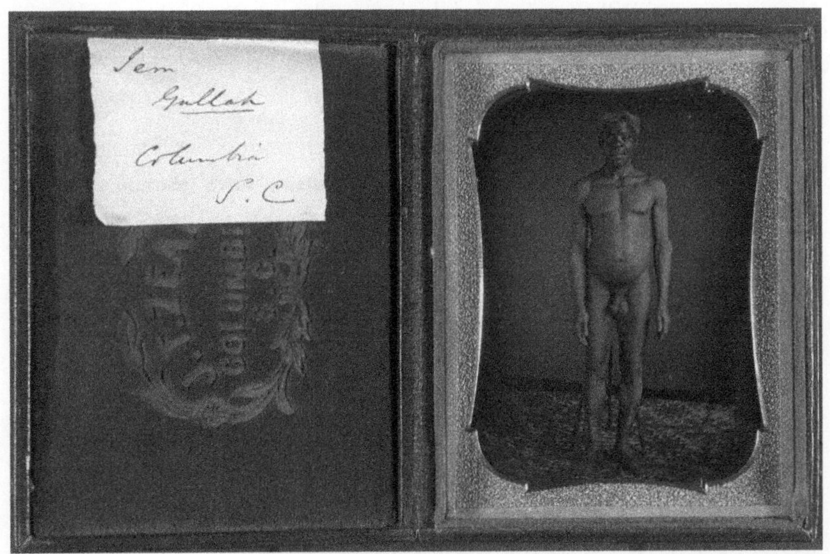

FIGURE 10. Photograph of Jem, Gulla, from a series of photographs of five enslaved men and two enslaved women, 1850. Courtesy of the Peabody Museum of Archaeology and Ethnology, Harvard University, PM# 35-5-10/53046.

FIGURE 11. Photograph of Alfred, Foulah, from a series of photographs of five enslaved men and two enslaved women, 1850. Courtesy of the Peabody Museum of Archaeology and Ethnology, Harvard University, PM# 35-5-10/53049.

> narration would fill a volume much larger than the present one. I aim only to give the reader a truthful impression of my slave life, without unnecessarily affecting him with harrowing details.[51]

Douglass's reluctance to detail his abuses stands in contrast to explanations and depictions that he has used effectively in his account to convey the abuses he witnessed and endured. Here, his silence on his own abuse at the hands of a sadistic man who sought total control over his body is suspect.

Similarly, the narrative of William Grimes, published decades before Douglass's, contains an extraordinary passage about an interaction with a new master, "Mr. A——, (for that was my new masters name, who was a Jew)." Early on, Grimes ran into problems with him: "I then started with my new master for Savannah, with a carriage and four horses: we travelled about twelve miles the first day. I was dissatisfied with him before I had got two miles." Grimes explained that the problems were serious enough for him to try to get out of the situation: "We travelled the next day twenty five miles, as far as Petersburgh. I was so much dissatisfied with him, that I offered a black man at that place, two silver dollars to take an axe and break my leg, in order that I could not go on to Savannah; but he refused." The man instead suggested to Grimes that he run away, but Grimes was unwilling to take that risk.[52] Nonetheless, his desire to end this association was severe enough that the following day he wrote:

> I then attempted to break my leg myself. Accordingly I took up an axe, and laying my leg on a log, I struck at it several times with an axe endeavouring to break it, at the same time I put up my fervent prayers to God to be my guide, saying, "if it be thy will that I break my leg in order that I may not go on to Georgia, grant that my blows may take effect; but thy will not mine be done." Finding I could not hit my leg after a number of fruitless attempts, I was convinced by my feelings then, that God had not left me in my sixth trouble, and would be with me in the seventh. Accordingly I tried no more to destroy myself. I then prayed to God, that if it was his will that I should go, that I might willingly.[53]

Grimes explains that his previous master had instilled in him a dislike for Georgia, yet that reasoning does not explain how he came to dislike his master after only two miles. Indeed, the reader is left to wonder what could possibly have been bad enough for him to take such extreme measures, yet not bad enough that he would risk running away. Given that Grimes does not refrain from descriptions of other abuses throughout the rest of his account, one can rule out nearly all possible explanations, and the odd silence becomes one that suggests unspoken queerness, like what Woodard finds for Douglass.

Physical punishments such as flogging and whipping were enhanced by being conducted in ways that heightened the degradation of enslaved men by incorporating sexualized elements. Masters and overseers would often strip men nude, contributing to the sexually abusive and invasive nature of the punishment. Whipping for Anglo-Americans had long been associated with eroticism and sexualized violence. As Colette Colligan explains, this was a function of the "combined stimulation to the genital area and public exposure of genitals and buttocks."[54]

Abolitionist literature contained commentary on the same-gender abuses of whipping enslaved men. Scholars have analyzed how the imagery within the literature functioned to engender a sense of sympathy and outrage for the abuses enslaved men endured.[55] We must also approach this literature not only as using same-gender abuses as a metaphor for the horrors of slavery but also as representing and capturing what was communal knowledge about the sexualized nature of these abuses. Recall Verdier's 1849 painting of a nude enslaved man staked to the ground, which illustrates the sexualized vulnerability of slavery's victims to black and white men (fig. 6). The image draws the eye to the exposed body of the vulnerable man. His exposed genitals, in the sight line of an enslaved couple in the background, are not gazed upon by them. The woman looks down, and the bound man looks at the man with the whip. A white man on the left side of the image, however, stands casually viewing the abuse, his gaze squarely on the nude man as he stands behind the man on the ground, who has his legs spread and his buttocks raised in the air. The white man's look fixes on the enslaved man's exposed buttocks and genitals, which are hidden from the viewer.

In another remarkable example, in English artist Charles Landseer's 1825 *Black Punishment at Rio Janeiro,* an enslaved man is tied against a pole with his buttocks exposed. Nearby on a hillside a well-muscled, shirtless laborer gazes at his body and the abuses with his head casually resting on his hand. A soldier on the right side of the image stands with his bayonet fully vertical in a phallic allusion. These two men smile along with the man getting ready to strike the enslaved man. A fourth man in the image, another enslaved man, also smiles as he holds the ends of the rope that holds the victim's ankles to the pole.[56]

Reducing enslaved men to their bodies served a critical calculus that supported slavery by emphasizing labor output potential, including (as we have seen in chapter 3) the power to reproduce. The objectification was deepened by sexualized violations that reinforced hierarchies of freedom and enslavement. Early abolitionist literature provides examples of masters who were said to be sexually abusing their slaves.[57] In one such widely translated and reprinted account, authored by Joseph LaVallée, a slave named Itanoko was subjected to rape by a white slaver named Urban. Urban was described as a "ravisher" who, Itanoko explained, was "struck by my comeliness," and he did "violate, what is most sacred among men." As John Saillant explains, although Itanoko was rescued, he found himself on a plantation in Saint-Domingue, where he met Theodore, "whose 'criminal complaisance with the overseer' allows him to give 'free scope to his irregular passions.'" Saillant continues: "The 'irregular passions' apparently include sexual activity with black men, which LaVallee calls 'crime,' 'vice,' and 'rapine,' all 'enormities' resulting from 'unbridled disorders' and 'passion.'"[58]

FAVORITES, VALETS, AND VULNERABILITY

In 1758 and 1764 Jamaican planter Thomas Thistlewood tersely noted in his diary two sexual assaults committed against enslaved men. In one entry he recorded: "Report of Mr. Watt Committing Sodomy with his Negroe waiting Boy." In the other, he wrote: "Strange reports about the parson and John his man."[59] That the acts occurred between a male slave owner and a close personal servant, "waiting Boy" and "his man," rather than with a field hand suggests that the abuse of enslaved men follows the broader pattern uncovered by the scholarship on the sexual violations of enslaved women: the closer the proximity to whites, the more likely it was that sexual violations would occur. This final section focuses on the sexual vulnerability of enslaved valets, an area of historical inquiry most recently advanced by literary scholar Woodard's *Delectable Negro*. In his introduction he asserted: "A master would often choose 'a favorite' male slave as the object of his cultivated delight. Black men in such contexts had to negotiate feelings of affection, hatred, shame, sexual degradation, and arousal toward white men."[60]

White planter-class men lived in a culture that was conducive to sexual exploitation and abuse of enslaved men. As scholars have well established, such men saw sexual access to enslaved women as their prerogative. Masters, slave drivers, and slave overseers similarly viewed enslaved men in the extreme hierarchy of enslavement, which allowed for a range of abuses and violations. At the same time, white planter-class men in the eighteenth century and antebellum period also embraced and celebrated a model of same-gender intimacy that included platonic loving bonds of friendship as well as same-gender physical sexual contact.[61] It is within these contexts that we can begin to view the interactions of masters and enslaved valets or body servants. Previous scholars have been reluctant to determine "whether participants in these sexual acts were willing or unwilling," and historically, the relationships have been romanticized by whites, but if we listen closely to the voices of enslaved people, we can begin to move beyond the claims of masters and view the same-gender intimacy experienced by valets through the lens of sexual exploitation and abuse that was inherent in the slave system.

Body servants or valets were enslaved men assigned to closely attend to their masters. Elite planters directed valets and body servants to serve them with intimate tasks such as dressing and bathing. Valets also labored closely with elite men during intensely emotional moments such as in warfare and attending to them when they were ill.[62] Whites characterized the relationships as tender and the orientation of masters toward body servants as paternal, thus hoping to soften criticism of the institution of slavery by positioning enslavers as beneficent and humane rather than sadistic and immoral.

Artists captured the intensity of the romanticized bond imagined existing between enslavers and the enslaved in this context. A large scene painting by John Trumbull, *The Death of General Warren at the Battle of Bunker Hill* (1786), for example, included in one corner American lieutenant Thomas Grosvenor, sword drawn as he watches British soldiers killing his general. Closely behind Grosvenor is a black body servant, peering over his soldier, musket drawn. The wartime bond between the men, symbolically highlighted by their physical proximity in the painting, was compelling enough for it to be reproduced eleven years later in Trumbull's *Lieutenant Thomas Grosvenor (1744–1825) and His Negro Servant* (1797) (fig. 12). In this version, the entire battlefield has been removed, and only the two men have been focused on and enlarged. In both paintings the two men are physically inseparable.[63]

This kind of tenderness was represented in other more popularly available art forms, such as figurines and public statuary. John Rogers's commercially successful figurine *The Wounded Scout* (1864), for example, depicts an escaped slave helping a wounded soldier back to his hiding place in a swamp (fig. 13). The soldier rests his entire body against the slave, the soldier's head on the man's chest, and the slave stands resolute and strong, holding the soldier's wrist for added support. Reproductions were sold in England and France, and in the United States the statuette was available for decades. Similar depictions of tenderness between white men and emancipated men appear in two other examples of statuary. The memorial for English abolitionist and member of Parliament Charles James Fox includes a muscular nearly nude African man kneeling mournfully, representing Africa. A similarly kneeling and barely clothed African man is positioned at the feet of a towering and fully clothed Abraham Lincoln in the 1876 statue that became a memorial in Washington, D.C. In one final example, a nearly naked young African man holds both hands over his heart as French abolitionist Victor Schoelcher embraces him with one arm, tenderly touching his shoulder. The two men gaze into each other's eyes. In these examples, the docile and appreciative

FIGURE 12. John Trumbull, *Lieutenant Thomas Grosvenor (1744–1825) and His Negro Servant*, 1797. John Trumbull's large oil painting of the Battle of Bunker Hill represented in one corner a man and the valet he had enslaved. The cultural celebration of the bond between masters and manservants was strong enough to warrant a reissue of a painting that showed just the figures of the two men. Yale University Art Gallery, Mabel Brady Garvan Collection.

FIGURE 13. This widely reproduced statuette of an escaped slave assisting a wounded soldier during the Civil War illustrated the cultural figure of the loyal slave. John Rogers, *The Wounded Scout: A Friend in the Swamp*, 1864, bronze, 22¼ × 10¼ × 8¼ in. Purchase, New York Historical Society, 1936.655. Photography © New-York Historical Society.

African man bears a resemblance to the idealized figure of the loyal and, for our purposes, vulnerable valet. The homoerotic bond between the men is also consistent.[64] Such bonds took place in a cultural context that objectified, eroticized, and dehumanized the bodies of enslaved men, whose bodies and genitals were long a site of exploitation and fixation by European American cultures. In all four statues, the men have idealized muscular bodies, with little clothing on.

Enslavers and their families recollected body servants and valets with great fondness and frequently characterized the bond between them as one of tenderness. Such sentiments were a common trope expressed in the antebellum period in artwork and in personal recollections of enslavers and their families. The daughter of Commodore of the Navy John Rodgers remembered her father's body servant, Butler, as a "devoted friend and servant of that loved master to the day of his death, and my father breathed his last in Butler's arms."[65] Similarly, Robert Phillip Howell, reflecting on a domestic servant who ran away, noted that it was particularly painful for him because "he was about my age and I always treated him more as a companion than a slave."[66]

Emancipation records similarly include mention of masters who freed their body servants, often late in life, with justifications to the state government that spoke of tender feelings and of being indebted to them for close personal attention. Some mentioned being nursed by their enslaved men after life-threatening illnesses. George Washington freed only one slave in his lifetime, his valet William Lee. Their relationship also lends itself to romanticization given his emancipation and his presence in important portraits of the president and his family, but we also know that, like all enslaved people, Billy Lee found his intimate relations with women the subject of Washington's scrutiny and control. In a letter to one Clement Biddle, Washington wrote:

> The mulatto fellow William, who has been with me all the War is attached (married he says) to one of his own colour a free woman, who, during the War was also of my family. . . . I had conceived that the connection between them had ceased, but I am mistaken; they are both applying to me to get her here, and tho' I never wished to see her more yet I cannot refuse his request (if it can be complied with on reasonable terms) as he has lived with me so long and followed my fortunes through the War with fidelity.[67]

Here Washington recognizes the relationship at the same time as he denigrates it—"(married he says)"—and demonstrates his desire to honor the bond he shares with Billy Lee. In a letter to Washington during the war, Lund Washington, a distant cousin and the steward of Mount Vernon, included news from

Mount Vernon for Billy Lee: "If it will give Will any pleasure, he may be told that his wife and child are both very well."[68]

Many masters expressed deep sentiments of attachment for the enslaved men who served them closely, but often the reality of the relationship was far more complex. Cultural items such as fiction, paintings, and statuary produced for and by whites emphasized a romanticized bond between enslaved men and the enslavers they served, but sources produced by enslaved men and women contradict this picture and point to the exploitation and abuses inherent in those relationships. Consider the example of John Randolph and his enslaved valet John. Randolph once wrote of John, "I know not at this time a better man. . . . I have not a truer friend." Such a declaration drew upon the cultural celebration of same-gender love that held sway in the late eighteenth and early nineteenth centuries. It crossed racial lines and by doing so further underscored the remarkableness of the feelings themselves. Such a statement could reinforce for a master his perception of himself as benevolent and humane.[69] Randolph also declared: "His attention and attachment to me resemble more those of a mother to a child, or rather a lover to his mistress, than a servant's to a master." That he would ultimately describe the relationship as "a lover to his mistress" placed Randolph in a feminine position—and as a mistress. This was not uncharacteristic for Randolph, who was known as effeminate in appearance and eccentric in mannerisms. In letters to intimate male friends, he wrote about "pure affection between man and man." In writing about his unhappiness, he referred to "the incubus that weighs me down," a reference to a male spirit who rapes sleeping women. In a political letter to Andrew Jackson, he wrote of Jackson as Alexander the Great and himself as Hephaestion, his male lover.[70] As Alan Taylor concludes, "Whether they had sex is unknowable and beside the point; emotionally John fulfilled the subordinate but nurturing role of a wife to Randolph."[71]

These sentiments tell us how Randolph felt, but we would be remiss to read into them too far to understand John's experience. For that we could consider that Randolph's biographers describe him as a "stern but not a cruel master" who was known for "occasional periods of derangement, when he could be brutal to all his intimates, white and black."[72] John's behaviors tell us something: he often drank to excess. John also ran away. Once John was caught, Randolph treated him cruelly, leaving him in prison for three months and then forcing him to work as a field hand for three years before allowing him to return to labor as a valet in the plantation house.

Such bonds, therefore, were often emotionally complicated and could be treacherous for enslaved men. James Madison's valet Paul Jennings, to take another example, described Madison in positive terms as "one of the best men that ever lived" and noted that he was not violent: "I never saw him in a passion, and never knew him to strike a slave, although he had over one hundred; neither would he allow an overseer to do it."[73] Jennings attended very closely to Madison, as did other enslaved valets. "I was always with Mr. Madison till he died, and shaved him every other day for sixteen years," he reflected. "For six months before his death, he was unable to walk, and spent most of his time reclined on a couch," wrote Jennings.[74] Jennings's care would have included toileting, bathing, and dressing Madison.

We should note that by praising Madison for not whipping enslaved people, Jennings was able to insert statements that served to indict enslavement in general. Although Jennings would appear to have had a privileged position, attending Madison in the White House, he was separated from his family and taken to Washington, a city he described as "a dreary place." Jennings also took pains to highlight the strength and capability of enslaved men while noting that Madison did not share this assessment. During the War of 1812, one commander's troops were described by Jennings as "tall, strapping negroes, mixed with white sailors and marines." And he noted Madison's failure to appreciate their strength and bravery: "Mr. Madison reviewed them just before the fight, and asked Com. Barney if his 'negroes would not run on the approach of the British?' 'No sir,' said Barney, 'they don't know how to run; they will die by their guns first.'" Jennings added: "They fought till a large part of them were killed or wounded." He also noted that the credit given to Dolly Madison for saving the Washington portrait actually partially belonged to an enslaved man: "It has often been stated in print, that when Mrs. Madison escaped from the White House, she cut out from the frame the large portrait of Washington (now in one of the parlors there), and carried it off. This is totally false.... John Susé (a Frenchman, then door-keeper, and still living) and Magraw, the President's gardener, took it down and sent it off on a wagon."[75]

In the hands of those who opposed slavery, the emasculation of men who served too closely to white masters stood as a symbol of their violations. Their unique enslavement allegedly stripped them of their manhood and included same-sex sexuality as an example of the types of abuses that occurred as well as serving metaphorically for the horrors of enslavement. *Uncle Tom's Cabin*, first published in 1852, vividly captured the peculiarity of the relationships that existed between enslaved valets and owners by depicting an effeminate slave owner and his slave in scenes that implied degeneracy and implicit sexual deviance. Stowe defended her work against proslavery critiques who decried it as wholly fictional. She argued that it was rooted in realities and that it captured the kinds of abuses that were known at the time, representing cultural knowledge of the potential for sexual abuse within the bonds shared between enslaved men and masters.[76]

Stowe's creation of a dandified enslaved valet named Adolph illustrated the corrupting influences of enslavement on masters and slaves. We are first introduced to Adolph with the following description: "Foremost among them was a highly-dressed young mulatto man, evidently a very distinguished personage, attired in the ultra extreme of the mode, and gracefully waving a scented cambric handkerchief in his hand." He is depicted as having an unhealthy devotion to his own appearance as well as to the welfare of his master—at the expense of his bond with the enslaved community: "'Back! All of you. I am ashamed of you,' he said, in a tone of authority" as he confronted domestic slaves who were anticipating greeting their master. The passage continued: "All looked abashed at this elegant speech, delivered with quite an air." He is described as fastidious and vain, "conspicuous in satin vest, gold guard-chain, and white pants, and bowing with inexpressible grace and suavity."[77]

The tenderness between master and slave, in conjunction with these aspects of the slave's character and appearance, draw a sharp line around their unwholesome bond: "'Ah, Adolph, is it you?' said his master, offering his hand to him; 'how are you, boy?' while Adolph poured forth, with great fluency, an extemporary speech, which he had been preparing, with great care, for a fortnight before."[78] In another scene, he scrutinizes another male slave, Tom, "through an opera-glass, with an air that would have done credit to any dandy living." His indulgent master is marked by a similar softness that immediately calls into question the nature of their bond. "'Puh! you puppy,' said his master, striking down the opera glass" and then "laying his finger on the elegant figured satin vest that Adolph was sporting," a stained garment that the master used to wear. In response, "Adolph tossed his head, and passed his fingers through his scented hair, with a grace."[79]

In very striking ways, Adolph's queerness also stood in contrast to traditions of homosocial bonding and same-gender intimacy and served to create tension rather than facilitate the type of same-gender bond that was an important part of survival for enslaved men and women. Adolph's effeminacy and closeness to his master cost him his manhood and instead made him vulnerable to conflicts with other enslaved men. Consider the following exchange, which occurs as he and other slaves are being sold away, one of the most traumatic experiences for enslaved communities. In the description of this scene, Sambo carelessly dismisses their sadness, "laying his hand freely on Adolph's shoulder." Adolph responds in a manner that speaks to his discomfort with homosocial bonding: "'Please to let me alone,' said Adolph, fiercely, straightening himself up with extreme disgust." In response he is mocked as "'white . . . kind o' cream color, ye know, scented!'"

"'I say, keep off, can't you?' said Adolph, enraged." His feminized response results in more mocking: "'Lor, now, how touchy we is—we white niggers! Look at us, now!' and Sambo gave a ludicrous imitation of Adolph's manner; 'here's de airs and graces. We's been in a good family, I specs.'" "'I belonged to the St. Clare family,' said Adolph, proudly."[80] Stowe's depiction of this fictional slave and his master was used to highlight the immorality of enslavement and its corrupting influence on masters and slaves alike. For our purposes, we might also read Stowe as a particular kind of evidence—of communal knowledge and of oral culture. Such characterizations and exploitative relations reflect the experiences of some enslaved men, albeit in varying degrees.

Black women also wrote about the particularly vulnerable position of enslaved valets. In her 1859 published account of travels through New Orleans, Eliza Potter, a free black woman, explained: "Almost all gentlemen in Louisiana and Mississippi have favorite body servants, and they are always very kind to them, more particularly so than to any other servant."[81] In the early part of a chapter entitled "Natchez New Orleans," Potter wrote about one particularly disturbing relationship, between "Mr. H.," a Natchez resident, and the man he enslaved, whom she described as "a companion" and the pair as "inseparable." Potter described a bond that results in violence and destruction for the white owner as his enslaved and abused valet resisted forcefully:

> It happened that, from some cause unknown, Mr. H. fell out with his body servant and chained him to a log of wood, and whipped him severely. He went out the next day to repeat the dose, when the despised slave, enraged at the treatment, broke loose from the log, seized it, and dashed Mr. H.'s brains out before the eyes of his family. It appears that, although a slave, he was descended from one of the highest southern families, and inherited all the proud feeling and independent spirit the Southerners generally pride themselves on.[82]

The experiences of the enslaved man underscore the especially volatile and emotionally complicated positions that valets and masters found themselves in.

As a published account, Potter's work also carried cultural resonance that symbolized the terror of slavery in addition to voicing the particular position of valets. Literary scholar Lisa Ze Winters argues: "The intimacy of the relationship, the suddenness of its dissolution, and the violence of its conclusion mark it as a sentimental romance." Winters argues that the scene is further sexualized by phallic symbolism in the account, as the "'log of wood' is literally attached to the enslaved man's body." She argues: "It is the site of Mr. H's assault on the captive slave and becomes, in the hands of the self-freed slave, an extension of his body. . . . [T]he log of wood is transformed into an exaggerated and deadly black phallus." As Winters reminds us, "It is precisely the body servant's enslavement that places him in an intimate bond with Mr. H."[83]

The abuse of enslaved valets was also vividly represented by Harriet Jacobs in her 1861 *Incidents in the Life of a Slave Girl.* Jacobs's autobiographical account graphically describes an incident between a slave named Luke and his young owner, a man who "became a prey to the vices growing out of the 'patriarchal institution'" and who had been "deprived of the use of his limbs, by excessive dissipation." Like many valets who attended ill owners, Luke was forced to "wait upon his bed-ridden master" and in a state of near undress: "Some days he was not allowed to wear anything but his shirt, in order to be in readiness to be flogged."[84] Jacobs continued:

> The fact that he was entirely dependent on Luke's care, and was obliged to be tended like an infant, instead of inspiring any gratitude or compassion towards his poor slave, seemed only to increase his irritability and cruelty. As he lay there on his bed, a mere wreck of manhood, he took into his head the strangest freaks of despotism; and if Luke hesitated to submit to his orders, the constable was immediately sent for. Some of these freaks were of a nature too filthy to be repeated. When I fled the house of bondage, I left poor Luke still chained to the bed of this cruel and disgusting wretch.[85]

Luke is depicted as especially vulnerable and regularly victimized, and his nakedness except for a long shirt underscored his sexual availability to his master. As Vincent Woodard argues, Luke's "rear parts serve as erotic spectacle." Woodard contends that although black women could appear in stories of rape and sexual assault as "honorable," for Luke, no such option existed, resulting instead in his total "emasculation."[86] The description of his master as a man who was a "wreck of manhood," one who had been disabled by his "excessive dissipation," signaled to readers that he was sexually depraved. The term "dissipation" carried specific sexual connotations at the time. Scholars have analyzed the passage about Luke as an example of same-gender sexual assault and have commented, as Woodard has, on the gendered rendering. As the evidence in this section makes clear, a key element to understanding the reference to Luke is his status as one who closely attends to his master's body, the particular sexual vulnerability of enslaved valets. Indeed, he was literally chained to his master's side.

For enslaved male valets or body servants, closeness to masters could present them with relatively better conditions and chances for labor of a different sort from exhausting agricultural labor, but it could also be emotionally suffocating and psychologically difficult, and it made them especially vulnerable to sexual violations. Although proslavery sources generally depict enslaved valets as tenderly and honorably serving their masters, other sources, especially those left to us by men and women who experienced enslavement, underscore the sexually vulnerable position of enslaved valets. By examining the ways in which literature, art, and firsthand accounts captured the representations and reports of intimate physical and psychological violence against enslaved body servants, this chapter suggests that future research in this area would likely prove to be fruitful. The violations and vulnerabilities of valets analyzed here were conducive to, not antithetical to, the growth and maintenance of hierarchies necessary to enslavement.

The system of slavery in America nurtured and developed same-gender loving bonds that sustained enslaved men and provided community and humanity. The confines and perversity of enslavement also gave rise to horrific abuses and intimate compromises, to tortures and physical assaults. For those men and their communities, their wives, sisters, mothers, fathers, brothers, friends, and enemies, same-gender intimacy was life-sustaining, and it was also one of many degradations that some endured.

What does all of this mean for Rufus? We do not know what interactions Rufus had with other men. We do know that Rose described him as a "bully." Perhaps he violated other men. Did he also develop intimate friendships? Was he leered at by white men when stripped naked or at other times? While we do not have answers to these questions, this chapter provides a general context within which Rufus was enslaved. Rufus, like all enslaved men, lived in a world that objectified his body and left him vulnerable to assaults that could be sexually degrading. The pressures and structures of enslavement fueled conflict among men but also intensified those bonds among enslaved men that nurtured and sustained some of them. Even positions that carried measures of relief from hard labor carried emotional, psychological, and physical risks, with increased vulnerability being a part of working closely with white men (and women).

When Rufus's master ordered him to establish a sexual relationship with Rose he was indirectly sexually violating Rufus, a kind of secondary sexual assault, even as we also acknowledge that Rufus may in turn have violated Rose. To recognize the interaction between Rufus and his master is to see one of the many ways that men were sexually assaulted by other men under slavery. This subordinate position may have drawn Rufus closer to Rose as he sought emotional support, but it may also have made him resent her and the situation. Thus, the psychic toll here may have also played itself out in Rufus's family and community and not simply within his own body, heart, and mind.

CONCLUSION

Rethinking Rufus

Rufus landed hard on the dirt floor. Rose had summoned up all her strength to kick him with both feet after he attempted to crawl into bed with her. She had always feared him. Rufus was used to getting his way. Rose and others thought of him as a bully. Now he had the full support of Master Hawkins to force himself on her, and she detested the idea. It wasn't the first time that she'd been attacked, and she was damned if it was going to happen tonight. She knew it was pointless, but still she needed to resist, or she didn't know what might come next. She vowed one thing that night: if she survived to freedom, she'd never again let any man come near her or touch her or think about her like that. Ever. No matter what.

For generations now, this has largely been the accepted version of Rose's and Rufus's experiences. As scholars have shown, Rose's experiences were shared by many enslaved women. Her interview poignantly reveals her thoughts and feelings regarding her own family and her forced coupling with a man she disliked. In the imagined version that begins this chapter, we learn little about Rufus, leaving gaps that to date had been filled with assumptions about his experiences in this situation. This book has argued that enslaved men like Rufus were also sexually exploited and abused in a range of ways.

One of the ways that enslaved men were sexually violated was through the social and cultural denigration of their bodies, which were objectified, fetishized, degraded, and abused. Enslaved men's genitalia were groped, scrutinized, imagined, and even tortured, all because black men's sexuality was symbolized by their genitals and thought of as a source of power—a strength that had to be possessed or put down. Enslaved men's bodies were also punished in ways that attested to their status as slaves, underscored by nudity—an aspect of whipping that enslaved men repeatedly noted as especially degrading.

Enslaved men spoke of many of the aspects of sexual abuse and exploitation described in this book. Their emphasis on independence of choice of intimate partner, of the dehumanization of being forced to partner with someone other than the one they chose, of the risks taken to see and be with women they loved and desired—all speak to their definition of manhood as one of independence and autonomy in the area of love and intimacy.

Many others reflected on the expectations to reproduce that all enslaved people found themselves operating under. Such expectations played themselves out in various ways, depending on the assertions of enslavers. Some allowed enslaved people to pair up as they desired—as long as they did indeed couple. Others took a more involved approach and coerced men and women to reproduce, paying little attention to the wants and desires of those involved and much more attention to strength, fitness, and financial bottom lines. The forced and coerced coupling of enslaved men, of course, did not affect men as it did women. Men did not get pregnant, their health jeopardized by childbirth, their hearts and minds forever impacted by the experience. But most men did experience the expectation to reproduce, and many experienced the trauma and violation of forced reproduction. Culturally, the ramifications for this emphasis on reproduction could be significant. The valuing of fertility and virility contributed to categories of manliness and of manhood that in some cases set up some men as inferior. Those deemed superior attained a different status in the community that could be isolating and carry its own burdens.

Those enslaved men who found themselves in relations with white women faced their own litany of hazards. To date, little attention has been paid to the vulnerable position of enslaved men in intimate relations with white women. The prevalence of these relationships has not alarmed scholars; instead, it has been pointed to as evidence of the permeability of rigid racial hierarchies and of the possibility for men and women to resist white patriarchal authority. But as this book has argued, the relations between white women and enslaved men need to be reconsidered and recontextualized in the setting of enslavement and sexual power. The image of hypersexualized enslaved men served to demonize and define the population of black men, but it also raised the radical possibility for some white women of the desirability of such men as highly sexual and accomplished—a model of masculinity that highlighted power, strength, and mastery rather than moderation and self-control. At a minimum, the sheer numbers of relations between white women and enslaved men should be understood in part as a product of the availability of enslaved men to white women's advances.

Of course, the desirability of enslaved men would not have only been limited to white women. Some white men also sexually abused enslaved men. Sexual abuse and exploitation of a wide variety of forms occurred under slavery as white men enacted and asserted their power over enslaved men in many situations. The culturally celebrated special bond between enslaved valets and enslavers masked a world of inequality and risks for enslaved men of the sort that the phrase "sexual vulnerability" can only just begin to describe. As this book has argued, enslaved men such as Rufus were themselves often subjected to sexual exploitation and abuses. Recognizing this aspect of slavery, rethinking Rufus expands our understanding of the experiences of all who were touched by enslavement.

Studying sexual violence against enslaved men helps underscore that sexual violations were about power. This point has been made since the advent of feminist theorizing about sexual violence against women, but it is often obscured by heterosexual interactions within slavery, especially those involving long-term relationships, which can appear to be about romantic desire as much as about power. Examining the sexual exploitation of enslaved men necessitates that we enlarge our frameworks for understanding sexual violence against enslaved people. To date, the study of women has largely focused on rape and reproduction. Examining enslaved men necessitates a broader view, incorporating sexual objectification, everyday interactions, same-sex sexual violations, and other less studied aspects of life.

Rethinking Rufus, therefore, also allows for rethinking Rose and the sexual violations of enslaved women. Reconsidering the position of Rose as a coerced partner of a man who was himself victimized raises additional questions to ponder. How complex was their relationship and their moments of trust and resentment if we view them not simply as perpetrator and victim but instead as two adults caught in multilayered webs of abuse and exploitation? How might Rose have thought about her own children and their vulnerability? Scholars have pointed to the abolitionist era lamentation that enslaved men suffered by their frustrated ability to protect their female dependents from sexual exploitation. This book argues that we must also imagine the worries, fears, and attempts of enslaved men and women to protect boys and young men from sexual violations.

Rethinking Rufus means rethinking the community of enslaved people. What impact did sexually violated men have on their communities as they sought to protect themselves and their loved ones? In what ways did enslaved men shield themselves from the pain of being denied autonomy in their intimate lives? How did this affect the families they did establish and the broader sense of kin and community that grew from that fragility? Undoubtedly, while some would be drawn to pull loved ones closer, others would respond with emotional barriers and distancing. Rethinking Rufus entails a vast restructuring of our understanding of the experiences of enslaved men and women, their communities, their kin, and even their enslavers.

Fully accounting for the position of Rufus has implications for rethinking the history of sexuality so as to be more cognizant of the influence of slavery. The traditional history of sexuality in America perhaps still emphasizes urban developments of middle-class whites. Understandings of how sexual othering affected mainstream concepts of sexuality have not fully examined how enslavement and abolition informed understandings of sexuality. This book suggests that because they touched virtually everyone in some manner, the conditions of slavery broadly informed the history of sexuality in America. As the evidence here implies, in myriad ways slavery affected experiences, identities, and even public discussions. For enslaved people, a host of aspects of life under the lash—objectification of bodies, coerced and forced coupling, the value of same-sex bonds—impacted understandings of normative behavior and even assessments of physical types, all of which refracted back and forth with enslavers and even, especially, with the popularizing of sexualized imagery put forth by abolitionists, the wider culture.

All of these aspects of sexual abuse and exploitation—objectification and fetishization, coerced reproduction, relations with white women and men—require a fundamental rethinking of the position of men like Rufus and of slavery in general. *Rethinking Rufus* suggests connections between sexual violations of enslaved men and the emerging scholarship on how slavery enabled the development of capitalism. As Edward Baptist, for example, has argued with regard to the sexual exploitation of enslaved women, their bodies were central to the productivity that fueled the nation's economic development. The exploitation of enslaved men's bodies operated in related ways. The intimacies and abuses analyzed here were conducive to, not antithetical to, the growth and maintenance of enslavement.[1] But as much as this book has implications for understanding more fully such institutions and discourses, its primary focus, of course, has been on the experiences of enslaved people, primarily sexually violated men, as a way of better understanding the past. Understanding those experiences more fully is one avenue for honoring those lives. The legacy of slavery continues to shape our economy, society, and culture in myriad ways. Examining this history of sexual violence against enslaved men allows us to also begin reconsidering how understandings of gender and sexuality continue to be shaped by the past.

APPENDIX

Full Text of WPA Interview with Rose Williams

ROSE WILLIAMS is over 90. She was owned by William Black, a trader whose plantation lay in Bell County, Texas. Rose and her parents were sold in 1860 to Hall Hawkins, of Bell County. Rose was forced to mate with a slave named Rufus when she was about sixteen, and had two children by him, one born after Rose was freed. She forced Rufus to leave her and never married. For the last ten years Rose has been blind. She lives at 1126 Hampton St., Fort Worth, Texas.

"What I say am de facts. If I's one day old, I's way over 90, and I's born in Bell County, right here in Texas, and am owned by Massa William Black. He owns mammy and pappy, too. Massa Black has a big plantation but he has more niggers dan he need for work on dat place, 'cause he am a nigger trader. He trade and buy and sell all de time.

"Massa Black am awful cruel and he whip de cullud folks and works 'em hard and feed dem poorly. We'uns have for rations de cornmeal and milk and 'lasses and some beans and peas and meat once a week. We'uns have to work in de field every day from daylight till dark and on Sunday we'uns do us washin'. Church? Shucks, we'uns don't know what dat mean.

"I has de correct mem'randum of when de war start. Massa Black sold we'uns right den. Mammy and pappy powerful glad to git sold, and dey and I is put on de block with 'bout ten other niggers. When we'uns gits to de tradin' block, dere lots of white folks dere what come to look us over. One man shows de intres' in pappy. His named Hawkins. He talk to pappy and pappy talk to him and say, 'Dem my woman and chiles. Please buy all of us and have mercy on we'uns.' Massa Hawkins say, 'Dat gal am a likely lookin' nigger, she am portly and strong, but three am more dan I wants, I guesses.'

"De sale start and 'fore long pappy am put on de block. Massa Hawkins wine

Rose Williams, in *Federal Writers' Project: Slave Narrative Project, Vol. 16, Texas, Part 4, Sanco–Young*, 1936, Manuscript / Mixed Material, https://www.loc.gov/item/mesn164/.

de bid for pappy and when mammy am put on de block, he wins de bid for her. Den dere am three or four other niggers sold befo' my time comes. Den massa Black calls me to de block and de auction man say, 'What am I offer for dis portly, strong young wench. She's never been 'bused and will make de good breeder.'

"I wants to hear Massa Hawkins bid, but him say nothin'. Two other men am biddin' 'gainst each other and I sho' has de worryment. Dere am tears comin' down my cheeks 'cause I's bein' sold to some man dat would make sep'ration from my mammy. One man bids $500 and de auction man ask, 'Do I hear more? She am gwine at $500.00.' Den someone say, $525.00 and de auction man say, 'She am sold for $525.00 to Massa Hawkins.' Am I glad and 'cited! Why, I's quiverin' all over.

"Massa Hawkins takes we'uns to his place and it am a nice plantation. Lots better am dat place dan Massa Black's. Dere is 'bout 50 niggers what is growed and lots of chillen. De first thing massa do when we'uns gits home am give we'uns rations and a cabin. You mus' believe dis nigger when I says dem rations a feast for us. Dere plenty meat and tea and coffee and white flour. I's never tasted white flour and coffee and mammy fix some biscuits and coffee. Well, de biscuits was yum, yum, yum to me, but de coffee I doesn't like.

"De quarters am purty good. Dere am twelve cabins all made from logs and a table and some benches and bunks for sleepin' and a fireplace for cookin' and de heat. Dere am no floor, jus' de ground.

"Massa Hawkins am good to he niggers and not force 'em work too hard. Dere am as much diff'ence 'tween him and old Massa Black in de way of treatment as 'twixt de Lawd and de devil. Massa Hawkins 'lows he niggers have reason'ble parties and go fishin', but we'uns am never tooken to church and has no books for larnin'. Dere am no edumcation for de niggers.

"Dere am one thing Massa Hawkins does to me what I can't shunt from my mind. I knows he don't do it for meanness, but I allus holds it 'gainst him. What he done am force me to live with dat nigger, Rufus, 'gainst my wants.

"After I been at the place 'bout a year, de massa come to me and say, 'You gwine live with Rufus in dat cabin over yonder. Go fix it for livin'.' I's 'bout sixteen year old and has no larnin', and I's jus' igno'mus chile. I's thought dat him mean for me to tend de cabin for Rufus and some other niggers. Well, dat am start de pestigation for me.

"I's took charge of de cabin after work am done and fixes supper. Now I don't like dat Rufus, 'cause he a bully. He am big and cause he so, he think everybody do what him say. We'uns has supper, den I goes here and dere talkin' till I's ready for sleep and den I gits in de bunk. After I's in, dat nigger come and crawl in de bunk with me 'fore I knows it. I says, 'What you means, you fool nigger?' He say for me to hush de mouth. 'Dis am my bunk, too,' he say.

"'You's teched in de head. Git out,' I's told him, and I puts de feet 'gainst him and give him a shove and out he go on de floor 'fore he know what I's doin'. Dat nigger jump up and he mad. He look like de wild bear. He starts for de bunk and I jumps quick for de poker. It am 'bout three foot long and when he comes at me I lets him have it over de head. Did dat nigger stop in he tracks? I's say he did. He looks at me steady for a minute and you's could tell he thinkin' hard. Den he go and set on de bench and say, 'Jus wait. You thinks it am smart, but you's am foolish in de head. Dey's gwine larn you somethin'.

"'Hush yous big mouth and stay 'way from dis nigger, dat all I wants,' I say, and jus' sets and hold dat poker in de hand. He jus' sets, lookin' like de bull. Dere we'uns sets and sets for 'bout an hour and den he go out and I bars de door.

"De nex' day I goes to de missy and tells her what Rufus wants and missy say dat am de massa's wishes. She say, 'Yous am de portly gal and Rufus am de portly man. De massa wants you-uns for to bring forth portly chillen.

"I's thinkin' 'bout what de missy say, but say to myse'f, 'I's not gwine live with dat Rufus.' Dat night when him come in de cabin, I grabs de poker and sits on de bench and says, 'Git 'way from me, nigger, 'fore I busts yous brains out and stomp on dem.' He say nothin' and git out.

"De nex' day de massa call me and tell me, 'Woman, I's pay big money for you and I's done dat for de cause I wants yous to raise me chillens. I's put yous to live with Rufus for dat purpose. Now, if you doesn't want whippin' at de stake, yous do what I wants.'

"I thinks 'bout massa buyin' me offen de block and savin' me from bein' sep'rated from my folks and 'bout bein' whipped at de stake. Dere it am. What am I's to do. So I 'cides to do as de massa wish and so I yields.

"When we'uns am given freedom, Massa Hawkins tells us we can stay and work for wages or share crop de land. Some stays and some goes. My folks and me stays. We works de land on shares for three years, den moved to other land near by. I stays with my folks till they dies.

"If my mem'randum am correct, it am 'bout thirty year since I come to Fort Worth. Here I cooks for white folks till I goes blind 'bout ten year ago.

"I never marries, 'cause one 'sperience am 'nough for dis nigger. After what I does for de massa, I's never wants no truck with any man. De Lawd forgive dis cullud woman, but he have to 'scuse me and look for some others for to 'plenish de earth."

NOTES

INTRODUCTION. The Rape of Rufus?

1. Wilma King, *Stolen Childhood: Slave Youth in Nineteenth-Century America* (Bloomington: Indiana University Press, 1995), 110.

2. Daina Ramey Berry, *"Swing the Sickle for the Harvest Is Ripe": Gender and Slavery in Antebellum Georgia* (Urbana: University of Illinois Press, 2007); Martha Hodes, *White Women, Black Men: Illicit Sex in the Nineteenth-Century South* (New Haven, Conn.: Yale University Press, 1999); Thelma Jennings, "'Us Colored Women Had to Go Though A Plenty': Sexual Exploitation of African-American Slave Women," *Journal of Women's History* 1, no. 3 (1990): 45–74; Brenda E. Stevenson, "What's Love Got to Do with It? Concubinage and Enslaved Black Women and Girls in the Antebellum South," *Journal of African American History* 98 (Winter 2013): 99–125; Deborah Gray White, *Ar'n't I a Woman? Female Slaves in the Plantation South*, rev. ed. (1985; New York: W. W. Norton, 1999).

3. For one example, women's sexual exploitation could lead to pregnancy and childbirth. See, for example, Cheryll Ann Cody, "Cycles of Work and of Childbearing: Seasonality in Women's Lives on Low Country Plantations," in *More Than Chattel: Black Women and Slavery in the Americas*, ed. David Barry Gaspar and Darlene Clark Hine (Bloomington: Indiana University Press, 1996), 61–78.

4. On the abuse of enslaved women, see, for example, Stevenson, "What's Love." On slave narratives as a source that differently portrays women's and men's abuses, see Frances Foster, "'In Respect to Females . . .': Differences in the Portrayals of Women by Male and Female Narrators," *Black American Literature Forum* 15 (Summer 1981): 66–70.

5. King, *Stolen Childhood*, 110.

6. Hodes, *White Women, Black Men*.

7. Berry, *Swing the Sickle*, 83.

8. bell hooks, *Ain't I a Woman: Black Women and Feminism* (1981; New York: Routledge, 2015), 24.

9. Saidiya V. Hartman, *Scenes of Subjection: Terror, Slavery, and Self-Making in Nineteenth-Century America* (New York: Oxford University Press, 1997), 81.

10. Sasha Turner, *Contested Bodies: Pregnancy, Childrearing, and Slavery in Jamaica* (Philadelphia: University of Pennsylvania Press, 2017), 63–64.

11. Wilma King, for example, reminds us that sexual assault was both raced and gendered in early America. Wilma King, "'Prematurely Knowing of Evil Things': The

Sexual Abuse of African American Girls and Young Women in Slavery and Freedom," *Journal of African American History* 99, no. 3 (Summer 2014): 173–96.

12. Sharon Block, *Rape and Sexual Power in Early America* (Chapel Hill: University of North Carolina Press, 2006).

13. Estelle B. Freedman, *Redefining Rape: Sexual Violence in the Era of Suffrage and Segregation* (Cambridge, Mass.: Harvard University Press, 2013), 3.

14. Block, *Rape and Sexual Power*, 2.

15. Hartman, *Scenes of Subjection*, 4.

16. Ibid., 80.

17. Block, *Rape and Sexual Power*, 2.

18. bell hooks, *Ain't I a Woman* (Boston: South End Press, 1991), 20.

19. Rebecca Fraser, "Negotiating Their Manhood: Masculinity amongst the Enslaved in the Upper South, 1830–1861," in *Black and White Masculinity in the American South, 1800–2000*, ed. Lydia Plath and Sergio Lussana (Newcastle upon Tyne: Cambridge Scholars Publishing, 2009), 87.

20. David Doddington, "Informal Economies and Masculine Hierarchies in Slave Communities of the U.S. South, 1800–1865," 2, in Gender and History File, 2015, http://orca.cf.ac.uk/74559/; David Stefan Doddington, *Contesting Masculinity in the American South* (Cambridge: Cambridge University Press, 2018).

21. Sergio Lussana, *My Brother Slaves: Friendship, Masculinity, and Resistance in the Antebellum South* (Lexington: University Press of Kentucky, 2016); Lussana, "To See Who Was Best on the Plantation: Enslaved Fighting Contests and Masculinity in the Antebellum South," *Journal of Southern History* 76, no. 4 (November 2010): 901–22; Lussana, "'No Band of Brothers Could Be More Loving': Enslaved Male Homosociality, Friendship, and Resistance in the Antebellum South," *Journal of Social History* 46, no. 4 (Summer 2013): 872–95. On slavery and black masculinity, see also Edward Baptist, "The Absent Subject: African American Masculinity and Forced Migration to the Antebellum Plantation Frontier," in *Southern Manhood: Perspectives on Masculinity in the Old South*, ed. Craig Thompson Friend and Lorri Glover (Athens: University of Georgia Press, 2004), 136–73; Daniel P. Black, *Dismantling Black Manhood: An Historical and Literary Analysis of the Legacy of Slavery* (New York: Garland Publishing, 1997); Kathleen M. Brown, "'Strength of the Lion . . . Arms Like Polished Iron': Embodying Black Masculinity in an Age of Slavery and Propertied Manhood," in *New Men: Manliness in Early America*, ed. Thomas A. Foster (New York: New York University Press, 2011), 172–94; Doddington, *Contesting Masculinity*; David Stefan Doddington, "Manhood, Sex, and Power in Antebellum Slave Communities," in *Sexuality and Slavery: Reclaiming Intimate Histories in the Americas*, ed. Daina Ramey Berry and Leslie M. Harris (Athens: University of Georgia Press, 2018), 148–58; Fraser, "Negotiating Their Manhood."

22. Sarah N. Roth, "'How a Slave Was Made a Man': Negotiating Black Violence and Masculinity in Antebellum Slave Narratives," *Slavery and Abolition* 28, no. 2 (August 2007): 255–75.

23. Gregory D. Smithers, *Slave Breeding: Sex, Violence, and Memory in African American History* (Gainesville: University Press of Florida, 2012), 103.

24. For a related argument, that in numerous instances throughout history "sexual violence [against men] was simply a form of warfare that aimed at complete subjugation of the enemy," see Amalendu Misra, *The Landscape of Silence: Sexual Violence against Men in War* (London: Hurst & Company, 2015), 10.

25. Treva B. Lindsey and Jessica Marie Johnson, "Searching for Climax: Black Erotic Lives in Slavery and Freedom," *Meridians: feminism, race, transnationalism* 12, no. 2 (2014): 187.

26. Amber Jamilla Musser has argued that "our understanding of pleasure" relies on "contemporary notions of individuality and personhood, which cannot be grafted onto the historical reality of slavery." Amber Jamilla Musser, *Sensational Flesh: Race, Power, and Masochism* (New York: New York University Press, 2014), 165.

27. Hooks and others like Frances Smith Foster argue that healing comes from telling. Frances Smith Foster, *'Til Death or Distance Do Us Part: Love and Marriage in African America* (Oxford: Oxford University Press, 2010), 118, 132.

28. Ann Cvetkovich, *An Archive of Feeling: Trauma, Sexuality, and Lesbian Public Cultures* (Durham, N.C.: Duke University Press, 2003); David L. Eng and David Kazanjian, eds., *Loss: The Politics of Mourning* (Berkeley: University of California Press, 2002); Ron Eyerman, *Cultural Trauma: Slavery and the Formation of African American Identity* (Cambridge: Cambridge University Press, 2001); Hartman, *Scenes of Subjection*; Dominick LaCapra, *Writing History, Writing Trauma* (Baltimore, Md.: Johns Hopkins University Press, 2001); Kidada E. Williams, *They Left Great Marks on Me: African American Testimonies of Racial Violence from Emancipation to World War I* (New York: New York University Press, 2012). Thanks to Leslie Harris for introducing me to this literature.

CHAPTER 1. "Remarkably Muscular and Well Made" or "Covered with Ulcers"

1. Kathleen M. Brown, "'Strength of the Lion . . . Arms Like Polished Iron': Embodying Black Masculinity in an Age of Slavery and Propertied Manhood," in *New Men: Manliness in Early America*, ed. Thomas A. Foster (New York: New York University Press, 2011), 173.

2. Richard Brilliant, *Portraiture* (Cambridge, Mass.: Harvard University Press, 1991), 35; Darcy Grimaldo Grigsby, *Extremities: Painting Empire in Post-revolutionary France* (New Haven, Conn.: Yale University Press, 2002), 55; Helen D. Weston, "Representing the Right to Present: The 'Portrait of Citizen Belley, Ex-Representative of the Colonies' by A.-L. Girodet," *RES: Anthropology and Aesthetics* 26 (Autumn 1994): 83–99.

3. John Saillant, "The Black Body Erotic and the Republican Body Politic," in *Long before Stonewall: Histories of Same-Sex Sexuality in Early America*, ed. Thomas A. Foster (New York: New York University Press, 2007), 314.

4. *Colored American*, October 5, 1839, http://www.accessible-archives.com/.

5. *North Star*, November 17, 1848, http://www.accessible-archives.com/.

6. *Frederick Douglass' Paper*, June 30, 1854, 1, http://www.accessible-archives.com/.

7. Sergio Lussana, "'To See Who Was Best on the Plantation': Enslaved Fighting Contests and Masculinity in the Antebellum Plantation South," *Journal of Southern*

History 76, no. 4 (November 2010): 901–22; Lussana, *My Brother Slaves: Friendship, Masculinity, and Resistance in the Antebellum South* (Lexington: University Press of Kentucky, 2016).

8. John Andrew Jackson, *The Experience of a Slave in South Carolina* (London, 1862), 29, http://docsouth.unc.edu/fpn/jackson/jackson.html.

9. Frederick Douglass, *The Heroic Slave* (Cleveland, 1853), 179, http://docsouth.unc.edu/neh/douglass1853/douglass1853.html. See Brown, "Strength of the Lion," 189.

10. Henson and Smith quoted in Lussana, "To See Who Was Best," 913–14.

11. *Federal Writers' Project: Slave Narrative Project, Vol. 14, South Carolina, Part 2, Eddington–Hunter*, 1936, Manuscript / Mixed Material, https://www.loc.gov/item/mesn142/. See also Jeff Forret, *Slave against Slave: Plantation Violence in the Old South* (Baton Rouge: Louisiana State University Press, 2015), 247–51.

12. Maurie D. McInnis, *Slaves Waiting for Sale: Abolitionist Art and the American Slave Trade* (Chicago: University of Chicago Press, 2011), 208.

13. Edward E. Baptist, "'Cuffy,' 'Fancy Maids,' and 'One-Eyed Men': Rape, Commodification, and the Domestic Slave Trade in the United States," *American Historical Review* 106, no. 5 (2001): 1621–22. On the cultural development of the figure of the quadroon as sexual exotic other, see Emily Clark, *The Strange History of the American Quadroon: Free Women of Color in the Revolutionary Atlantic World* (Chapel Hill: University of North Carolina Press, 2013); Sarah N. Roth, *Gender and Race in Antebellum Popular Culture* (Cambridge: Cambridge University Press, 2014), 12–14.

14. Baptist, "Cuffy," 1648.

15. Lewis Bourne Papers, Louisa County, 1825, Legislative Petitions Digital Collection, Library of Virginia, Richmond.

16. Lisa Ze Winters, "'More Desultory and Unconnected Than Any Other': Geography, Desire, and Freedom in Eliza Potter's *A Hairdresser's Experience in High Life*," *American Quarterly* 61, no. 3 (September 2009): 467. For another example, see Armstrong V. Hodges, cited in Martha Hodes, *White Women, Black Men: Illicit Sex in the Nineteenth-Century South* (New Haven, Conn.: Yale University Press, 1999).

17. Letters Received by the Office of the Adjutant General, M619, RG 94, NA, reel 201, National Archives, Washington, D.C.

18. Ibid.

19. Ibid.

20. Ibid.

21. John Andrew Jackson, *The Experience of a Slave in South Carolina* (London, 1862), 12, http://docsouth.unc.edu/fpn/jackson/jackson.html#123#.

22. L. A. Chamerovzow, ed., *Slave Life in Georgia: A Narrative of the Life, Sufferings, and Escape of John Brown, a Fugitive Slave, Now in England* (London, 1855), 11, http://docsouth.unc.edu/neh/jbrown/jbrown.html.

23. Larry E. Hudson, *To Have and to Hold: Slave Work and Family Life in Antebellum South Carolina* (Athens: University of Georgia Press, 1997), 131–32.

24. Richard S. Dunn, *A Tale of Two Plantations: Slave Life and Labor in Jamaica and Virginia* (Cambridge, Mass.: Harvard University Press, 2014), 156.

25. These descriptions quoted in Dea H. Boster, *African American Slavery and*

Disability: Bodies, Property, and Power in the Antebellum South, 1800–1860 (New York: Routledge, 2013), 39.

26. Drew Gilpin Faust, *James Henry Hammond and the Old South: A Design for Mastery* (Baton Rouge: Louisiana State University Press, 1982), 72, 75–76, 81.

27. Richard S. Dunn, *A Tale of Two Plantations: Slave Life and Labor in Jamaica and Virginia* (Cambridge, Mass.: Harvard University Press, 2014), 156–57.

28. I would like to thank Jenny Reynaerts (Rijksmuseum, Amsterdam) and other participants of the "Male Bonds in Nineteenth-Century Art" conference (Museum of Fine Arts, Ghent, Belgium, May 15–16, 2018) for their insights into the presence of the marble bust and the significance of the original title for the purposes of the catalog.

29. Richard Brilliant makes no mention of the genital outline but still concludes that the overall image is one that "reveals a prejudiced attitude" by its "relaxed pose, small head, and sloping profile," all of which had "racial and ethnic" "negative implications." Richard Brilliant, *Portraiture* (Cambridge, Mass.: Harvard University Press, 1991), 35. See also Helen D. Weston, "Representing the Right to Present: The 'Portrait of Citizen Belley, Ex-Representative of the Colonies' by A.-L. Girodet," *RES: Anthropology and Aesthetics* 26 (Autumn 1994): 83–99; Darcy Grimaldo Grigsby, *Extremities: Painting Empire in Post-revolutionary France* (New Haven, Conn.: Yale University Press, 2002), 55. On Edward W. Clay's antebellum depictions of black male sexuality as "masterful and potent, lacking in inhibition," see Roth, *Gender and Race*, 70. On fetishizing black male bodies via a racist gaze, see Maurice O. Wallace, *Constructing the Black Masculine: Identity and Ideality in African American Men's Literature and Culture, 1775–1995* (Durham, N.C.: Duke University Press, 2002), chap. 1.

30. Philip D. Morgan, *Slave Counterpoint: Black Culture in the Eighteenth-Century Chesapeake and Lowcountry* (Chapel Hill: University of North Carolina Press, 1998), 398–99.

31. William Seals Brown, Courtesy of © John B. Cade Slave Narratives Collection, box 1, Location Indian Territory, folder 024, Archives and Manuscripts Department, John B. Cade Library, Southern University and A&M College, Baton Rouge, Louisiana, http://star.lib.subr.edu/starweb/l.skca-catalog/servlet.starweb?path=l.skca-catalog/skcacatalog.web.

32. Chamerovzow, *Slave Life in Georgia*, 4–5, http://docsouth.unc.edu/neh/jbrown/jbrown.html.

33. Stephanie M. H. Camp, "The Pleasures of Resistance: Enslaved Women and Body Politics in the Plantation South, 1830–1861," *Journal of Southern History* 68 (August 2002): 559.

34. Quoted in [François-Jean,] Marquis de Chastellux, *Travels in North America in the Years 1780, 1781, and 1782* (London, 1787), 83, http://books.google.com/books/about/Travels_in_North_America_in_the_years_17.html?id=tPToMGiYPn4C. See also Kirsten Fischer, *Suspect Relations: Sex, Race, and Resistance in Colonial North Carolina* (Ithaca, N.Y.: Cornell University Press, 2002), 163.

35. Winthrop Jordan, *White over Black: American Attitudes toward the Negro, 1550–1812* (Chapel Hill: University of North Carolina Press for the Institute of Early American History and Culture, 1968), 34–35.

36. Land Records (Deeds and Wills), 1677–92, part 1, c, Henrico County Microfilm Collection, reel 4, pp. 192–96, account of the Katherine Watkins case, Library of Virginia County and City Records, Richmond, microfilm. See also Warren M. Billings, ed., *The Old Dominion in the Seventeenth Century: A Documentary History of Virginia, 1606–1689* (Chapel Hill: University of North Carolina Press, 1975), 161–63; Mechal Sobel, *The World They Made Together: Black and White Values in Eighteenth-Century Virginia* (Princeton, N.J.: Princeton University Press, 1987), 149.

37. Military journal of Lt. William Feltman, June 22, 1781, Historical Society of Pennsylvania, as quoted in Jordan, *White over Black*, 159. Jordan notes that the passage was not included in the 1853 published version of the journal.

38. Charles White, *An Account of the Regular Gradation in Man* (London, 1799), 61, https://archive.org/details/b24924507. See Craig Steven Wilder, *Ebony and Ivy: Race, Slavery, and the Troubled History of America's Universities* (New York: Bloomsbury, 2013), 209.

39. Amber Jamilla Musser, *Sensational Flesh: Race, Power, and Masochism* (New York: New York University Press, 2014), 49.

40. Chamerovzow, *Slave Life in Georgia*, 4–5, http://docsouth.unc.edu/neh/jbrown/jbrown.html.

41. *Inspection and Sale of a Negro* (New York, 1854, reproduced between 1960 and 1980), http://www.loc.gov/pictures/item/98510180/.

42. See McInnis, *Slaves Waiting*, 127–30.

43. Art and Picture Collection, New York Public Library, *Dealers Inspecting a Negro at a Slave Auction in Virginia*, New York Public Library Digital Collections, http://digitalcollections.nypl.org/items/510d47e1-4092-a3d9-e040-e00a18064a99.

44. *National Era*, March 17, 1859, 1, http://www.accessible-archives.com/.

45. Gilberto Freyre, *The Masters and the Slaves: A Study in the Development of Brazilian Civilization*, trans. Samuel Putnam, abridged from the revised edition (1946; New York: Alfred A. Knopf, 1956), 379–80.

46. Walter Johnson, *Soul by Soul: Life inside the Antebellum Slave Market* (Cambridge, Mass.: Harvard University Press, 2000), 144–45.

47. Jones, "Contesting the Boundaries," 223; Hilary McD. Beckles, "White Women and Slavery in the Caribbean," *History Workshop Journal* 36 (Autumn 1993): 68.

48. Thomas Johns, in *Federal Writers' Project: Slave Narrative Project, Vol. 16, Texas, Part 2, Easter–King*, 1936, Manuscript / Mixed Material, https://www.loc.gov/item/mesn162/.

49. Isaac Williams account in *A North-Side View of Slavery*, ed. Benjamin Drew (Boston, 1856), 59–60, http://docsouth.unc.edu/neh/drew/drew.html.

50. McInnis, *Slaves Waiting*, 127; [G. H. Andrews], "Slave Auctions in Richmond, Virginia," *Illustrated London News*, February 16, 1861, 138, http://cdm15942.contentdm.oclc.org/cdm/ref/collection/p15942coll18/id/15. See also Gerald G. Eggert, "A Pennsylvanian Visits a Richmond Slave Market," Notes & Documents, *Pennsylvania Magazine of History and Biography* 109, no. 4 (October 1985): 571–76.

51. William Benemann, *Male-Male Intimacy in Early America: Beyond Romantic Friendships* (New York: Harrington Park, 2006), 68–69; Colette Colligan, "Anti-Abolition

Writes Obscenity: The English Vice, Transatlantic Slavery, and England's Obscene Print Culture," in *International Exposure: Perspectives on Modern Pornography, 1800–2000*, ed. Lisa Z. Sigel (New Brunswick, N.J.: Rutgers University Press, 2005), 67–99.

52. Karen Halttunen, "Humanitarianism and the Pornography of Pain in Anglo-American Culture," *American Historical Review* 100, no. 2 (April 1995): 325. On "white fantasies of black lives and suffering," see Marcus Wood, *Slavery, Empathy, and Pornography* (Oxford: Oxford University Press, 2002), quote from 21.

53. McInnis, *Slaves Waiting*, 128–30.

54. Charles Ball, *Fifty Years in Chains; or, The Life of an American Slave* (Indianapolis, 1859), 86–88, http://docsouth.unc.edu/fpn/ball/ball.html.

55. Henry Banks in Drew, *North-Side View*, 73–76.

56. Solomon Northrup, *Twelve Years a Slave* (London, 1853), 44, http://docsouth.unc.edu/fpn/northup/northup.html.

57. Henry Bibb, *Narrative of the Life and Adventures of Henry Bibb, an American Slave, Written by Himself* (New York, 1849), 13–15, http://docsouth.unc.edu/neh/bibb/bibb.html. See also Clifton, "Rereading Voices," 356.

58. *A Narrative of the Adventures and Escape of Moses Roper, from American Slavery* (Philadelphia, 1838), 42, http://docsouth.unc.edu/fpn/roper/roper.html.

59. Jonathan Plummer, "Dying Confession of POMP" (Newburyport, Mass., 1795), http://docsouth.unc.edu/neh/pomp/pomp.html.

60. Bibb, *Narrative*, 132, http://docsouth.unc.edu/neh/bibb/bibb.html.

61. Chamerovzow, *Slave Life in Georgia*, 62–63, http://docsouth.unc.edu/neh/jbrown/jbrown.html.

62. Bibb, *Narrative*, 132, http://docsouth.unc.edu/neh/bibb/bibb.html.

63. *The Light and the Truth of Slavery, Aaron's History* (Worcester, Mass., [1845]), 29, http://docsouth.unc.edu/neh/aaron/aaron.html.

64. John Andrew Jackson, *The Experience of a Slave in South Carolina* (London, 1862), 32, http://docsouth.unc.edu/fpn/jackson/jackson.html.

65. *Star* (Raleigh, N.C.), October 13, 1815, 3, http://www.accessible-archives.com/.

66. Dunn, *Two Plantations*, 150.

67. Bibb, *Narrative*, 103–5, http://docsouth.unc.edu/neh/bibb/bibb.html.

68. Chamerovzow, *Slave Life in Georgia*, 62–63, http://docsouth.unc.edu/neh/jbrown/jbrown.html.

69. Baltimore city register of wills (petitions), *Martin v. Johnson* (1862), MSA T621-184, Maryland State Archives, Annapolis.

70. Plummer, "Dying Confession of POMP," http://docsouth.unc.edu/neh/pomp/pomp.html.

71. *City Gazette* (Charleston, S.C.), September 3, 1812, 3.

72. Henry Banks in Drew, *North-Side View*, 73–76; see also *The Light and the Truth of History: Aaron's History* (Worcester, Mass., 1845), 29, http://docsouth.unc.edu/neh/aaron/aaron.html; and Chamerovzow, *Slave Life in Georgia*, 39, http://docsouth.unc.edu/neh/jbrown/jbrown.html.

73. *Gordon as he entered our lines. Gordon under medical inspection. Gordon in his uniform as a U.S. soldier* (1863), http://www.loc.gov/pictures/item/89716298.

74. *City Gazette*, September 3, 1812, 3, http://www.accessible-archives.com/.

75. Sharon Block, *Colonial Complexions: Race and Bodies in Eighteenth-Century America* (Philadelphia: University of Pennsylvania Press, 2018), 110, 135–36.

76. Chamerovzow, *Slave Life in Georgia*, 62, http://docsouth.unc.edu/neh/jbrown/jbrown.html.

77. *Boston News-Letter*, March 3, 1718. See Foster, *Sex*, 152.

78. SS XVIII, box 1, Magistrates and Freeholders Court, Secretary of State Collection, series 18, box 1, State Archives of North Carolina, Raleigh, Courtesy of the State Archives of North Carolina. See also Fischer, *Suspect Relations*, 185.

79. Freyre, *Masters and the Slaves*, 353.

80. Testimony of Dr. Jackson, M.D., in Lambert, *House of Commons Sessional Papers*, 82:56. See Marisa J. Fuentes, *Dispossessed Lives: Enslaved Women, Violence, and the Archive* (Philadelphia: University of Pennsylvania Press, 2016), 135.

81. Elaine Forman Crane, *Witches, Wife Beaters, and Whores: Common Law and Common Folk in Early America* (Ithaca, N.Y.: Cornell University Press, 2011), 138–39, on Cuff's case, see chapter 4; *Boston Post-Boy*, June 18, 1744, image of ad reproduced on page 139 of Crane.

82. Judith K. Schafer, "Sexual Cruelty to Slaves: The Unreported Case of *Humphreys v. Utz*," in "Symposium on the Law of Slavery: Criminal and Civil Law of Slavery," special issue, *Chicago-Kent Law Review* 68 (1992): 1515, 1313, http://scholarship.kentlaw.iit.edu/cgi/viewcontent.cgi?article=2910&context=cklawreview.

83. S. H. Melcher to Lieut. J. F. Alden, January 16, 1866, Registered Letters Received, series 3379, TN Assistant Commissioner Bureau of Refugees, Freedmen, Abandoned Lands, RG 105, National Archives, Washington, D.C. I first encountered this case as "Affidavit of a Tennessee Freedman" (September 13, 1865), Freedmen & Southern Society Project, http://www.freedmen.umd.edu/Vaughn.html.

84. Maude H. Woodfin, ed., and Marion Tinling, trans., *Another Secret Diary of William Byrd of Westover, 1739–1741* (Richmond: Dietz Press, 1942), 123; Louis B. Wright and Marion Tinling, eds., *The Secret Diary of William Byrd of Westover, 1709–1712* (Richmond: Dietz Press, 1941), 113.

85. January 28, May 26, July 23, July 30, 1756, in *In Miserable Slavery: Thomas Thistlewood in Jamaica, 1750–86*, ed. Douglas Hall (London: Macmillan, 1992), 72–73.

86. Melcher to Alden, January 16, 1866. See also "Affidavit of a Tennessee Freedman" (1865), http://www.freedmen.umd.edu/Vaughn.html.

87. Stewart case, Richmond County, divorces for surname "S," State Archives of North Carolina, Raleigh, Courtesy of the State Archives of North Carolina.

88. Chancery book, 1839–41, 364, Shelby County Historical Society, Columbiana, Ala.

89. Governor and Council (Pardon Papers) Petitions for William Holland, March 1787, box 4, folder 47, 02/46/01/003, S1061-3, Maryland State Archives, Annapolis. See Sharon Block, *Rape and Sexual Power in Early America* (Chapel Hill: University of North Carolina Press, 2006), 85.

90. *National Era*, August 4, 1853, http://www.accessible-archives.com/.

91. Winthrop D. Jordan, *White over Black: American Attitudes toward the Negro, 1550–1812* (Chapel Hill: University of North Carolina Press, 1968), 151.

92. See, for example, Leslie Harris, "From Abolitionist Amalgamators to 'Rulers of the Five Points': The Discourse of Interracial Sex and Reform in Antebellum New York City," in *Sex, Love, Race: Crossing Boundaries in North American History*, ed. Martha Hodes (New York: New York University Press, 1999), 191–212.

CHAPTER 2. "No Man Can Be Prevented from Visiting His Wife"

1. John W. Lewis, *The Life, Labors, and Travels of Elder Charles Bowles, of the Free Will Baptist Denomination* (Watertown: Ingalls & Stowell's Steam Press, 1852), 194–95, http://docsouth.unc.edu/neh/lewisjw/lewisjw.html. I use "autonomy" as a personal ideal of enslaved men. On the term as a political ideal and "not an analytical tool" for historians of slavery, see Anthony E. Kaye, "The Problem of Autonomy: Toward a Political History," in *New Directions in Slavery Studies: Commodification, Community, and Comparison*, ed. Jeff Forret and Christine E. Sears (Baton Rouge: Louisiana State University Press, 2015), 164.

2. On black masculinity and varieties of norms and ideals, see, for example, Edward E. Baptist, "The Absent Subject: African American Masculinity and Forced Migration to the Antebellum Plantation Frontier," in *Southern Manhood: Perspectives on Masculinity in the Old South*, ed. Craig Thompson Friend and Lorri Glover (Athens: University of Georgia Press, 2004), 136–73; Kathleen Brown, "'Strength of the Lion . . . Arms Like Polished Iron': Embodying Black Masculinity in an Age of Slavery and Propertied Manhood," in *New Men: Manliness in Early America*, ed. Thomas A. Foster (New York: New York University Press, 2011), 172–94; and Sergio Lussana, "'To See Who Was Best on the Plantation': Enslaved Fighting Contests and Masculinity in the Antebellum Plantation South," *Journal of Southern History* 76, no. 4 (November 2010): 901–22. On white southern manhood and romantic love, see, for example, Stephen W. Berry II, *All That Makes a Man: Love and Ambition in the Civil War South* (Oxford: Oxford University Press, 2005).

3. Daniel P. Black, *Dismantling Black Manhood: An Historical and Literary Analysis of the Legacy of Slavery* (New York: Garland Publishing, 1997), esp. chap. 5.

4. Tera W. Hunter, *Bound in Wedlock: Slave and Free Black Marriage in the Nineteenth Century* (Cambridge, Mass.: Harvard University Press, 2017), 20. On marital discord, see, for example, Randy M. Browne, *Surviving Slavery in the British Caribbean* (Philadelphia: University of Pennsylvania Press, 2017), chap. 4.

5. Kenneth E. Marshall, *Manhood Enslaved: Bondmen in Eighteenth- and Early Nineteenth-Century New Jersey* (Rochester, N.Y.: University of Rochester Press, 2011).

6. Many masters articulated what they saw as their Christian responsibility for the morality of those they enslaved. See, for example, Rebecca Fraser, *Courtship and Love among the Enslaved in North Carolina* (Jackson: University Press of Mississippi, 2007), 41–45.

7. Although marriage was often written about as a manly right denied them by

slavery, monogamy should not be conflated with marriage. Some enslaved men also practiced polygyny. Historian Terri Snyder speculates that some men may have seen it as their masculine entitlement to engage in the African practice of polygyny. Richard Dunn in his study of a Virginian plantation noted that among eighteenth-century Moravian missionaries it was "frequently reported" that enslaved men had multiple wives, engaging in polygyny. In her study of James Henry Hammond's enslaved people, Drew Faust found that monogamy was the norm among enslaved men and women but that some men did have multiple wives. Enslaved men, especially in the eighteenth century, might have followed West African courtship rituals and those infused with a variety of African traditions. See Richard S. Dunn, *A Tale of Two Plantations: Slave Life and Labor in Jamaica and Virginia* (Cambridge, Mass.: Harvard University Press, 2014), 158; Drew Gilpin Faust, *James Henry Hammond and the Old South: A Design for Mastery* (Baton Rouge: Louisiana State University Press, 1982), 84; Terri L. Snyder, *The Power to Die: Slavery and Suicide in British North America* (Chicago: University of Chicago Press, 2015), 78; James H. Sweet, "Defying Social Death: The Multiple Configurations of African Slavery in the Atlantic World," *William and Mary Quarterly* 70, no. 2 (April 2013): 251–72; Sweet, *Recreating Africa: Culture, Kinship, and Religion in the African-Portuguese World* (Chapel Hill: University of North Carolina Press, 2003); Emily West, *Chains of Love: Slave Couples in Antebellum South Carolina* (Urbana: University of Illinois Press, 2004), 19–42.

8. Warren M. Billings, ed., *The Old Dominion in the Seventeenth Century: A Documentary History of Virginia, 1606–1689* (Chapel Hill: University of North Carolina Press, 1975), 161.

9. Suffolk County Court General Sessions, 1705, Massachusetts State Archives, Boston, cited in Thomas A. Foster, *Sex and the Eighteenth-Century Man: Massachusetts and the History of Sexuality in America* (Boston: Beacon Press, 2006), 145–46.

10. Ibid.

11. Rebecca Griffin, "Courtship Contests and the Meaning of Conflict in the Folklore of Slaves," *Journal of Southern History* 71, no. 4 (November 2005): 798–99.

12. Stephanie M. H. Camp, "The Pleasures of Resistance: Enslaved Women and Body Politics in the Plantation South, 1830–1861," *Journal of Southern History* 68 (August 2002): 540, 534. See also Camp, *Closer to Freedom: Enslaved Women and Everyday Resistance in the Plantation South* (Chapel Hill: University of North Carolina Press, 2004).

13. Quoted in Rebecca J. Griffin, "'Goin' Back Over There to See That Girl': Competing Social Spaces in the Lives of the Enslaved in Antebellum North Carolina," *Slavery and Abolition* 25, no. 1 (April 2004): 107.

14. Ibid., 109. Stephanie Camp shows that socializing and dancing were part of an autonomous world of slave courtship and heterosocializing. Camp, "The Pleasures of Resistance."

15. Herbert G. Gutman, *The Black Family in Slavery and Freedom, 1750–1925* (New York: Pantheon Books, 1976), 351; Roi Ottley and W. J. Weatherby, eds., *The Negro in New York: An Informal Social History* (New York: New York Public Library, 1967), 1–8.

16. Gutman, *The Black Family*, 350; *Collections of the Massachusetts Historical Society*, 5th series, III (1877): 432–37. See also John Wood Sweet, *Bodies Politic: Negotiating Race in the American North, 1730–1830* (Baltimore, Md.: Johns Hopkins University Press, 2003), 157–58; Foster, *Sex*, 20–21; Hunter, *Bound in Wedlock*, 66–67.

17. *Freedom's Journal*, April 6, 1827, 1, https://web.archive.org/web/20150211175514/http://www.wisconsinhistory.org/pdfs/la/FreedomsJournal/v1n04.pdf.

18. Hunter, *Bound in Wedlock*, 34.

19. Brenda E. Stevenson, *Life in Black and White: Family and Community in the Slave South* (New York: Oxford University Press, 1997), 231.

20. Henry Bibb, *Narrative of the Life and Adventures of Henry Bibb, an American Slave, Written by Himself* (New York, 1849), 192, http://docsouth.unc.edu/neh/bibb/bibb.html.

21. On *The Hunted Slaves*, see Maurie D. McInnis, *Slaves Waiting for Sale: Abolitionist Art and the American Slave Trade* (Chicago: University of Chicago Press, 2011), 204–9.

22. Charles Stearns, *Narrative of Henry Fox Brown, Who Escaped from Slavery Enclosed in a Box 3 Feet Long and 2 Wide. Written from a Statement of Facts Made by Himself* (Boston: Brown & Stearns, 1849), 22–23, http://docsouth.unc.edu/neh/boxbrown/boxbrown.html.

23. Daina Ramey Berry, *"Swing the Sickle for the Harvest Is Ripe": Gender and Slavery in Antebellum Georgia* (Urbana: University of Illinois Press, 2010), 77. On the importance of family units for enslaved people, see Frances Smith Foster, *'Til Death or Distance Do Us Part: Love and Marriage in African America* (Oxford: Oxford University Press, 2010); Rebecca Fraser, *Courtship and Love among the Enslaved in North Carolina* (Jackson: University Press of Mississippi, 2007); Larry E. Hudson, *To Have and to Hold: Slave Work and Family Life in Antebellum South Carolina* (Athens: University of Georgia Press, 1997), esp. chap. 4, 141–76; Tera W. Hunter, *Bound in Wedlock: Slave and Free Black Marriage in the Nineteenth Century* (Cambridge, Mass.: Harvard University Press, 2017); West, *Chains of Love*.

24. Berry, *Swing the Sickle*, 81, quoting from Albert, *The House of Bondage* (1890), 108.

25. George P. Rawick, ed., *The American Slave: A Composite Autobiography* (Westport, Conn.: Greenwood Press, 1972–79), vol. 7, 161.

26. Hall, *In Miserable Slavery*, 205, 296–97.

27. Rosa Starke, in *Federal Writers' Project: Slave Narrative Project, Vol. 14, South Carolina, Part 1, Abrams–Durant*, 148, 1936, Manuscript / Mixed Material, https://www.loc.gov/item/mesn141/.

28. Charles Ball, *Fifty Years in Chains; or, The Life of an American Slave* (New York, 1869), 28–29, http://docsouth.unc.edu/fpn/ball/ball.html.

29. December 11 and 14, 1774, and December 6, 1777, in Hall, *In Miserable Slavery*, 205, 253.

30. L. A. Chamerovzow, ed., *Slave Life in Georgia: A Narrative of the Life, Sufferings, and Escape of John Brown, a Fugitive Slave, Now in England* (London, 1855), 62–63, http://docsouth.unc.edu/neh/jbrown/jbrown.html.

31. William Byrd, February 22, 1709, June 17, 1710, May 22, 1712, all in *Documenting Intimate Matters: Primary Sources for a History of Sexuality in America*, ed. Thomas A. Foster (Chicago: University of Chicago Press, 2012), 19–21.

32. Thistlewood, March 16, 1752, in Hall, *In Miserable Slavery*, 44.

33. Drew Gilpin Faust, *James Henry Hammond and the Old South: A Design for Mastery* (Baton Rouge: Louisiana State University Press, 1982), 85.

34. Bibb, *Narrative*, 36–37, http://docsouth.unc.edu/neh/bibb/bibb.html.

35. Heather Andrea Williams, *Help Me to Find My People: The African American Search for Family Lost in Slavery* (Chapel Hill: University of North Carolina Press, 2012), 57.

36. James Mellon, ed., *Bullwhip Days: The Slaves Remember* (New York: Weidenfeld & Nicolson, 1988), 296.

37. Ambrose Douglass, in *Federal Writers' Project: Slave Narrative Project, Vol. 3, Florida, Anderson–Wilson with Combined Interviews of Others*, 101, 1936, Manuscript / Mixed Material, https://www.loc.gov/item/mesn030/.

38. John Andrew Jackson, *The Experience of a Slave in South Carolina* (London: Passmore & Alabaster, 1862), 21–22, http://docsouth.unc.edu/fpn/jackson/jackson.html.

39. Ibid., 29–30.

40. Ibid., 29.

41. Chamerovzow, *Slave Life in Georgia*, 37–38, http://docsouth.unc.edu/neh/jbrown/jbrown.html.

42. Ibid., 38–39.

43. Ibid., 39.

44. Ibid., 40.

45. Ibid., 40–41.

46. Ibid., 43.

47. Foster, *Sex*, 21–22.

48. Bibb, *Narrative*, 40, http://docsouth.unc.edu/neh/bibb/bibb.html.

49. May 6, 1771, in Hall, *In Miserable Slavery*, 181–82.

50. Hunter, *Bound in Wedlock*, 23.

51. Black, *Dismantling Black Manhood*, 169.

52. Camp, *Closer to Freedom*, 37, 45, 123.

53. Jackson, *The Experience*, 29–30.

54. Snyder, *Power to Die*, 131.

55. *The Dying Negro, a Poem* (London, 1775), http://www.brycchancarey.com/slavery/dying.htm.

56. Snyder, *The Power to Die*, 52, quote at 78.

57. William Wells Brown, *Narrative of William W. Brown* (Boston, 1847), 85–86, http://docsouth.unc.edu/neh/brown47/brown47.html.

58. Ibid., 86–87.

59. Ibid., 87.

60. Ibid., 88.

61. Ibid.

CHAPTER 3. "Just Like Raising Stock and Mating It"

1. Ambrose Douglass, in *Federal Writers' Project: Slave Narrative Project, Vol. 3, Florida, Anderson–Wilson with Combined Interviews of Others*, 101, 1936, Manuscript / Mixed Material, https://www.loc.gov/item/mesn030/.

2. Richard Sutch, "The Breeding of Slaves for Sale and the Westward Expansion of Slavery, 1850–1860," in *Race and Slavery in the Western Hemisphere: Quantitative Studies*, ed. Stanley L. Engerman and Eugene D. Genovese (Princeton, N.J.: Princeton University Press, 1975), 173–210.

3. Sutch, "The Breeding of Slaves," 191.

4. Robert William Fogel and Stanley L. Engerman, *Time on the Cross: The Economics of American Negro Slavery* (Boston: Little, Brown and Company, 1974), 78–79.

5. Richard G. Lowe and Randolph B. Campbell, "The Slave-Breeding Hypothesis: A Demographic Comment on the 'Buying' and 'Selling' States," *Journal of Southern History* 42 (August 1976): 401–12.

6. David Lowenthal and Colin G. Clarke, "Slave-Breeding in Barbuda: The Past of a Negro Myth," in *Comparative Perspectives on Slavery in New World Plantation Societies*, ed. Vera Rubin and Arthur Tuden (New York: New York Academy of Sciences, 1977), 510–35.

7. Richard S. Dunn, *A Tale of Two Plantations: Slave Life and Labor in Jamaica and Virginia* (Cambridge, Mass.: Harvard University Press, 2014), 311.

8. Even scholars who examine the implications of the practice generally conclude it was rare: "Not many planters tried to breed slaves through forced pairings" and "forced pairings were uncommon," concludes Marie Jenkins Schwartz, *Birthing a Slave: Motherhood and Medicine in the Antebellum South* (Cambridge, Mass.: Harvard University Press, 2006), 25, 22.

9. One recent nonacademic book takes slave breeding as central to slavery, thus virtually renaming the institution the "slave-breeding industry": "*Every* farm where the enslaved had children was a slave-breeding farm, if only because every newborn slave child increased an estate's net worth." Ned and Constance Sublette, *The American Slave Coast: A History of the Slave-Breeding Industry* (Chicago: Chicago Review Press, 2016), xiii, 31. See also the collection of WPA interviews compiled by Donna Wyant Howell, *I Was a Slave: Book 4: The Breeding of Slaves* (Washington, D.C.: American Legacy Books, 1996), which contains several examples of "male breeders."

10. Fogel and Engerman, *Time on the Cross*, 127.

11. Jones, *Labor of Love*, 34.

12. Schwartz, *Birthing a Slave*, 10. See also bell hooks, *Ain't I a Woman: Black Women and Feminism* (1981; New York: Routledge, 2015); Jacqueline Jones, *Labor of Love, Labor of Sorrow: Black Women, Work, and the Family from Slavery to the Present* (New York: Basic Books, 1985), 11–43; Sasha Turner, *Contested Bodies: Pregnancy, Childrearing, and Slavery in Jamaica* (Philadelphia: University of Pennsylvania Press, 2017), chap. 2.

13. His figures seem to undercount the total incidence, finding only seven examples of masters renting a man (or men) from another plantation and sixteen cases of masters

using enslaved men to impregnate through visiting or polygamy, and he does not distinguish between men and women for other examples of forced pairing. He also conceded that "reticence" on the part of former slaves to speak openly about such trauma "likely . . . caused some underreporting" in the interviews. Paul D. Escott, *Slavery Remembered: A Record of Twentieth-Century Slave Narratives* (Chapel Hill: University of North Carolina Press, 1979), 45.

14. Gregory D. Smithers, *Slave Breeding: Sex, Violence, and Memory in African American History* (Gainesville: University Press of Florida, 2012). Other recent books also focus almost exclusively on enslaved women. See, for example, Eddie Donoghue, *Black Breeding Machines: The Breeding of Negro Slaves in the Diaspora* (Bloomington, Ind.: AuthorHouse, 2008). In a notable exception, Daina Berry examines how "forced breeding" affected "familial connections." Berry notes that southern planters referred to slave breeding in agricultural journals, mentioning the same practices they engaged in with animals. "Reproductive abuse," Berry argues, affected both men and women. Daina Ramey Berry, *"Swing the Sickle for the Harvest Is Ripe": Gender and Slavery in Antebellum Georgia* (Urbana: University of Illinois Press, 2007), 77, 79. Gregory D. Smithers's examination of the memory of forced reproduction captures its larger, post-slavery significance, noting that since the nineteenth century "slave breeding became critical to historical explanations of the racial and sexual objectification of black bodies; of the distortion of ideals regarding gender roles between black men and black women; of the fragile nature of black family life; and of the need for African Americans to craft narratives that make sense of the brutal ways in which life can be conceived and snuffed out—for instance, through interracial rape and lynchings—in a racist society." Smithers does an excellent examination of the meaning and resonance of terms like "stud," "buck," and "wench." He concludes that slaves used the words as agricultural metaphors and sexualized terms of women, respectively, of the nineteenth and early twentieth centuries. Smithers rightly notes that scholars "define slave breeding in much narrower terms" than he does, leading to their conclusions that it did not occur. Smithers, *Slave Breeding*, 10, 3.

15. Smithers, *Slave Breeding*, 103.

16. West, *Chains of Love*, 26.

17. Isaac Williams, *Sunshine and Shadow of Slave Life* (East Saginaw, Mich., 1885), 6, http://docsouth.unc.edu/neh/iwilliams/iwilliams.html.

18. Jennifer L. Morgan, *Laboring Women: Reproduction and Gender in New World Slavery* (Philadelphia: University of Pennsylvania Press, 2004), 83.

19. John W. Blassingame, *The Slave Community: Plantation Life in the Antebellum South*, rev. and enlarged ed. (1972; New York: Oxford University Press, 1979), 151.

20. Thelma Jennings, "'Us Colored Women Had to Go Though A Plenty': Sexual Exploitation of African-American Slave Women," *Journal of Women's History* 1, no. 3 (1990): 45–74, 46.

21. Ibid., 50. See also, for example, Berry, *Swing the Sickle*, 76–103.

22. Ida Blackshear Hutchinson, in *Federal Writers' Project: Slave Narrative Project, Vol. 2, Arkansas, Part 3, Gadson–Isom*, 374, 1936, Manuscript / Mixed Material, https://www.loc.gov/item/mesn023/.

23. John Josselyn, *An Account of Two Voyages to New England* (Boston, 1638, 1865), 24, http://archive.org/details/accountoftwovoyaoojoss. On the woman's "rape" by this enslaved man, see Wendy Anne Warren, "'The Cause of Her Grief': The Rape of a Slave in Early New England," *Journal of American History* 93, no. 4 (March 2007): 1031–49.

24. Morgan, *Laboring Women*, 91, 100–101.

25. Planters' manuals discussed the value in reproduction. See *Practical Rules for the Management and Medical Treatment of Negro Slaves in the Sugar Colonies* (London: J. Barfield, 1811; repr., Freeport, N.Y.: Books for Libraries, 1971), 9–10, 18, 131, 133 ("it is much cheaper to breed than to purchase" [131]).

26. See Steven Deyle, *Carry Me Back: The Domestic Slave Trade in American Life* (Oxford: Oxford University Press, 2005), 46–49. See also Stanley, "Slave Breeding."

27. Thomas Weld, *American Slavery as It Is: Testimony of a Thousand Witnesses* (New York: American Anti-slavery Society, 1839), 182, http://docsouth.unc.edu/neh/weld/weld.html#p182.

28. Ibid., 183.

29. Donoghue, *Black Breeding*, 347–48. See also Barbara Bush, "Hard Labor: Women, Childbirth, and Resistance in British Caribbean Slave Societies," in *More Than Chattel: Black Women and Slavery in the Americas*, ed. David Barry Gaspar and Darlene Clark Hine (Bloomington: Indiana University Press, 1996), 198–201.

30. William J. Anderson, *Life and Narrative of William J. Anderson* (Chicago, 1857), 24, https://docsouth.unc.edu/neh/andersonw/andersonw.html.

31. Henry Bibb, *Narrative of the Life and Adventures of Henry Bibb, an American Slave, Written by Himself* (New York, 1849), 40, http://docsouth.unc.edu/neh/bibb/bibb.html.

32. David W. Blight, ed., *Narrative of the Life of Frederick Douglass, an American Slave, Written by Himself*, 2nd ed. (New York: Bedford, 2003), 82–83.

33. Quoted in Smithers, *Slave Breeding*, 11n29; Christopher Morris, *Becoming Southern: The Evolution of a Way of Life, Warren County and Vicksburg, Mississippi, 1770–1860* (New York: Oxford University Press, 1995), 71.

34. Octavia V. Rogers Albert, *The House of Bondage or Charlotte Brooks and Other Slaves* (New York: Oxford University Press, 1988), 107.

35. Tom Douglas, in *Federal Writers' Project: Slave Narrative Project, Vol. 2, Arkansas, Part 2, Cannon–Evans*, 195, 1936, Manuscript / Mixed Material, https://www.loc.gov/item/mesn022/. See also numerous examples in *Opinions Regarding Slavery*, http://star.lib.subr.edu/star/findingaids/Opinions.xml, including Maria Carter, Georgia; Louis Williams, Louisiana; Henery Hickmon, Missouri; Mr. P. T. Harper, North Carolina; Mrs. Minnerva Handley, Texas; William Seals Brown, Indian Territory; David Walker, Kentucky, http://star.lib.subr.edu/starweb/l.skca-catalog/servlet.starweb?path=l.skca-catalog/skcacatalog.web#.

36. *Federal Writers' Project: Slave Narrative Project, Vol. 2, Arkansas, Part 5, McClendon–Prayer*, 181, 1936, Manuscript / Mixed Material, https://www.loc.gov/item/mesn025/.

37. Willie Williams, in *Federal Writers' Project: Slave Narrative Project, Vol. 16, Texas, Part 4, Sanco–Young*, 1936, Manuscript / Mixed Material, https://www.loc.gov/item

/mesn164/. See also Willie Williams, in *The American Slave: A Composite Autobiography*, ed. George P. Rawick (Westport, Conn.: Greenwood Press, 1972–79), Supplemental Series 2, vol. 10, pt. 9, p. 4158; Schwartz, *Birthing a Slave*, 24.

38. J. M. Parker, in *Federal Writers' Project: Slave Narrative Project, Vol. 2, Arkansas, Part 5, McClendon–Prayer*, 243, 1936, Manuscript / Mixed Material, https://www.loc.gov/item/mesn025/.

39. Amsy O. Alexander, in *Federal Writers' Project: Slave Narrative Project, Vol. 2, Arkansas, Part 1, Abbott–Byrd*, November–December 25, 1936, Manuscript / Mixed Material, https://www.loc.gov/item/mesn021/.

40. Ida Blackshear Hutchinson, in *Federal Writers' Project: Slave Narrative Project, Vol. 2, Arkansas, Part 3, Gadson–Isom*, 370, 1936, Manuscript / Mixed Material, https://www.loc.gov/item/mesn023/.

41. Barney Stone, in *Federal Writers' Project: Slave Narrative Project, Vol. 5, Indiana, Arnold–Woodson*, 186, 1936, Manuscript / Mixed Material, https://www.loc.gov/item/mesn050/.

42. Sarah Ford, in *Federal Writers' Project: Slave Narrative Project, Vol. 16, Texas, Part 2, Easter–King*, 42, 1936, Manuscript / Mixed Material, https://www.loc.gov/item/mesn162/.

43. Carl F. Hall, in *Federal Writers' Project: Slave Narrative Project, Vol. 7, Kentucky, Bogie–Woods with Combined Interviews of Others*, 72, 1936, Manuscript / Mixed Material, https://www.loc.gov/item/mesn070/.

44. *Federal Writers' Project: Slave Narrative Project, Vol. 2, Arkansas, Part 6, Quinn–Tuttle*, 243, 1936, Manuscript / Mixed Material, https://www.loc.gov/item/mesn026/.

45. Ibid., 73.

46. Lulu Wilson, *Federal Writers' Project: Slave Narrative Project, Vol. 16, Texas, Part 4, Sanco–Young*, 1936, Manuscript / Mixed Material, https://www.loc.gov/item/mesn164/. Similar interviews refer to "breeding" women as a type of enslaved person. See, for example, Josephine Howell, in *Federal Writers' Project: Slave Narrative Project, Vol. 2, Arkansas, Part 3, Gadson–Isom*, 339, 1936, Manuscript / Mixed Material,http://www.loc.gov/item/mesn023/; *Federal Writers' Project: Slave Narrative Project, Vol. 2, Arkansas, Part 2, Cannon–Evans*, 132, 1936, Manuscript / Mixed Material, https://www.loc.gov/item/mesn022/; Alice Wright, in *Federal Writers' Project: Slave Narrative Project, Vol. 2, Arkansas, Part 7, Vaden–Young*, 246, 1936, Manuscript / Mixed Material, https://www.loc.gov/item/mesn027/.

47. See, for example, Robert W. Slenes, "Black Homes, White Homilies: Perceptions of the Slave Family and of Slave Women in Nineteenth-Century Brazil," in *More Than Chattel: Black Women and Slavery in the Americas*, ed. David Barry Gaspar and Darlene Clark Hine (Bloomington: Indiana University Press, 1996), 131.

48. Thomas Hall, in Rawick, *The American Slave*, North Carolina Narratives, vol. 14, pt. 1, p. 360.

49. James Mellon, ed., *Bullwhip Days: The Slaves Remember* (New York: Weidenfeld & Nicolson, 1988), 296.

50. Carl F. Hall, in *Federal Writers' Project: Slave Narrative Project, Vol. 7, Kentucky,*

Bogie–Woods with Combined Interviews of Others, 72, 1936, Manuscript / Mixed Material, https://www.loc.gov/item/mesn070/.

51. Katie Darling, in *Federal Writers' Project: Slave Narrative Project, Vol. 16, Texas, Part 1, Adams–Duhon*, 279, 1936, Manuscript / Mixed Material, https://www.loc.gov/item/mesn161/.

52. Frances Anne Kemble, *Journal of a Residence on a Georgian Plantation in 1838–1839*, ed. John A. Scott (London, 1863; Athens: University of Georgia Press, 1984), 95–96.

53. Eliza Jones, in *Federal Writers' Project: Slave Narrative Project, Vol. 2, Arkansas, Part 4, Jackson–Lynch*, 143, 1936, Manuscript / Mixed Material, https://www.loc.gov/item/mesn024/.

54. Thomas Johns, in *Federal Writers' Project: Slave Narrative Project, Vol. 16, Texas, Part 2, Easter–King*, 204, 1936, Manuscript / Mixed Material, https://www.loc.gov/item/mesn162/.

55. Willie McCullough, in *Federal Writers' Project: Slave Narrative Project, Vol. 11, North Carolina, Part 2, Jackson–Yellerday*, 78, 1936, Manuscript / Mixed Material, https://www.loc.gov/item/mesn112/.

56. Sam Everett, in *Federal Writers' Project: Slave Narrative Project, Vol. 3, Florida, Anderson–Wilson with Combined Interviews of Others*, 127, 1936, Manuscript / Mixed Material, https://www.loc.gov/item/mesn030/.

57. Dora Jerman, in *Federal Writers' Project: Slave Narrative Project, Vol. 2, Arkansas, Part 4, Jackson–Lynch*, 50, 1936, Manuscript / Mixed Material, https://www.loc.gov/item/mesn024/.

58. Cornelia Andrews, in Rawick, *The American Slave*, North Carolina Narratives, vol. 14, pt. 1, p. 30.

59. Carl F. Hall, in *Federal Writers' Project: Slave Narrative Project, Vol. 7, Kentucky, Bogie–Woods with Combined Interviews of Others*, 72, 1936, Manuscript / Mixed Material, https://www.loc.gov/item/mesn070/.

60. G. W. Hawkins, in *Federal Writers' Project: Slave Narrative Project, Vol. 2, Arkansas, Part 3, Gadson–Isom*, 218, 1936, Manuscript / Mixed Material, https://www.loc.gov/item/mesn023/.

61. Julia Cole, in *Federal Writers' Project: Slave Narrative Project, Vol. 4, Georgia, Part 1, Adams–Furr*, 228, 1936, Manuscript / Mixed Material, https://www.loc.gov/item/mesn041/.

62. John R. Cox, in *Federal Writers' Project: Slave Narrative Project, Vol. 7, Kentucky, Bogie–Woods with Combined Interviews of Others*, 34, 1936, Manuscript / Mixed Material, https://www.loc.gov/item/mesn070/.

63. F. Roy Johnson, "A Sampling of Eastern Oral Folk Humor," *North Carolina Folklore Journal* 23 (1975): 5, https://archive.org/stream/northcarolinafol2324nort/northcarolinafol2324nort_djvu.txt. See also Bill Cecil-Fronsman, *Common Whites: Class and Culture in Antebellum North Carolina* (Lexington: University Press of Kentucky, 1992), 75.

64. Quoted in Charles L. Perdue Jr., Thomas E. Barden, and Robert K. Phillips, eds.,

Weevils in the Wheat: Interviews with Virginia Ex-slaves (Charlottesville: University of Virginia Press, 1976), 291.

65. Willie McCullough, in *Federal Writers' Project: Slave Narrative Project, Vol. 11, North Carolina, Part 2, Jackson–Yellerday*, 82, 1936, Manuscript / Mixed Material, https://www.loc.gov/item/mesn112/. For other examples, see Bill Simms, *Federal Writers' Project: Slave Narrative Project, Vol. 6, Kansas, Holbert–Williams*, 12, 1936, Manuscript / Mixed Material, https://www.loc.gov/item/mesn060/; Julia Malone, *Federal Writers' Project: Slave Narrative Project, Vol. 16, Texas, Part 3, Lewis–Ryles*, 44, 1936, Manuscript / Mixed Material, https://www.loc.gov/item/mesn163/; William Mathews, *Federal Writers' Project: Slave Narrative Project, Vol. 16, Texas, Part 3, Lewis–Ryles*, 69, 1936, Manuscript / Mixed Material, https://www.loc.gov/item/mesn163/.

66. Ida Blackshear Hutchinson, in *Federal Writers' Project: Slave Narrative Project, Vol. 2, Arkansas, Part 3, Gadson–Isom*, 370, 1936, Manuscript / Mixed Material, https://www.loc.gov/item/mesn023/.

67. Jeptha Choice, in *Federal Writers' Project: Slave Narrative Project, Vol. 16, Texas, Part 1, Adams–Duhon*, 218, 1936, Manuscript / Mixed Material, https://www.loc.gov/item/mesn161/.

68. Quoted in Jennings, "Us Colored Women," 50.

69. Henry Nelson, in *Federal Writers' Project: Slave Narrative Project, Vol. 2, Arkansas, Part 5, McClendon–Prayer*, 197, 1936, Manuscript / Mixed Material, https://www.loc.gov/item/mesn025/.

70. G. W. Hawkins, in *Federal Writers' Project: Slave Narrative Project, Vol. 2, Arkansas, Part 3, Gadson–Isom*, 218, 1936, Manuscript / Mixed Material, https://www.loc.gov/item/mesn023/.

71. Fred Brown, in *Federal Writers' Project: Slave Narrative Project, Vol. 16, Texas, Part 1, Adams–Duhon*, 158, 1936, Manuscript / Mixed Material, https://www.loc.gov/item/mesn161/.

72. Katie Darling, in ibid., 279.

73. Lulu Wilson, in *Federal Writers' Project: Slave Narrative Project, Vol. 16, Texas, Part 4, Sanco–Young*, 1, 1936, Manuscript / Mixed Material, https://www.loc.gov/item/mesn164/. Similar interviews refer to "breeding" women as a type of enslaved person. See, for example, Josephine Howell, in *Federal Writers' Project: Slave Narrative Project, Vol. 2, Arkansas, Part 3, Gadson–Isom*, 339, 1936, Manuscript / Mixed Material, https://www.loc.gov/item/mesn023/; Alice Wright, in *Federal Writers' Project: Slave Narrative Project, Vol. 2, Arkansas, Part 7, Vaden–Young*, 246, 1936, Manuscript / Mixed Material, https://www.loc.gov/item/mesn027/.

74. Mary Reynolds, in *Federal Writers' Project: Slave Narrative Project, Vol. 16, Texas, Part 3, Lewis–Ryles*, 236, 1936, Manuscript / Mixed Material, https://www.loc.gov/item/mesn163/.

75. Benjamin Russell, in *Federal Writers' Project: Slave Narrative Project, Vol. 14, South Carolina, Part 4, Raines–Young*, 53, 1936, Manuscript / Mixed Material, https://www.loc.gov/item/mesn144/.

76. Bill Simms, *Federal Writers' Project: Slave Narrative Project, Vol. 6, Kansas,*

Holbert–Williams, 12, 1936, Manuscript / Mixed Material, https://www.loc.gov/item/mesn060/.

77. Ibid.

78. Thomas Johns, in *Federal Writers' Project: Slave Narrative Project, Vol. 16, Texas, Part 2, Easter–King*, 203, 1936, Manuscript / Mixed Material, https://www.loc.gov/item/mesn162/.

79. Howell, *I Was a Slave*, 11.

80. Cornelia Andrews, in Rawick, *The American Slave*, North Carolina Narratives, vol. 14, pt. 1, p. 31.

81. Willie Williams, in *Federal Writers' Project: Slave Narrative Project, Vol. 16, Texas, Part 4, Sanco–Young*, 1936, Manuscript / Mixed Material, https://www.loc.gov/item/mesn164/.

82. Irene Robertson, in Rawick, *The American Slave*, vol. 10, pt. 6, p. 223. See also Schwartz, *Birthing a Slave*, 24.

83. Jones, "Contesting the Boundaries," 223; Hilary McD. Beckles, "White Women and Slavery in the Caribbean," *History Workshop Journal* 36 (Autumn 1993): 68; Gilberto Freyre, *The Masters and the Slaves: A Study in the Development of Brazilian Civilization*, trans. Samuel Putnam, abridged from the revised edition (1946; New York: Alfred A. Knopf, 1956), 379–80.

84. Henery Hickman, Courtesy of © John B. Cade Slave Narratives Collection, box 1, Location Missouri, folder 078, Archives and Manuscripts Department, John B. Cade Library, Southern University and A&M College, Baton Rouge, Louisiana, http://star.lib.subr.edu/starweb/l.skca-catalog/servlet.starweb?path=l.skca-catalog/skcacatalog.web.

85. On slavery and childhood, see Wilma King, *Stolen Childhood: Slave Youth in Nineteenth-Century America* (Bloomington: Indiana University Press, 1995). See Rose Williams for an example of a sixteen-year-old girl being forcibly paired with an enslaved man.

86. Jordan Smith, in *Federal Writers' Project: Slave Narrative Project, Vol. 16, Texas, Part 4, Sanco–Young*, 37–38, 1936, Manuscript / Mixed Material, https://www.loc.gov/item/mesn164/.

87. George Austin, in Rawick, *The American Slave*, Supplemental Series 2, vol. 2, pt. 1, pp. 105–6. See also Schwartz, *Birthing a Slave*, 24.

88. Fred Brown, in *Federal Writers' Project: Slave Narrative Project, Vol. 16, Texas, Part 1, Adams–Duhon*, 158, 1936, Manuscript / Mixed Material, https://www.loc.gov/item/mesn161/.

89. J. W. Whitfield, in *Federal Writers' Project: Slave Narrative Project, Vol. 2, Arkansas, Part 7, Vaden–Young*, 139, 1936, Manuscript / Mixed Material, https://www.loc.gov/item/mesn027/.

90. Ida Blackshear Hutchinson, in *Federal Writers' Project: Slave Narrative Project, Vol. 2, Arkansas, Part 3, Gadson–Isom*, 374, 1936, Manuscript / Mixed Material, https://www.loc.gov/item/mesn023/.

91. Blassingame, *The Slave Community*; Frances Smith Foster, *'Til Death or Distance*

Do Us Part: Love and Marriage in African America (New York: Oxford University Press, 2010); Herbert G. Gutman, *The Black Family in Slavery and Freedom, 1750–1925* (New York: Pantheon Books, 1976); Ann Patton Malone, *Sweet Chariot: Slave Family and Household Structure in Nineteenth-Century Louisiana* (Chapel Hill: University of North Carolina Press, 1992), 5, 14; Philip D. Morgan, *Slave Counterpart: Black Culture in the Eighteenth-Century Chesapeake and Lowcountry* (Chapel Hill: University of North Carolina Press, 1998), 501; Emily West, *Chains of Love: Slave Couples in Antebellum South Carolina* (Urbana: University of Illinois Press, 2004).

92. Malone, *Sweet Chariot*, 2.

93. West, *Chains of Love*, 39.

94. Stevenson, *Life in Black and White*, 212.

95. Blassingame, *The Slave Community*, 149–91.

96. Heather Andrea Williams, *Help Me to Find My People: The African American Search for Family Lost in Slavery* (Chapel Hill: University of North Carolina Press, 2012), 32. On family bonds, see also Foster, *'Til Death*; Gutman, *The Black Family*; and West, *Chains of Love*.

97. Williams, *Help Me*, 53, 55.

98. Gomez, *Exchanging*, 239, 40, 41.

99. Ibid., 50.

100. See, for example, Daniel P. Black, *Dismantling Black Manhood: An Historical and Literary Analysis of the Legacy of Slavery* (New York: Garland, 1997); Gutman, *The Black Family*.

101. Jacob Manson, in *Federal Writers' Project: Slave Narrative Project, Vol. 11, North Carolina, Part 2, Jackson–Yellerday*, 98, 1936, Manuscript / Mixed Material, https://www.loc.gov/item/mesn112/.

102. Jennings, "Us Colored Women," 51.

103. Willie Williams, in *Federal Writers' Project: Slave Narrative Project, Vol. 16, Texas, Part 4, Sanco–Young*, 1936, Manuscript / Mixed Material, https://www.loc.gov/item/mesn164/.

104. George Austin, in Rawick, *The American Slave*, Supplemental Series 2, vol. 2, pt. 1, pp. 105–6. See also Schwartz, *Birthing a Slave*, 24.

105. Ida Blackshear Hutchinson, in *Federal Writers' Project: Slave Narrative Project, Vol. 2, Arkansas, Part 3, Gadson–Isom*, 370, 1936, Manuscript / Mixed Material, https://www.loc.gov/item/mesn023/.

106. Lewis Jones, in *Federal Writers' Project: Slave Narrative Project, Vol. 16, Texas, Part 2, Easter–King*, 237, 1936, Manuscript / Mixed Material, https://www.loc.gov/item/mesn162/.

107. Jeptha Choice, in *Federal Writers' Project: Slave Narrative Project, Vol. 16, Texas, Part 1, Adams–Duhon*, 218, 1936, Manuscript / Mixed Material, https://www.loc.gov/item/mesn161/.

108. Quoted in Perdue, Barden, and Phillips, *Weevils in the Wheat*, 291.

109. Oscar Felix Junell, in *Federal Writers' Project: Slave Narrative Project, Vol. 2, Arkansas, Part 4, Jackson–Lynch*, 174, 1936, Manuscript / Mixed Material, https://www.loc.gov/item/mesn024/.

110. Ida Blackshear Hutchinson, in *Federal Writers' Project: Slave Narrative Project, Vol. 2, Arkansas, Part 3, Gadson–Isom*, 370, 1936, Manuscript / Mixed Material, https://www.loc.gov/item/mesn023/.

111. Willie Williams, in *Slave Narratives: A Folk History of Slavery in the United States from Interviews with Former Slaves*, vol. 16, Texas Narratives, pt. 4, www.gutenberg.org.

112. George Austin, in Rawick, *The American Slave*, Supplemental Series 2, vol. 2, pt. 1, pp. 105–6. See also Schwartz, *Birthing a Slave*, 24.

113. Irene Robertson, in Rawick, *The American Slave*, vol. 10, pt. 6, p. 223. See also Schwartz, *Birthing a Slave*, 24.

114. Daina Ramey Berry, *"Swing the Sickle for the Harvest Is Ripe": Gender and Slavery in Antebellum Georgia* (Urbana: University of Illinois Press, 2007), 53, 60–61.

115. Emma Barr, in *Federal Writers' Project: Slave Narrative Project, Vol. 2, Arkansas, Part 1, Abbott–Byrd*, November–December 1936, Manuscript / Mixed Material, http://www.loc.gov/item/mesn021/.

116. George Austin, in Rawick, *The American Slave*, Supplemental Series 2, vol. 2, pt. 1, pp. 105–6. See also Schwartz, *Birthing a Slave*, 24.

117. Irene Robertson, in Rawick, *The American Slave*, vol. 10, pt. 6, p. 223. See also Schwartz, *Birthing a Slave*, 24.

118. Julia Cole, in *Federal Writers' Project: Slave Narrative Project, Vol. 4, Georgia, Part 1, Adams–Furr*, 228, 1936, Manuscript / Mixed Material, https://www.loc.gov/item/mesn041/.

119. George P. Rawick, ed., *The American Slave: A Composite Autobiography*, Texas Narratives, Supplemental Series 2, vol. 2, pt. 1 (Westport, Conn.: Greenwood Press, 1979), 309.

120. Barney Stone, in *Federal Writers' Project: Slave Narrative Project, Vol. 5, Indiana, Arnold–Woodson*, 186, 1936, Manuscript / Mixed Material, https://www.loc.gov/item/mesn050/.

121. John R. Cox, in *Federal Writers' Project: Slave Narrative Project, Vol. 7, Kentucky, Bogie–Woods with Combined Interviews of Others*, 34, 1936, Manuscript / Mixed Material, https://www.loc.gov/item/mesn070/.

122. Quoted in Perdue, Barden, and Phillips, *Weevils in the Wheat*, 291.

123. Sarah Ford, in *Federal Writers' Project: Slave Narrative Project, Vol. 16, Texas, Part 2, Easter–King*, 42, 1936, Manuscript / Mixed Material, https://www.loc.gov/item/mesn162/. See also Betty Powers, in *Federal Writers' Project: Slave Narrative Project, Vol. 16, Texas, Part 3, Lewis–Ryles*, 191–92, 1936, Manuscript / Mixed Material, https://www.loc.gov/item/mesn163/.

124. Thomas Johns, in *Federal Writers' Project: Slave Narrative Project, Vol. 16, Texas, Part 2, Easter–King*, 203, 1936, Manuscript / Mixed Material, https://www.loc.gov/item/mesn162/.

125. G. W. Hawkins, in *Federal Writers' Project: Slave Narrative Project, Vol. 2, Arkansas, Part 3, Gadson–Isom*, 218, 1936, Manuscript / Mixed Material, https://www.loc.gov/item/mesn023/.

126. Willie McCullough, in *Federal Writers' Project: Slave Narrative Project, Vol. 11,*

North Carolina, Part 2, Jackson–Yellerday, 1936, Manuscript / Mixed Material, https://www.loc.gov/item/mesn112/.

127. John Henry Kemp, in *Federal Writers' Project: Slave Narrative Project, Vol. 3, Florida, Anderson–Wilson with Combined Interviews of Others*, 184–85, 1936, Manuscript / Mixed Material, https://www.loc.gov/item/mesn030/.

128. Sam and Louisa Everett, in *Federal Writers' Project: Slave Narrative Project, Vol. 3, Florida, Anderson–Wilson with Combined Interviews of Others*, 127–28, 1936, Manuscript / Mixed Material, https://www.loc.gov/item/mesn030/.

129. Ibid.

130. Jacob Branch, in *Federal Writers' Project: Slave Narrative Project, Vol. 16, Texas, Part 1, Adams–Duhon*, 137–38, 1936, Manuscript / Mixed Material, https://www.loc.gov/item/mesn161/.

131. Sam and Louisa Everett, in *Federal Writers' Project: Slave Narrative Project, Vol. 3, Florida, Anderson–Wilson with Combined Interviews of Others*, 127–28, 1936, Manuscript / Mixed Material, https://www.loc.gov/item/mesn030/.

132. Rose Williams, in *Federal Writers' Project: Slave Narrative Project, Vol. 16, Texas, Part 4, Sanco–Young*, 174–78, 1936, Manuscript / Mixed Material, https://www.loc.gov/item/mesn164/.

133. Wilma King, "'Suffer with Them till Death': Slave Women and Their Children in Nineteenth-Century America," in *More Than Chattel: Black Women and Slavery in the Americas*, ed. David Barry Gaspar and Darlene Clark Hine (Bloomington: Indiana University Press, 1996), 159.

134. Jennings, "Us Colored Women," 49.

135. George P. Rawick, ed., *The American Slave: A Composite Autobiography* (Westport, Conn.: Greenwood Press, 1972–79), Supplemental Series 2, vol. 5, pt. 4, p. 1453.

136. Irene Robertson, in Rawick, *The American Slave*, vol. 10, pt. 6, p. 223. See also Schwartz, *Birthing a Slave*, 24.

137. Quoted in White, *Ar'n't I a Woman?*, 156–57.

138. Ibid., 149.

139. Silvia King, in *Federal Writers' Project: Slave Narrative Project, Vol. 16, Texas, Part 2, Easter–King*, 291, 1936, Manuscript / Mixed Material, https://www.loc.gov/item/mesn162/.

140. John Brickell, *Natural History of North Carolina* (Dublin, 1737), 274–75, http://books.google.com/books?id=p4c5AAAAcAAJ&printsec=frontcover&vq=fifth&source=gbs_ge_summary_r&cad=0#v=onepage&q=fifth&f=false. See Kirsten Fischer, *Suspect Relations: Sex, Race, and Resistance in Colonial North Carolina* (Ithaca, N.Y.: Cornell University Press, 2002), 165. See also Jennifer L. Morgan, *Laboring Women: Reproduction and Gender in New World Slavery* (Philadelphia: University of Pennsylvania Press, 2004), 100.

141. Morgan, *Laboring Women*, 100.

142. James Mellon, ed., *Bullwhip Days: The Slaves Remember* (New York: Weidenfeld & Nicolson, 1988), 296.

143. Kemble, *Journal of a Residence*, 207.

144. Berry, *Swing the Sickle*, 81, quoting from Albert, *The House of Bondage* (1890), 108.

145. Sam and Louisa Everett, in *Federal Writers' Project: Slave Narrative Project, Vol. 3, Florida, Anderson–Wilson with Combined Interviews of Others*, 127–28, 1936, Manuscript / Mixed Material, https://www.loc.gov/item/mesn030/.

146. See, for example, Rawick, *The American Slave*, Texas Narratives, Supplemental Series 2, vol. 8, pt. 7, p. 3332, and vol. 6, pt. 5, p. 1950; Smithers, *Slave Breeding*, 104, 108; Barney Stone, in *Federal Writers' Project: Slave Narrative Project, Vol. 5, Indiana, Arnold–Woodson*, 186, 1936, Manuscript / Mixed Material, https://www.loc.gov/item/mesn050/; Julia Cole, in *Federal Writers' Project: Slave Narrative Project, Vol. 4, Georgia, Part 1, Adams–Furr*, 228, 1936, Manuscript / Mixed Material, https://www.loc.gov/item/mesn041/.

CHAPTER 4. "Frequently Heard Her Threaten to Sell Him"

1. Elizabeth Fox-Genovese, *Within the Plantation Household: Black and White Women of the Old South* (Chapel Hill: University of North Carolina Press, 1988), 81.

2. See, for example, Thavolia Glymph, *Out of the House of Bondage: The Transformation of the Plantation Household* (Cambridge: Cambridge University Press, 2008).

3. Cecily Jones, "Contesting the Boundaries of Gender, Race and Sexuality in Barbadian Plantation Society," *Women's History Review* 12, no. 2 (2003): 197.

4. Gilberto Freyre, *The Masters and the Slaves: A Study in the Development of Brazilian Civilization*, trans. Samuel Putnam, abridged from the revised edition (1946; New York: Alfred A. Knopf, 1956), 351–52.

5. Jones, "Contesting the Boundaries," 197.

6. Hilary McD. Beckles, "White Women and Slavery in the Caribbean," *History Workshop* 36 (Autumn 1993): 72; Marisa J. Fuentes, *Dispossessed Lives: Enslaved Women, Violence, and the Archive* (Philadelphia: University of Pennsylvania Press, 2016); Emily West with R. J. Knight, "Mother's Milk: Slavery, Wet-Nursing, and Black and White Women in the Antebellum South," *Journal of Southern History* 83, no. 1 (February 2017): 37–68. See also Stephanie E. Jones-Rogers, "Rethinking Sexual Violence and the Marketplace of Slavery: White Women, the Slave Market, and Enslaved People's Sexualized Bodies in the Nineteenth-Century South," in *Sexuality and Slavery: Reclaiming Intimate Histories in the Americas*, ed. Daina Ramey Berry and Leslie M. Harris (Athens: University of Georgia Press, 2018), 109–23; Jones-Rogers, "'[S]he Could . . . Spare One Ample Breast for the Profit of Her Owner': White Mothers and Enslaved Wet Nurses' Invisible Labor in American Slave Markets," *Slavery and Abolition* 38, No. 2 (April 2017): 337–355.

7. Madison Hemings, "Life among the Lowly, No. 1," *Pike County (Ohio) Republican*, March 13, 1873, https://www.encyclopediavirginia.org/media_player?mets_filename=evr6448mets.xml.

8. Eugene D. Genovese, *Roll, Jordan, Roll: The World the Slaves Made* (New York: Pantheon Books, 1974), 422.

9. Ibid.

10. Richard S. Dunn, *Sugar and Slaves: The Rise of the Planter Class in the English West Indies, 1624–1713* (Chapel Hill: University of North Carolina Press for the Institute of Early American History and Culture, 2000), 228.

11. Martha Hodes, *White Women, Black Men: Illicit Sex in the Nineteenth-Century South* (New Haven, Conn.: Yale University Press, 1999), 19.

12. Hartwood Baptist Church, June 25, 1785, quoted in Philip D. Morgan, *Slave Counterpoint: Black Culture in the Eighteenth-Century Chesapeake and Lowcountry* (Chapel Hill: University of North Carolina Press, 1998), 402. Numerous examples can be found in James Hugo Johnston, *Race Relations in Virginia and Miscegenation in the South, 1776–1860* (Amherst: University of Massachusetts Press, 1970), 165–90.

13. Bill Cecil-Fronsman, *Common Whites: Class and Culture in Antebellum North Carolina* (Lexington: University Press of Kentucky, 1992), 68.

14. Kathleen M. Brown, *Good Wives, Nasty Wenches, and Anxious Patriarchs: Gender, Race, and Power in Colonial Virginia* (Chapel Hill: University of North Carolina Press for the Institute of Early American History and Culture, 1996), 197–99. There is a large body of work on sex between white men and enslaved women. See, for example, Sharony Green, *Remember Me to Miss Louisa: Hidden Black-White Intimacies in Antebellum America* (DeKalb: Northern Illinois University Press, 2015).

15. Kirsten Fischer, *Suspect Relations: Sex, Race, and Resistance in Colonial North Carolina* (Ithaca, N.Y.: Cornell University Press, 2002), 123–24. See also Cecil-Fronsman, *Common Whites*, 71. On the higher execution rate of black men accused of rape than white in occupied Virginia during the Civil War, see E. Susan Barber and Charles F. Ritter, "'Physical Abuse . . . and Rough Handling': Race, Gender, and Justice in the Occupied South," in *Occupied Women: Gender, Military Occupation, and the American Civil War*, ed. LeeAnn Whites and Alecia P. Long (Baton Rouge: Louisiana State University Press, 2009), 63.

16. Trevor Burnard, "'A Matron in Rank, a Prostitute in Manners': The Manning Divorce of 1741 and Class, Gender, Race and the Law in Eighteenth-Century Jamaica," in *Working Slavery, Pricing Freedom: Perspectives from the Caribbean, Africa and the African Diaspora*, ed. Verene A. Shepherd (New York: Palgrave, 2002), 133–52.

17. A.F.C., "An Early Portuguese Trading Voyage to the Forcados River," *Journal of the Historical Society of Nigeria* 1, no. 4 (December 1959): 298n1. See also C. R. Boxer, *Race Relations in the Portuguese Colonial Empire, 1415–1825* (New York: Oxford University Press, 1963), 15.

18. Ira Berlin, "Time, Space, and Evolution of Afro-American Society on British Mainland North America," *American Historical Review* 85 no. 1 (1980): 69.

19. Brown, *Good Wives*, 197–99.

20. Warren M. Billings, ed., *The Old Dominion in the Seventeenth Century: A Documentary History of Virginia, 1606–1689* (Chapel Hill: University of North Carolina Press, 1975), 163.

21. Mechal Sobel, *The World They Made Together: Black and White Values in Eighteenth-Century Virginia* (Princeton, N.J.: Princeton University Press, 1987), 149. See also Berlin, "Time, Space," 69; Allan Kulikoff, *Tobacco and Slaves: The Development

of Southern Cultures in the Chesapeake, 1680–1800 (Chapel Hill: University of North Carolina Press for the Institute of Early American History and Culture), 387, 395–96.

22. Kulikoff, *Tobacco and Slaves*, 395.

23. Morgan, *Slave Counterpoint*, 400, emphasis added.

24. Kulikoff, *Tobacco and Slaves*, 386–87.

25. Ibid., 395; *Maryland Gazette*, October 12, 1769.

26. Glenda Riley, *Divorce: An American Tradition* (New York: Oxford University Press, 1991), 35. Riley cites from George E. Howard, *A History of Matrimonial Institutions*, 3 vols. (Chicago, 1904), 2:32–35.

27. Riley, *Divorce*, 36.

28. Loren Schweninger, *Families in Crisis in the Old South: Divorce, Slavery, and the Law* (Chapel Hill: University of North Carolina Press, 2012), 25.

29. Cecil-Fronsman, *Common Whites*, 91; Guion Griffis Johnson, *Ante-bellum North Carolina: A Social History; Electronic Edition* (Chapel Hill: University of North Carolina Press, 1937), 211, https://docsouth.unc.edu/nc/johnson/titlepage.html. We might question the validity of the claim. One formerly enslaved woman recalled that her master wanted her to claim that his wife "had black men," but she refused, despite being brutally beaten. George Townsend, *The Swamp Outlaws: Or the Lowery Bandits of North Carolina: Being a Complete History of the Modern Rob Roys and Robin Hoods* (New York: Robert M. DeWitt Publisher, 1872), 27. Thanks to Seth Rockman and James Schuelke for sharing this case with me.

30. Thomas E. Buckley, S.J., *The Great Catastrophe of My Life: Divorce in the Old Dominion* (Chapel Hill: University of North Carolina Press, 2002), 123. See also Joshua D. Rothman, *Notorious in the Neighborhood: Sex and Families across the Color Line in Virginia, 1787–1861* (Chapel Hill: University of North Carolina Press, 2003), 170.

31. Riley, *Divorce*, 35.

32. Peter Neilson, *Recollections of a Six Years Residence in the United States of America* (Glasgow, 1830), 297. See Johnston, *Race Relations*, 264.

33. Henry Bibb, *Narrative of the Life and Adventures of Henry Bibb, an American Slave, Written by Himself* (New York, 1849), 16, http://docsouth.unc.edu/neh/bibb/bibb.html.

34. Land Records (Deeds and Wills), 1677–92, part 1, c, Henrico County Microfilm Collection, reel 4, pp. 192–96, account of the Katherine Watkins case, Library of Virginia County and City Records, Richmond, microfilm. See also Billings, *Old Dominion*, 161–63; and Sobel, *The World They Made*, 149.

35. [François-Jean,] Marquis de Chastellux, *Travels in North America in the Years, 1780, 1781, and 1782* (London, 1787), 83, http://books.google.com/books/about/Travels_in_North_America_in_the_years_17.html?id=tPT0MGiYPn4C. See also Fischer, *Suspect Relations*, 163.

36. Jones, "Contesting the Boundaries," 210. On the power imbalance inherent in slavery, see, for example, Orlando Patterson, *Slavery and Social Death: A Comparative Study* (Cambridge, Mass.: Harvard University Press, 1982).

37. Jones, "Contesting the Boundaries," 223; Beckles, "White Women," 68.

38. Burnard, *Mastery, Tyranny and Desire*, 216; see June 11, 1758, in *In Miserable Slavery: Thomas Thistlewood in Jamaica, 1750–86*, ed. Douglas Hall (London: Macmillan, 1992), 84.

39. *Anne Batson v. John Fitchet and Wife Mary* (1731), quoted in Morgan, *Slave Counterpoint*, 401–2.

40. Stephen Bordley to Matt Harris, Annapolis, Maryland, January 30, 1739, quoted in Jordan, *White over Black*, 154.

41. *Maryland Gazette*, October 12, 1769, https://msa.maryland.gov/megafile/msa/speccol/sc4800/sc4872/001281/html/m1281-0893.html.

42. *Daily New Orleanian*, February 12, 1852. See Robert C. Reinders, "Slavery in New Orleans in the Decade before the Civil War," *Mid-America: An Historical Journal* 44 (1962): 219.

43. Divorce Graves, Montgomery County Divorce Records, 1848–1907, State Archives of North Carolina, Raleigh, Courtesy of the State Archives of North Carolina.

44. *Kennedy Williams v. Mary Williams*, 1858, Yadkin County Divorce Records, 1851–1931, State Archives of North Carolina, Raleigh, Courtesy of the State Archives of North Carolina.

45. *Rhodias Riley v. Nancy Riley*, 1858, Randolph County Divorce Records, 1804–1927, Presnell–York, State Archives of North Carolina, Raleigh, Courtesy of the State Archives of North Carolina.

46. *Henry Shouse v. Ann Shouse*, 1848, Stokes County Divorce Records, 1816–1941, State Archives of North Carolina, Raleigh, Courtesy of the State Archives of North Carolina.

47. *William Hickman v. Nancy Hickman*, 1832, Granville County Divorce Records, 1819–1895, 1914, State Archives of North Carolina, Raleigh, Courtesy of the State Archives of North Carolina.

48. Lewis Bourne Papers, Louisa County, 1825, Legislative Petitions Digital Collection, Library of Virginia, Richmond. See Hodes, *White Women, Black Men*, 68–95. Dianne Sommerville similarly finds that during slavery, the figure of the black rapist had not yet taken hold. On the varied legal reactions to rape cases involving black men and white women accusers, see Dianne Miller Sommerville, *Rape and Race in the Nineteenth-Century South* (Chapel Hill: University of North Carolina Press, 2004).

49. Harriet Jacobs, *Incidents in the Life of a Slave Girl* (Mineola, NY: Dover Publications, 2001), 46; J. W. Lindsay interview, in Blassingame, *Slave Testimony*, 400–401.

50. Letters Received by the Office of the Adjutant General, M619, RG 94, NA, reel 201, National Archives, Washington, D.C. I first encountered the testimony in the AFIC records about white women and enslaved men in Hodes, *White Women, Black Men*, 128–29.

51. Ibid.

52. Ibid.

53. Brown, *Good Wives*, 239.

54. *James Larrimore v. Catherine Larrimore*, 1823, Stokes County Divorce Records, 1816–1941, State Archives of North Carolina, Raleigh, Courtesy of the State Archives of North Carolina.

55. Stephen and Mary Cole, Divorce "C," Richmond County Divorce Records, 1816–1910, State Archives of North Carolina, Raleigh, Courtesy of the State Archives of North Carolina.

56. Betty Wood, "Servant Women and Sex in the Seventeenth-Century Chesapeake," in *Women in Early America*, ed. Thomas A. Foster (New York: New York University Press, 2015), 111.

57. Brown, *Good Wives*, 209.

58. Sharon Block, *Rape and Sexual Power in Early America* (Chapel Hill: University of North Carolina Press, 2006). For other examples, see Thomas A. Foster, *Sex and the Eighteenth-Century Man: Massachusetts and the History of Sexuality in America* (Boston: Beacon Press, 2006), chap. 3; Terri L. Snyder, "Sexual Consent and Sexual Coercion in Seventeenth-Century Virginia," in *Sex without Consent: Rape and Sexual Coercion in America*, ed. Merril D. Smith (New York: New York University Press, 2001), 46–60.

59. Letters Received by the Office of the Adjutant General, M619, RG 94, NA, reel 201, National Archives, Washington, D.C.

60. Petition of William McClure to the County Court, Montgomery County, Tennessee, July 16, 1822, in Legislative Petitions, Tennessee State Library and Archives, Nashville, from Schweninger, *Families in Crisis*, 100–101.

61. Ann Patton Malone, *Sweet Chariot: Slave Family and Household Structure in Nineteenth-Century Louisiana* (Chapel Hill: University of North Carolina Press, 1992), 219.

62. *Daily New Orleanian*, January 15, 1852. See also Reinders, "Slavery in New Orleans," 219; *Weekly Picayune*, June 18, July 23, August 27, 1855.

63. Letters Received by the Office of the Adjutant General, M619, RG 94, NA, reel 201, National Archives, Washington, D.C. See also Hodes, *White Women, Black Men*, 39–67, and for other examples of women accused in this manner once bringing rape charges, see 62–63.

64. Hodes, *White Women, Black Men*, 57.

65. Ibid., 130.

66. Ibid.

67. James Hugo Johnston, *Race Relations in Virginia and Miscegenation in the South, 1776–1860* (Amherst: University of Massachusetts Press, 1970), 179; Minutes of the Chester County Courts, 1697–1710, p. 24, as recorded by Edward Raymond Turner, *The Negro in Pennsylvania: Slavery, Servitude, Freedom, 1639–1861* (Washington, D.C.: American Historical Association, 1911), 30.

68. Letters Received, October 2, 1813, Executive Papers, Archives of Virginia. See Johnston, *Race Relations in Virginia*, 261–62.

69. Letters Received, June 10, 1826, Executive Papers, Archives of Virginia. See Johnston, *Race Relations in Virginia*, 267.

70. Armstrong v. Hodges, 41 Ky. 69 (1841) (from Franklin County). I first encountered this case in Hodes, *White Women, Black Men*, 133–34.

71. *Sarah Jane Thomas v. William M. Thomas*, 1859, Davidson County Divorce Records, 1831–1944, State Archives of North Carolina, Raleigh, Courtesy of the State Archives of North Carolina.

72. *A Narrative of the Adventures and Escape of Moses Roper, from American Slavery* (Philadelphia, 1838), 15, http://docsouth.unc.edu/fpn/roper/roper.html.

73. Edward Everett Brown, *Sketch of the Life of Mr. Lewis Charlton, and Reminiscences of Slavery* (Portland, Maine, undated), 1–2, http://docsouth.unc.edu/neh/charlton/charlton.html.

74. Letters Received by the Office of the Adjutant General, M619, RG 94, NA, reel 201, National Archives, Washington, D.C.

75. Jacobs, *Incidents in the Life*, 46.

76. Letters Received by the Office of the Adjutant General, M619, RG 94, NA, reel 201, National Archives, Washington, D.C.

77. Ibid.

78. Samuel Gridley Howe, *The Refugees from Slavery in Canada West: Report to the Freedmen's Inquiry Commission* (1864; New York: Arno Press and New York Times, 1969).

79. *Josiah Houston v. Matilda Houston*, Talladega County Judicial Building, Talladega, Alabama. See Schweninger, *Families in Crisis*, 105, 196n13.

CHAPTER 5. "Till I Had Mastered Every Part"

1. Notable exceptions are William Benemann, *Male-Male Intimacy in Early America: Beyond Romantic Friendships* (New York: Harrington Park Press, 2006), chap. 6; Charles Clifton, "Rereading Voices from the Past: Images of Homo-eroticism in the Slave Narrative," in *The Greatest Taboo: Homosexuality in Black Communities*, ed. Delroy Constantine-Simms (Los Angeles: Alyson Books, 2000), 358; John Saillant, in *Long before Stonewall: Histories of Same-Sex Sexuality in Early America*, ed. Thomas A. Foster (New York: New York University Press, 2007); and Vincent Woodard, *The Delectable Negro: Human Consumption and Homoeroticism within U.S. Slave Culture* (New York: New York University Press, 2014). Activist Charles Clifton, in one of the first essays on same-sex sexuality and enslaved men, hoped that his essay would have "created an opening for the future explorations in gay and lesbian historiography and for a more complete understanding of black sexuality and manhood as denoted in these narratives" ("Rereading Voices," 358). This chapter takes up his call for further research and continues the project of rereading extant sources for queer experiences. It also builds on literary scholar Vincent Woodard's *Delectable Negro*. Woodard's analysis focused on real and imagined cannibalism and how that very consumption by white men of male bodies was also always homoerotic.

2. P. Gabrielle Foreman, "Manifest Signs: The Politics of Sex and Representation in *Incidents in the Life of a Slave Girl*," in *Harriet Jacobs and Incidents in the Life of a Slave Girl: New Critical Essays*, ed. Deborah M. Garfield and Rafia Zafar (Cambridge: Cambridge University Press, 1996), 77; Frances Foster, "'In Respect to Females . . .': Differences in the Portrayals of Women by Male and Female Narrators," *Black American Literature Forum* 15 (Summer 1981): 67.

3. Richard Goddard and Noel Polk, "Reading the Ledgers," *Mississippi Quarterly* 55 (2002): 308n7.

4. William Styron, *The Confessions of Nat Turner* (1966; New York: Random House, 1967), 226–40. Michael Bibler's analysis of the fictional Nat Turner notes that there are limits to homoness serving as a bond between men. Michael P. Bibler, *Cotton's Queer Relations: Same-Sex Intimacy and the Literature of the Southern Plantation, 1936–1968* (Charlotte: University of Virginia Press, 2009), 208.

5. Charles I. Nero, "Toward a Black Gay Aesthetic: Signifying in Contemporary Black Gay Literature," in *Brother to Brother: New Writings by Black Gay Men*, ed. Essex Hemphill and Joseph Beam (Boston: Alyson Publications, 1991), 232–33; Natasha Tinsley, "Black Atlantic, Queer Atlantic: Queer Imaginings of the Middle Passage," *GLQ* 14, no. 2–3 (2008): 192; Woodard, *The Delectable Negro*. In contrast, Bibler's analysis of twentieth-century plantation literature, for example, finds expressions of the radical possibilities for equality among same-gender loving individuals. Bibler, *Cotton's Queer Relations*; Goddard and Polk, "Reading the Ledgers."

6. Sergio A. Lussana, *My Brother Slaves: Friendship, Masculinity, and Resistance in the Antebellum South* (Lexington: University Press of Kentucky, 2016). Scholarship on same-gender sexual contact within the context of slavery has focused almost exclusively on interactions between white and black men, in particular on abuse at the hands of white enslavers and overseers. Aliyyah I. Abdur-Rahman, "'The Strangest Freaks of Despotism': Queer Sexuality in Antebellum African American Slave Narratives," *African American Review* 40 (2006): 223–37; Clifton, "Rereading Voices, 342–61; Jim Downs, "With Only a Trace: Same-Sex Sexual Desire and Violence on Slave Plantations, 1607–1865," in *Connexions: Histories of Race and Sex in North America*, ed. Jennifer Brier, Jim Downs, and Jennifer Morgans (Springfield: University of Illinois Press, 2016), 15–37; Robert Richmond Ellis, "Reading through the Veil of Juan Francisco Manzano: From Homoerotic Violence to the Dream of a Homoracial Bond," *PMLA* 113 (1998): 422–35; Woodard, *The Delectable Negro*.

7. Ellis, "Reading through the Veil," 431.

8. Caleb Crain, *American Sympathy: Men, Friendship, and Literature in the New Nation* (New Haven, Conn.: Yale University Press, 2001); Martin Bauml Duberman, "'Writhing Bedfellows' in Antebellum South Carolina: Historical Interpretation and the Politics of Evidence," in *Hidden from History: Reclaiming the Gay and Lesbian Past*, ed. Martin Bauml Duberman, Martha Vicinus, and George Chauncey Jr. (New York: NAL Books, 1989), 153–69; Richard Godbeer, *The Overflowing of Friendship: Love between Men and the Creation of the American Republic* (Baltimore, Md.: Johns Hopkins University Press, 2009); Karen V. Hansen, "'Our Eyes Behold Each Other': Masculinity and Intimate Friendship in Antebellum New England," in *Men's Friendships: Research on Men and Masculinities*, ed. Peter M. Nardi (London: Sage Publications, 1992), 35–58; Anya Jabour, "Male Friendship and Masculinity in the Early National South: William Wirt and His Friends," *Journal of the Early Republic* 20 (2000): 83–111; Carroll Smith-Rosenberg, "The Female World of Love and Ritual: Relations between Women in Nineteenth-Century America," *Signs* 1, no. 1 (1975): 1–29.

9. Karen V. Hansen, "'No Kisses Like Yours': An Erotic Friendship between Two African-American Women during the Mid-Nineteenth Century," *Gender & History* 7 (1995): 153–82.

10. Delroy Constantine-Simms, ed., *The Greatest Taboo: Homosexuality in Black Communities* (Los Angeles: Alyson Books, 2000), 147.

11. Woodard, *The Delectable Negro*, 236.

12. David Bindman and Henry Louis Gates Jr., eds., *The Image of the Black in Western Art*, vol. 4, *From the American Revolution to World War I*, pt. 2, *Black Models and White Myths*, 2nd ed. (Cambridge, Mass.: Belknap Press, 2012), 60.

13. Robert Aldrich, *Colonialism and Homosexuality* (London: Routledge, 2003), 153.

14. Tinsley, "Black Atlantic," 145, 192.

15. Sergio Lussana, "'No Band of Brothers Could Be More Loving': Enslaved Male Homosociality, Friendship, and Resistance in the Antebellum American South," *Journal of Social History* 46 (2013): 875; Lussana, "To See Who Was Best on the Plantation: Enslaved Fighting Contests and Masculinity in the Antebellum Plantation South," *Journal of Southern History* 76 (2010): 901–22. See also David Doddington, "Informal Economies and Masculine Hierarchies in Slave Communities of the U.S. South, 1800–1865," in Gender and History File, 2015, http://orca.cf.ac.uk/74559/; Jeff Forret, "Conflict and the 'Slave Community': Violence among Slaves in Upcountry South Carolina," *Journal of Southern History* 74 (2008): 551–88.

16. Jonathan Ned Katz, *Gay/Lesbian Almanac: A New Documentary* (New York: Carroll & Graf, 1994), 61.

17. Joseph Addison, Richard Steele, et al., "Tuesday, November 6, 1711," *Spectator* 1, no. 215 (1853): 195. See also Terri L. Snyder, *The Power to Die: Slavery and Suicide in British North America* (Chicago: University of Chicago Press, 2015), 101.

18. Robert J. Allison, ed., *The Interesting Narrative of the Life of Olaudah Equiano, Written by Himself* (Boston: Medford Books of St. Martin's Press, 1995), 61.

19. Lussana, "No Band," 881. On friendship and running away, see Lussana, *My Brother Slaves*, 114–24.

20. Solomon Northup, *Twelve Years a Slave* (Auburn: Durby and Miller, 1853), 221–22, http://docsouth.unc.edu/fpn/northup/northup.html.

21. Lussana, "No Band," 884; Isaac Mason, *Life of Isaac Mason as a Slave* (1893), 37, http://docsouth.unc.edu/fpn/mason/mason.html.

22. William Parker, "The Freedman's Story in Two Parts," *Atlantic Monthly Magazine* 17 (1866): 155–56, https://docsouth.unc.edu/neh/parker1/parker.html.

23. Louis Hughes, *Thirty Years a Slave: From Bondage to Freedom; The Institution of Slavery as Seen on the Plantation and in the Home of the Planter* (Milwaukee, 1897), 100, https://docsouth.unc.edu/fpn/hughes/hughes.html.

24. Lussana, "No Band," 884, 887.

25. Charles I. Nero, "Toward a Black Gay Aesthetic: Signifying in Contemporary Black Gay Literature," in Hemphill and Beam, *Brother to Brother*, 233–34.

26. Esteban Montejo, *Biography of a Runaway Slave*, ed. Miguel Barnet, trans. W. Nick Hill (Willimantic, Conn.: Curbstone Press, 1994), 40; Woodward, *The Delectable Negro*, 235.

27. Robert Richmond Ellis, "Reading through the Veil of Juan Francisco Manzano: From Homoerotic Violence to the Dream of a Homoracial Bond," *PMLA* 113 (1998): 432.

28. Heather Martel, "Colonial Allure: Normal Homoeroticism and Sodomy in French and Timucuan Encounters in Sixteenth-Century Florida," *Journal of the History of Sexuality* 22, no. 1 (January 2013): 34–64.

29. Christina Snyder, *Slavery in Indian Country: The Changing Face of Captivity in Early America* (Cambridge, Mass.: Harvard University Press, 2010), 145; Bernard Romans, *A Concise Natural History of East and West Florida*, ed. Kathryn E. Holland Braund (Tuscaloosa: University of Alabama Press, 1999), 128.

30. Ramón A. Gutiérrez, "Warfare, Homosexuality, and Gender Status Among American Indian Men in the Southwest," in Foster, *Long before Stonewall*, 19–31.

31. Stephanie M. H. Camp, *Closer to Freedom: Enslaved Women and Everyday Resistance in the Plantation South* (Chapel Hill: University of North Carolina Press, 2004), 43; Jeff Forret, *Slave against Slave: Plantation Violence in the Old South* (Baton Rouge: Louisiana State University Press, 2015).

32. Genovese, *Roll*, 371.

33. Genovese argues that jealousies led to fights at times. Ibid., 632.

34. Gilberto Freyre, *The Masters and the Slaves: A Study in the Development of Brazilian Civilization*, trans. Samuel Putnam, abridged from the revised edition (1946; New York: Alfred A. Knopf, 1956), 72.

35. Ibid., 285–86.

36. Genovese, *Roll*, 423.

37. Kenneth Scott and Kenn Stryker-Rodda, eds., *New York Historical Manuscripts: Dutch*, vol. 4, *Council Minutes, 1638–1649* (Baltimore, Md.: Genealogical Publishing, 1974), 326–27; Katz, *Gay/Lesbian Almanac*, 61, 90.

38. Jason R. Zeledon, "The United States and the Barbary Pirates: Adventures in Sexuality, State-Building, and Nationalism, 1784–1815" (PhD diss., University of California at Santa Barbara, 2016), 61.

39. See Marcus Rediker, *The Slave Ship: A Human History* (New York: Penguin, 2007); Sowande' M. Muskateem, *Slavery at Sea: Terror, Sex, and Sickness in the Middle Passage* (Urbana: University of Illinois Press, 2016), 86–90; Stephanie E. Smallwood, *Saltwater Slavery: A Middle Passage from Africa to American Diaspora* (Cambridge, Mass.: Harvard University Press, 2007).

40. Arthur N. Gilbert, "Buggery and the British Navy, 1700–1861," *Journal of Social History* 10, no. 1 (1976): 72–98, http://www.jstor.org/stable/3786421.

41. B. R. Burg, *Boys at Sea: Sodomy, Indecency, and Courts Martial in Nelson's Navy* (New York: Palgrave Macmillan, 2007).

42. Jacob A. Hazen, *Five Years before the Mast or Life in the Forecastle aboard a Whaler and Man-of-War*, 2nd ed. (Chicago: Belford, Clarke, & Co., 1858), 227; see also William Benemann, *Men in Eden: William Drummond Stewart and Same-Sex Desire in the Rocky Mountain Fur Trade* (Lincoln: University of Nebraska Press, 2012), chap. 3; Clifton, "Rereading Voices," 347.

43. Harold Langley, *Social Reform in the United States Navy, 1798–1862* (Annapolis, Md.: Naval Institute Press, 2015), 172–74.

44. Darcy Grimaldo Grigsby, *Extremities: Painting Empire in Post-revolutionary France* (New Haven, Conn.: Yale University Press, 2002), 55.

45. See David Bindman and Henry Louis Gates Jr., *The Image of the Black in Western Art*, vol. 4, *From the American Revolution to World War I*, pt. 2, *Black Models and White Myths*, 2nd ed. (Cambridge, Mass.: Belknap Press, 2012), 26–30.

46. Malcolm Elwin, *The Autobiography and Journals of Benjamin Robert Haydon, 1786–1846* (1853; London: MacDonald, 1950), 123–24.

47. Ibid., 123–24, 144.

48. Molly Rogers, *Delia's Tears: Race, Science, and Photography in Nineteenth-Century America* (New Haven, Conn.: Yale University Press, 2010).

49. Solomon Northrup, *Twelve Years a Slave* (London, 1853), 283–84, http://docsouth.unc.edu/fpn/northup/northup.html.

50. Woodard, *Delectable Negro*, 96, 105, 106.

51. Frederick Douglass, *My Bondage and My Freedom* (New York: Miller, Orton, & Mulligan, 1855), 222; Woodard, *Delectable Negro*, 107.

52. William Grimes, *Life of William Grimes, the Runaway Slave, Written by Himself* (1825), 22, http://docsouth.unc.edu/neh/grimes25/menu.html. I thank David Blight and the participants of the Yale Slave Narratives Seminar (June 2015), especially Martha Eads and Kevin McGruder, for their comments regarding Grimes's narrative.

53. Ibid.

54. Colette Colligan, "Anti-abolition Writes Obscenity: The English Vice, Transatlantic Slavery, and England's Obscene Print Culture," in *International Exposure: Perspectives on Modern European Pornography, 1800–2000*, ed. Lisa Z. Sigel (New Brunswick, N.J.: Rutgers University Press, 2005), 69; Amber Jamilla Musser, *Sensational Flesh: Race, Power, and Masochism* (New York: New York University Press, 2014), 47, especially Musser's use of Fanon and the claim that "sadism" is erotic.

55. William Benemann, *Male-Male Intimacy in Early America: Beyond Romantic Friendships* (New York: Harrington Park, 2006), 68–69; Colligan, "Anti-abolition Writes Obscenity"; Foster, "Sexual Abuse," 450.

56. Honour, *The Image of the Black*, vol. 4, part 1, 119.

57. Saillant, "The Black Body Erotic," 303–30.

58. Ibid., 310.

59. Trevor Burnard, *Mastery, Tyranny, and Desire: Thomas Thistlewood and His Slaves in the Anglo-Jamaican World* (Chapel Hill: University of North Carolina Press, 2004), 216. While the term "strange reports" is not precise, Trevor Burnard interprets it as meaning same-sex sexual assault.

60. Woodard, *The Delectable Negro*, 14. See also Downs, "With Only a Trace."

61. See, for example, Richard Godbeer, *The Overflowing of Friendship: Love between Men and the Creation of the American Republic* (Baltimore, Md.: Johns Hopkins University Press, 2009).

62. Rictor Norton notes that similar interactions occurred between British masters and body servants. Examples include William Beckford's homoerotic fantasizing about his boy servants; libels against the Duke of Cumberland for murdering one manservant in order to conceal his buggering of another manservant; and the dramatist Samuel Foote, who was charged with buggering his coachman. See http://rictornorton.co.uk/eighteen/1823news.htm. Thanks to Rictor Norton for pointing me to these cases.

63. Bindman and Gates, *The Image of the Black*, 25–26.

64. Ibid., 194, 75–78, 228–29, 232.

65. Charles Oscar Paullin, *Commodore John Rodgers, Captain, Commodore, Senior Officer of the American Navy, 1773–1838* (Cleveland: Arthur H. Clark Company, 1910), 369.

66. Robert Phillip Howell, "Memoirs," in *Southern Historical Collection*, in C. W. Harper, "Black Aristocrats: Domestic Servants on the Antebellum Plantation," *Phylon* 46 (1985): 132.

67. "From George Washington to Clement Biddle, 28 July 1784," *Founders Online*, National Archives, http://founders.archives.gov/documents/Washington/04-02-02-0014. Original source, *The Papers of George Washington*, Confederation Series, vol. 2, *18 July 1784–18 May 1785*, ed. W. W. Abbot (Charlottesville: University Press of Virginia, 1992), 14.

68. Ibid.

69. Alan Taylor, *The Internal Enemy: Slavery and War in Virginia, 1772–1832* (New York: W. W. Norton, 2013), 79; W. C. Bruce, *John Randolph of Roanoke, 1773–1833*, 2 vols. (New York: G. P. Putnam's Sons, 1922), 2:700; Robert Dawidoff, *Education of John Randolph* (New York: W. W. Norton, 1979), 52–53.

70. Benemann, *Male-Male Intimacy*, 191.

71. Taylor, *The Internal Enemy*, 79.

72. Dawidoff, *Education*, 52.

73. Paul Jennings, *A Colored Man's Reminiscences of James Madison* (Brooklyn: George C. Beadle, 1865), 15, http://docsouth.unc.edu/neh/jennings/jennings.html.

74. Ibid., 18.

75. Ibid., 6, 7–8, 12–13.

76. Harriet Beecher Stowe, *The Key to "Uncle Tom's Cabin"; Presenting the Original Facts and Documents Upon Which the Story Is Founded, Together with Corroborative Statements Verifying the Truth of the Work* (Boston: John P. Jewett and Company, 1854), http://utc.iath.virginia.edu/uncletom/key/kyhp.html. On vernacular history, see Edward E. Baptist, "'Stol' and Fetched Here': Enslaved Migration, Ex-slave Narratives, and Vernacular History," in *New Studies in the History of American Slavery*, ed. Edward E. Baptist and Stephanie M. H. Camp (Athens: University of Georgia Press, 2006), 243–74. For a queer reading of Tom and St. Clare, see P. Gabrielle Foreman, "'This Promiscuous Housekeeping': Death, Transgression, and Homoeroticism in *Uncle Tom's Cabin*," *Representations* 43 (Summer 1993): 51–72.

77. Harriet Beecher Stowe, *Uncle Tom's Cabin* (Boston: Jewett & Co., 1852), chap. 15, http://utc.iath.virginia.edu/uncletom/uthp.html.

78. Ibid.

79. Ibid. See also Benneman, *Male-Male Intimacy*, 144–49; David Greven, *Gender Protest and Same-Sex Desire in Antebellum American Literature* (Burlington, Vt.: Ashgate Press, 2014), 179.

80. Stowe, *Uncle Tom's Cabin*, chap. 30.

81. Eliza Potter, *A Hairdresser's Experience in High Life*, ed. Xiomara Santamarina (Chapel Hill: University of North Carolina Press), second page of chap. 8. I would like to thank Lisa Ze Winters for pointing me to this source.

82. Ibid., 145–46.

83. Lisa Ze Winters, "'More Desultory and Unconnected Than Any Other': Geography, Desire, and Freedom in Eliza Potter's *A Hairdressers Experience in High Life*," *American Quarterly* 61, no. 3 (September 2009): 466, 467.

84. Linda Brent [Harriet Jacobs], *Incidents in the Life of a Slave Girl, Written by Herself*, ed. Jennifer Fleischner (Boston, 1861; New York: Bedford, 2010), 203; Daina Ramey Berry, *"Swing the Sickle for the Harvest Is Ripe": Gender and Slavery in Antebellum Georgia* (Urbana: University of Illinois Press, 2007), 86.

85. Ibid.

86. Woodard, *Delectable Negro*, 146, 135, 138, 127–70.

CONCLUSION. Rethinking Rufus

1. Edward Baptist, *The Half Has Never Been Told: Slavery and the Making of American Capitalism* (New York: Basic Books, 2014).

BIBLIOGRAPHY

Abdur-Rahman, Aliyyah I. "'The Strangest Freaks of Despotism': Queer Sexuality in Antebellum African American Slave Narratives." *African American Review* 40 (2006): 223–37.

Aldrich, Robert. *Colonialism and Homosexuality*. London: Routledge, 2003.

Baptist, Edward E. "The Absent Subject: African American Masculinity and Forced Migration to the Antebellum Plantation Frontier." In *Southern Manhood: Perspectives on Masculinity in the Old South*, edited by Craig Thompson Friend and Lorri Glover, 136–73. Athens: University of Georgia Press, 2004.

———. "'Cuffy,' 'Fancy Maids,' and 'One-Eyed Men': Rape, Commodification, and the Domestic Slave Trade in the United States." *American Historical Review* 106, no. 5 (2001): 1619–50.

———. *The Half Has Never Been Told: Slavery and the Making of American Capitalism*. New York: Basic Books, 2014.

———. "'Stol' and Fetched Here': Enslaved Migration, Ex-slave Narratives, and Vernacular History." In *New Studies in the History of American Slavery*, edited by Edward E. Baptist and Stephanie M. H. Camp, 243–74. Athens: University of Georgia Press, 2006.

Barber, Susan E., and Charles F. Ritter. "'Physical Abuse . . . and Rough Handling': Race, Gender, and Justice in the Occupied South." In *Occupied Women: Gender, Military Occupation, and the American Civil War*, edited by LeeAnn Whites and Alecia P. Long, 63. Baton Rouge: Louisiana State University Press, 2009.

Beckles, Hilary M. "White Women and Slavery in the Caribbean." *History Workshop Journal* 36 (Autumn 1993): 66–82.

Benemann, William. *Male-Male Intimacy in Early America: Beyond Romantic Friendships*. New York: Harrington Park, 2006.

———. *Men in Eden: William Drummond Stewart and Same-Sex Desire in the Rocky Mountain Fur Trade*. Lincoln: University of Nebraska Press, 2012.

Berlin, Ira. "Time, Space, and Evolution of Afro-American Society on British Mainland North America." *American Historical Review* 85, no. 1 (1980): 44–78.

Berry, Daina Ramey. *The Price for Their Pound of Flesh: The Value of the Enslaved, from Womb to Grave, in the Building of a Nation*. Boston: Beacon Press, 2017.

———. *"Swing the Sickle for the Harvest Is Ripe": Gender and Slavery in Antebellum Georgia*. Urbana: University of Illinois Press, 2007.

Berry, Daina Ramey, and Leslie M. Harris, eds. *Sexuality and Slavery: Reclaiming Intimate Histories in the Americas*. Athens: University of Georgia Press, 2018.

Berry, Stephen W., II. *All That Makes a Man: Love and Ambition in the Civil War South*. Oxford: Oxford University Press, 2005.

Bibler, Michael P. *Cotton's Queer Relations: Same-Sex Intimacy and the Literature of the Southern Plantation, 1936–1968*. Charlottesville: University of Virginia Press, 2009.

Bindman, David, and Henry Louis Gates Jr., eds. *The Image of the Black in Western Art*, vol. 4, *From the American Revolution to World War I*, pt. 1, *Slaves and Liberators*. 2nd ed. Cambridge, Mass.: Belknap Press, 2012.

———. *The Image of the Black in Western Art*, vol. 4, *From the American Revolution to World War I*, pt. 2, *Black Models and White Myths*. 2nd ed. Cambridge, Mass.: Belknap Press, 2012.

Black, Daniel P. *Dismantling Black Manhood: An Historical and Literary Analysis of the Legacy of Slavery*. New York: Garland Publishing, 1997.

Blassingame, John W. *The Slave Community: Plantation Life in the Antebellum South*. Revised and enlarged edition. 1972; New York: Oxford University Press, 1979.

Block, Sharon. *Colonial Complexions: Race and Bodies in Eighteenth-Century America*. Philadelphia: University of Pennsylvania Press, 2018.

———. *Rape and Sexual Power in Early America*. Chapel Hill: University of North Carolina Press, 2006.

Boster, Dea H. *African American Slavery and Disability: Bodies, Property, and Power in the Antebellum South, 1800–1860*. New York: Routledge, 2013.

Boxer, C. R. *Race Relations in the Portuguese Colonial Empire, 1415–1825*. New York: Oxford University Press, 1963.

Brilliant, Richard. *Portraiture*. Cambridge, Mass.: Harvard University Press, 1991.

Brown, Kathleen M. *Good Wives, Nasty Wenches, and Anxious Patriarchs: Gender, Race, and Power in Colonial Virginia*. Chapel Hill: University of North Carolina Press for the Institute of Early American History and Culture, 1996.

———. "'Strength of the Lion . . . Arms Like Polished Iron': Embodying Black Masculinity in an Age of Slavery and Propertied Manhood." In *New Men: Manliness in Early America*, edited by Thomas A. Foster, 172–94. New York: New York University Press, 2011.

Browne, Randy M. *Surviving Slavery in the British Caribbean*. Philadelphia: University of Pennsylvania Press, 2017.

Buckley, Thomas E., S.J. *The Great Catastrophe of My Life: Divorce in the Old Dominion*. Chapel Hill: University of North Carolina Press, 2002.

Burg, B. R. *Boys at Sea: Sodomy, Indecency, and Courts Martial in Nelson's Navy*. New York: Palgrave Macmillan, 2007.

Burnard, Trevor. *Mastery, Tyranny, and Desire: Thomas Thistlewood and His Slaves in the Anglo-Jamaican World*. Chapel Hill: University of North Carolina Press, 2004.

———. "'A Matron in Rank, a Prostitute in Manners': The Manning Divorce of 1741 and Class, Gender, Race and the Law in Eighteenth-Century Jamaica." In *Working Slavery, Pricing Freedom: Perspectives from the Caribbean, Africa and the African Diaspora*, edited by Verene A. Shepherd, 133–52. New York: Palgrave, 2002.

Bush, Barbara. "Hard Labor: Women, Childbirth, and Resistance in British Caribbean Slave Societies." In *More Than Chattel: Black Women and Slavery in the Americas*, edited by David Barry Gaspar and Darlene Clark Hine, 198–201. Bloomington: Indiana University Press, 1996.

Camp, Stephanie. *Closer to Freedom: Enslaved Women and Everyday Resistance in the Plantation South*. Chapel Hill: University of North Carolina Press, 2004.

———. "The Pleasures of Resistance: Enslaved Women and Body Politics in the Plantation South, 1830–1861." *Journal of Southern History* 68 (August 2002): 533–72.

Cecil-Fronsman, Bill. *Common Whites: Class and Culture in Antebellum North Carolina*. Lexington: University Press of Kentucky, 1992.

Clark, Emily. *The Strange History of the American Quadroon: Free Women of Color in the Revolutionary Atlantic World*. Chapel Hill: University of North Carolina Press, 2013.

Clifton, Charles. "Rereading Voices from the Past: Images of Homo-eroticism in the Slave Narrative." In *The Greatest Taboo: Homosexuality in Black Communities*, edited by Delroy Constantine-Simms, 342–61. Los Angeles: Alyson Books, 2000.

Cody, Cheryll Ann. "Cycles of Work and of Childbearing: Seasonality in Women's Lives on Low Country Plantations." In *More Than Chattel: Black Women and Slavery in the Americas*, edited by David Barry Gaspar and Darlene Clark Hine, 61–78. Bloomington: Indiana University Press, 1996.

Colligan, Colette. "Anti-Abolition Writes Obscenity: The English Vice, Transatlantic Slavery, and England's Obscene Print Culture." In *International Exposure: Perspectives on Modern Pornography, 1800–2000*, edited by Lisa Z. Sigel, 67–99. New Brunswick, N.J.: Rutgers University Press, 2005.

Constantine-Simms, Delroy, ed. *The Greatest Taboo: Homosexuality in Black Communities*. New York: Alyson Books, 2001.

Crain, Caleb. *American Sympathy: Men, Friendship, and Literature in the New Nation*. New Haven, Conn.: Yale University Press, 2001.

Crane, Elaine Forman. *Witches, Wife Beaters, and Whores: Common Law and Common Folk in Early America*. Ithaca, N.Y.: Cornell University Press, 2011.

Curry, Tommy J. *The Man-Not: Race, Class, Genre, and the Dilemmas of Black Manhood*. Philadelphia: Temple University Press, 2017.

Cvetkovich, Ann. *An Archive of Feeling: Trauma, Sexuality, and Lesbian Public Cultures*. Durham, N.C.: Duke University Press, 2003.

Dawidoff, Robert. *Education of John Randolph*. New York: W. W. Norton, 1979.

D'Emilio, John. "Capitalism and Gay Identity." In *Making Trouble: Essays on Gay History, Politics, and the University*. New York: Routledge, 1992.

Deyle, Steven. *Carry Me Back: The Domestic Slave Trade in American Life*. Oxford: Oxford University Press, 2005.

Doddington, David. *Contesting Masculinity in the American South*. Cambridge: Cambridge University Press, 2018.

———. "Informal Economies and Masculine Hierarchies in Slave Communities of the U.S. South, 1800–1865." In *Gender and History File*, 2015, http://orca.cf.ac.uk/74559/.

Donoghue, Eddie. *Black Breeding Machines: The Breeding of Negro Slaves in the Diaspora*. Bloomington: AuthorHouse, 2008.

Downs, Jim. "With Only a Trace: Same-Sex Sexual Desire and Violence on Slave Plantations, 1607–1865." In *Connexions: Histories of Race and Sex in North America*, edited by Jennifer Brier, Jim Downs, and Jennifer Morgan, 15–37. Springfield: University of Illinois Press, 2016.

Duberman, Martin Bauml. "'Writhing Bedfellows' in Antebellum South Carolina: Historical Interpretation and the Politics of Evidence." In *Hidden from History: Reclaiming the Gay and Lesbian Past*, edited by Martin Bauml Duberman, Martha Vicinus, and George Chauncey Jr., 153–69. New York: NAL Books, 1989.

Dunn, Richard S. *Sugar and Slaves: The Rise of the Planter Class in the English West Indies, 1624–1713*. Chapel Hill: University of North Carolina Press for the the Institute of Early American History and Culture, 2000.

———. *A Tale of Two Plantations: Slave Life and Labor in Jamaica and Virginia*. Cambridge, Mass.: Harvard University Press, 2014.

Eggert, Gerald G. "A Pennsylvanian Visits a Richmond Slave Market." Notes & Documents, *Pennsylvania Magazine of History and Biography* 109, no. 4 (October 1985): 571–76.

Ellis, Robert Richmond. "Reading through the Veil of Juan Francisco Manzano: From Homoerotic Violence to the Dream of a Homoracial Bond." *PMLA* 113 (1998): 422–35.

Eng, David L., and David Kazanjian, eds. *Loss: The Politics of Mourning*. Berkeley: University of California Press, 2002.

Escott, Paul D. *Slavery Remembered: A Record of Twentieth-Century Slave Narratives*. Chapel Hill: University of North Carolina Press, 1979.

Eyerman, Ron. *Cultural Trauma: Slavery and the Formation of African American Identity*. Cambridge: Cambridge University Press, 2001.

Faust, Drew Gilpin. *James Henry Hammond and the Old South: A Design for Mastery*. Baton Rouge: Louisiana State University Press, 1982.

Fede, Andrew. "Legitimized Violent Slave Abuse in the American South, 1619–1865: A Case Study of Law and Social Change in Six Southern States." *American Journal of Legal History* 29, no. 2 (April 1985): 93–150.

Fischer, Kirsten. *Suspect Relations: Sex, Race, and Resistance in Colonial North Carolina*. Ithaca, N.Y.: Cornell University Press, 2002.

Fogel, William Robert, and Stanley L. Engerman. *Time on the Cross: The Economics of American Negro Slavery*. Boston: Little, Brown and Company, 1974.

Foreman, P. Gabrielle. "Manifest Signs: The Politics of Sex and Representation in *Incidents in the Life of a Slave Girl*." In *Harriet Jacobs and "Incidents in the Life of a Slave Girl": New Critical Essays*, edited by Deborah M. Garfield and Rafia Zafar, 76–99. Cambridge: Cambridge University Press, 1996.

———. "'This Promiscuous Housekeeping': Death, Transgression, and Homoeroticism in *Uncle Tom's Cabin*." *Representations* 43 (Summer 1993): 51–72.

Forret, Jeff. "Conflict and the 'Slave Community': Violence among Slaves in Upcountry South Carolina." *Journal of Southern History* 74 (2008): 551–88.

———. *Slave against Slave: Plantation Violence in the Old South*. Baton Rouge: Louisiana State University Press, 2015.

Foster, Frances Smith. "'In Respect to Females . . .': Differences in the Portrayals of Women by Male and Female Narrators." *Black American Literature Forum* 15 (Summer 1981): 66–70.

———. *'Til Death or Distance Do Us Part: Love and Marriage in African America*. Oxford: Oxford University Press, 2010.

Foster, Thomas A. *Sex and the Eighteenth-Century Man: Massachusetts and the History of Sexuality in America*. Boston: Beacon Press, 2006.

———. "Sexual Abuse of Black Men under American Slavery." *Journal of the History of Sexuality* 20, no. 3 (2011): 445–64.

Fox-Genovese, Elizabeth. *Within the Plantation Household: Black and White Women of the Old South*. Chapel Hill: University of North Carolina Press, 1988.

Fraser, Rebecca. *Courtship and Love among the Enslaved in North Carolina*. Jackson: University Press of Mississippi, 2007.

———. "Negotiating Their Manhood: Masculinity amongst the Enslaved in the Upper South, 1830–1861." In *Black and White Masculinity in the American South, 1800–2000*, edited by Lydia Plath and Sergio Lussana, 76–94. Newcastle upon Tyne: Cambridge Scholars Publishing, 2009.

Freedman, Estelle B. *Redefining Rape: Sexual Violence in the Era of Suffrage and Segregation*. Cambridge, Mass.: Harvard University Press, 2013.

Freyre, Gilberto. *The Masters and the Slaves: A Study in the Development of Brazilian Civilization*. Translated by Samuel Putnam, abridged from the revised edition. 1946; New York: Alfred A. Knopf, 1956.

Fuentes, Marisa J. *Dispossessed Lives: Enslaved Women, Violence, and the Archive*. Philadelphia: University of Pennsylvania Press, 2017.

Genovese, Eugene G. *Roll, Jordan, Roll: The World the Slaves Made*. New York: Pantheon Books, 1974.

Gilbert, Arthur N. "Buggery and the British Navy, 1700–1861." *Journal of Social History* 10, no. 1 (1976): 72–98.

Glymph, Thavolia. *Out of the House of Bondage: The Transformation of the Plantation Household*. Cambridge: Cambridge University Press, 2008.

Godbeer, Richard. *The Overflowing of Friendship: Love between Men and the Creation of the American Republic*. Baltimore, Md.: Johns Hopkins University Press, 2009.

Goddard, Richard, and Noel Polk. "Reading the Ledgers (Faulkner)." *Mississippi Quarterly* 55 (2002): 301–59.

Gomez, Michael A. *Exchanging Our Country Marks: The Transformation of African Identities in the Colonial and Antebellum South*. Chapel Hill: University of North Carolina Press, 1998.

Green, Sharony. *Remember Me to Miss Louisa: Hidden Black-White Intimacies in Antebellum America*. DeKalb: Northern Illinois University Press, 2015.

Greven, David. *Gender Protest and Same-Sex Desire in Antebellum American Literature*. Burlington, Vt.: Ashgate, 2014.

Griffin, Rebecca. "Courtship Contests and the Meaning of Conflict in the Folklore of Slaves." *Journal of Southern History* 71, no. 4 (November 2005): 769–802.

———. "'Goin' Back Over There to See That Girl': Competing Social Spaces in the Lives of the Enslaved in Antebellum North Carolina." *Slavery and Abolition* 25, no. 1 (April 2004): 94–113.

Grigsby, Darcy Grimaldo. *Extremities: Painting Empire in Post-revolutionary France*. New Haven, Conn.: Yale University Press, 2002.

Gutiérrez, Ramón A. "Warfare, Homosexuality, and Gender Status among American Indian Men in the Southwest." In *Long before Stonewall: Histories of Same-Sex Sexuality in Early America*, edited by Thomas A. Foster, 19–31. New York: New York University Press, 2007.

Gutman, Herbert G. *The Black Family in Slavery and Freedom, 1750–1925*. New York: Pantheon Books, 1976.

Hall, Douglas, ed. *In Miserable Slavery: Thomas Thistlewood in Jamaica, 1750–86*. London: Macmillan, 1992.

Halttunen, Karen. "Humanitarianism and the Pornography of Pain in Anglo-American Culture." *American Historical Review* 100, no. 2 (April 1995): 303–34.

Hansen, Karen V. "'No Kisses Is Like Youres': An Erotic Friendship between Two African-American Women during the Mid-Nineteenth Century." *Gender & History* 7, no. 2. (August 1995): 153–82.

———. "'Our Eyes Behold Each Other': Masculinity and Intimate Friendship in Antebellum New England." In *Men's Friendships: Research on Men and Masculinities*, edited by Peter M. Nardi, 35–58. London: Sage Publications, 1992.

Harris, Leslie. "From Abolitionist Amalgamators to 'Rulers of the Five Points': The Discourse of Interracial Sex and Reform in Antebellum New York City." In *Sex, Love, Race: Crossing Boundaries in North American History*, edited by Martha Hodes, 191–212. New York: New York University Press, 1999.

Hartman, Saidiya V. *Scenes of Subjection: Terror, Slavery, and Self-Making in Nineteenth-Century America*. New York: Oxford University Press, 1997.

Higgins, Kathleen J. *"Licentious Liberty" in a Brazilian Gold-Mining Region: Slavery, Gender, and Social Control in Eighteenth-Century Sabara, Minas Gerais*. University Park: Pennsylvania State University Press, 1999.

Hodes, Martha. *White Women, Black Men: Illicit Sex in the Nineteenth-Century South*. New Haven, Conn.: Yale University Press, 1999.

hooks, bell. *Ain't I a Woman: Black Women and Feminism*. 1981; New York: Routledge, 2015.

Howell, Donna Wyant, comp. *I Was a Slave: Book 4: The Breeding of Slaves*. Washington, D.C.: American Legacy Books, 1996.

Hudson, Larry E. *To Have and to Hold: Slave Work and Family Life in Antebellum South Carolina*. Athens: University of Georgia Press, 1997.

Hunter, Tera W. *Bound in Wedlock: Slave and Free Black Marriage in the Nineteenth Century*. Cambridge, Mass.: Harvard University Press, 2017.

Jabour, Anya. "Male Friendship and Masculinity in the Early National South: William Wirt and His Friends." *Journal of the Early Republic* 20 (2000): 83–111.

Jennings, Thelma. "'Us Colored Women Had to Go Though A Plenty': Sexual Exploitation of African-American Slave Women." *Journal of Women's History* 1, no. 3 (1990): 45–74.

Johnson, Guion Griffis. *Ante-bellum North Carolina: A Social History; Electronic Edition*. Chapel Hill: University of North Carolina Press, 1937. https://docsouth.unc.edu/nc/johnson/titlepage.html.

Johnson, Walter. *Soul by Soul: Life inside the Antebellum Slave Market*. Cambridge, Mass.: Harvard University Press, 2000.

Johnston, James Hugo. *Race Relations in Virginia and Miscegenation in the South, 1776–1860*. Amherst: University of Massachusetts Press, 1970.

Jones, Cecily. "Contesting the Boundaries of Gender, Race and Sexuality in Barbadian Plantation Society." *Women's History Review* 12, no. 2 (2003): 195–232.

Jones, Jacqueline. *Labor of Love, Labor of Sorrow: Black Women, Work, and the Family from Slavery to the Present*. New York: Basic Books, 1985.

Jones-Rogers, Stephanie E. "'[S]he Could . . . Spare One Ample Breast for the Profit of Her Owner': White Mothers and Enslaved Wet Nurses' Invisible Labor in American Slave Markets." *Slavery and Abolition* 38, no. 2 (April 2017): 337–55.

Jordan, Winthrop D. *White over Black: American Attitudes toward the Negro, 1550–1812*. Chapel Hill: University of North Carolina Press for the Institute of Early American History and Culture, 1968.

Katz, Jonathan Ned. *Gay/Lesbian Almanac: A New Documentary*. New York: Carroll & Graf, 1994.

Kaye, Anthony E. "The Problem of Autonomy: Toward a Political History." In *New Directions in Slavery Studies: Commodification, Community, and Comparison*, edited by Jeff Forret and Christine E. Sears, 150–78. Baton Rouge: Louisiana State University Press, 2015.

King, Wilma. "'Prematurely Knowing of Evil Things': The Sexual Abuse of African American Girls and Young Women in Slavery and Freedom." *Journal of African American History* 99, no. 3 (Summer 2014): 173–96.

———. *Stolen Childhood: Slave Youth in Nineteenth-Century America*. Bloomington: Indiana University Press, 1995.

———. "'Suffer with Them till Death': Slave Women and Their Children in Nineteenth-Century America." In *More Than Chattel: Black Women and Slavery in the Americas*, edited by David Barry Gaspar and Darlene Clark Hine, 147–68. Bloomington: Indiana University Press, 1996.

Kulikoff, Allan. *Tobacco and Slaves: The Development of Southern Cultures in the Chesapeake, 1680–1800*. Chapel Hill: University of North Carolina Press for the Institute of Early American History and Culture, 1998.

LaCapra, Dominick. *Writing History, Writing Trauma*. Baltimore, Md.: Johns Hopkins University Press, 2001.

Langley, Harold. *Social Reform in the United States Navy, 1798–1862*. Annapolis, Md.: Naval Institute Press, 2015.

Lebsock, Suzanne. *The Free Women of Petersburg: Status and Culture in a Southern Town, 1784–1860*. New York: W. W. Norton & Co., 1985.

Lindsey, Treva B., and Jessica Marie Johnson. "Searching for Climax: Black Erotic Lives in Slavery and Freedom." *Meridians: feminism, race, transnationalism* 12, no. 2 (2014): 169–95.

Long, Alecia P. *The Great Southern Babylon: Sex, Race, and Respectability in New Orleans, 1865–1920*. Baton Rouge: Louisiana State University Press, 2004.

Lowe, Richard G., and Randolph B. Campbell. "The Slave-Breeding Hypothesis: A Demographic Comment on the 'Buying' and 'Selling' States." *Journal of Southern History* 42 (August 1976): 401–12.

Lowenthal, David, and Colin G. Clarke. "Slave-Breeding in Barbuda: The Past of a Negro Myth." In *Comparative Perspectives on Slavery in New World Plantation Societies*, edited by Vera Rubin and Arthur Tuden, 510–35. New York: New York Academy of Sciences, 1977.

Lussana, Sergio A. *My Brother Slaves: Friendship, Masculinity, and Resistance in the Antebellum South*. Lexington: University Press of Kentucky, 2016.

———. "'No Band of Brothers Could Be More Loving': Enslaved Male Homosociality, Friendship, and Resistance in the Antebellum South." *Journal of Social History* 46, no. 4 (Summer 2013): 872–95.

———. "To See Who Was Best on the Plantation: Enslaved Fighting Contests and Masculinity in the Antebellum South." *Journal of Southern History* 76, no. 4 (November 2010): 901–22.

Malone, Ann Patton. *Sweet Chariot: Slave Family and Household Structure in Nineteenth-Century Louisiana*. Chapel Hill: University of North Carolina Press, 1992.

Mandell, Daniel R. "The Saga of Sarah Muckamugg: Indian and African American Intermarriage in Colonial New England." In *Sex, Love, Race: Crossing Boundaries in North American History*, edited by Martha Hodes, 72–90. New York: New York University Press, 1999.

Marshall, Kenneth E. *Manhood Enslaved: Bondmen in Eighteenth- and Early Nineteenth-Century New Jersey*. Rochester, N.Y.: University of Rochester Press, 2011.

Martel, Heather. "Colonial Allure: Normal Homoeroticism and Sodomy in French and Timucuan Encounters in Sixteenth-Century Florida." *Journal of the History of Sexuality* 22, no. 1 (January 2013): 34–64.

McInnis, Maurie D. *Slaves Waiting for Sale: Abolitionist Art and the American Slave Trade*. Chicago: University of Chicago Press, 2011.

Miller Sommerville, Dianne. *Rape and Race in the Nineteenth-Century South*. Chapel Hill: University of North Carolina Press, 2004.

Misra, Amalendu. *The Landscape of Silence: Sexual Violence against Men in War*. London: Hurst & Company, 2015.

Montejo, Esteban. *Biography of a Runaway Slave*. Edited by Miguel Barnet, translated by W. Nick Hill. Willimantic, Conn.: Curbstone Press, 1994.

Morgan, Jennifer L. *Laboring Women: Reproduction and Gender in New World Slavery*. Philadelphia: University of Pennsylvania Press, 2004.

———. "*Partus sequitur ventrem*: Law, Race, and Reproduction in Colonial Slavery." *Small Axe* 22, no. 1 (2018): 1–17. https://doi.org/10.1215/07990537-4378888.

Morgan, Philip D. *Slave Counterpoint: Black Culture in the Eighteenth-Century Chesapeake and Lowcountry*. Chapel Hill: University of North Carolina Press, 1998.

Morris, Christopher. *Becoming Southern: The Evolution of a Way of Life, Warren County and Vicksburg, Mississippi, 1770–1860*. New York: Oxford University Press, 1995.

Muskateem, Sowande' M. *Slavery at Sea: Terror, Sex, and Sickness in the Middle Passage*. Urbana: University of Illinois Press, 2016.

Musser, Amber Jamilla. *Sensational Flesh: Race, Power, and Masochism*. New York: New York University Press, 2014.

Nero, Charles I. "Toward a Black Gay Aesthetic: Signifying in Contemporary Black Gay Literature." In *Brother to Brother: New Writings by Black Gay Men*, edited by Essex Hemphill and Joseph Beam, 229–51. Boston: Alyson Publications, 1991.

Nyong'o, Tavia. *The Amalgamation Waltz: Race, Performance, and the Ruses of Memory*. Minneapolis: University of Minnesota Press, 2009.

Ottley, Roi, and W. J. Weatherby, eds. *The Negro in New York: An Informal Social History*. New York: New York Public Library, 1967.

Patterson, Orlando. *Slavery and Social Death: A Comparative Study*. Cambridge, Mass.: Harvard University Press, 1982.

Perdue, Charles L., Jr., Thomas E. Barden, and Robert K. Phillips, eds. *Weevils in the Wheat: Interviews with Virginia Ex-slaves*. Charlottesville: University of Virginia Press, 1976.

Rediker, Marcus. *The Slave Ship: A Human History*. New York: Penguin, 2007.

Riley, Glenda. *Divorce: An American Tradition*. New York: Oxford University Press, 1991.

Rogers, Molly. *Delia's Tears: Race, Science, and Photography in Nineteenth-Century America*. New Haven, Conn.: Yale University Press, 2010.

Rogers Albert, Octavia V. *The House of Bondage or Charlotte Brooks and Other Slaves*. New York: Oxford University Press, 1988.

Roth, Sarah N. *Gender and Race in Antebellum Popular Culture*. Cambridge: Cambridge University Press, 2014.

———. "'How a Slave Was Made a Man': Negotiating Black Violence and Masculinity in Antebellum Slave Narratives." *Slavery and Abolition* 28, no. 2 (August 2007): 255–75.

Ryder, A. F. C. "An Early Portuguese Trading Voyage to the Forcados River." *Journal of the Historical Society of Nigeria* 1, no. 4 (December 1959): 294–321.

Saillant, John. "The Black Body Erotic and the Republican Body Politic, 1790–1820." In *Long before Stonewall: Histories of Same-Sex Sexuality in Early America*, edited by Thomas A. Foster, 303–30. New York: New York University Press, 2007.

Schafer, Judith K. "Sexual Cruelty to Slaves: The Unreported Case of *Humphreys v. Utz*." In "Symposium on the Law of Slavery: Criminal and Civil Law of Slavery." Special issue, *Chicago-Kent Law Review* 68 (1992): 1313–40.

Schwartz, Marie Jenkins. *Birthing a Slave: Motherhood and Medicine in the Antebellum South*. Cambridge, Mass.: Harvard University Press, 2006.

Schweninger, Loren. *Families in Crisis in the Old South: Divorce, Slavery, and the Law*. Chapel Hill: University of North Carolina Press, 2012.

Shaw, Stephanie J. "Using the WPA Ex-slave Narrative to Study the Impact of the Great Depression." *Journal of Southern History* 69, no. 3 (August 2003): 623–58.

Sielke, Sabine. *Reading Rape: The Rhetoric of Sexual Violence in American Literature and Culture, 1790–1990*. Princeton, N.J.: Princeton University Press, 2002.

Slenes, Robert W. "Black Homes, White Homilies: Perceptions of the Slave Family and of Slave Women in Nineteenth-Century Brazil." In *More Than Chattel: Black Women and Slavery in the Americas*, edited by David Barry Gaspar and Darlene Clark Hine, 126–46. Bloomington: Indiana University Press, 1996.

Smallwood, Stephanie E. *Saltwater Slavery: A Middle Passage from Africa to American Diaspora*. Cambridge, Mass.: Harvard University Press, 2007.

Smith, Merril D., ed. *Sex without Consent: Rape and Sexual Coercion in America*. New York: New York University Press, 2001.

Smith-Rosenberg, Carroll. "The Female World of Love and Ritual: Relations between Women in Nineteenth-Century America." *Signs* 1, no. 1 (1975): 1–29.

Smithers, Gregory D. *Slave Breeding: Sex, Violence, and Memory in African American History*. Gainesville: University Press of Florida, 2012.

Snyder, Christina. *Slavery in Indian Country: The Changing Face of Captivity in Early America*. Cambridge, Mass.: Harvard University Press, 2010.

Snyder, Terri L. "Marriage on the Margins: Free Wives, Enslaved Husbands, and the Law in Early Virginia." *Law and History Review* 30, no. 1 (February 2012): 141–71.

———. *The Power to Die: Slavery and Suicide in British North America*. Chicago: University of Chicago Press, 2015.

———. "Sexual Consent and Sexual Coercion in Seventeenth-Century Virginia." In *Sex without Consent: Rape and Sexual Coercion in America*, edited by Merril D. Smith, 46–60. New York: New York University Press, 2001.

Sobel, Mechal. *The World They Made Together: Black and White Values in Eighteenth-Century Virginia*. Princeton, N.J.: Princeton University Press, 1987.

Spindel, Donna J. "Assessing Memory: Twentieth-Century Slave Narratives Reconsidered." *Journal of Interdisciplinary History* 27, no. 2 (Autumn 1996): 247–61.

Stanley, Amy Dru. "Slave Breeding and Free Love: An Antebellum Argument over Slavery, Capitalism, and Personhood." In *Capitalism Takes Command: The Social Transformation of Nineteenth-Century America*, edited by Michael Zakim and Gary J. Kornblith, 119–44. Chicago: University of Chicago Press, 2012.

Stevenson, Brenda E. *Life in Black and White: Family and Community in the Slave South*. New York: Oxford University Press, 1997.

———. "What's Love Got to Do with It? Concubinage and Enslaved Black Women and Girls in the Antebellum South." *Journal of African American History* 98 (Winter 2013): 99–125.

Styron, William. *The Confessions of Nat Turner*. 1966; New York: Random House, 1967.

Sublette, Ned, and Constance Sublette. *The American Slave Coast: A History of the Slave-Breeding Industry*. Chicago: Chicago Review Press, 2016.

Sutch, Richard. "The Breeding of Slaves for Sale and the Westward Expansion of Slavery, 1850–1860." In *Race and Slavery in the Western Hemisphere: Quantitative Stud-*

ies, edited by Stanley L. Engerman and Eugene D. Genovese, 173–210. Princeton, N.J.: Princeton University Press, 1975.

Sweet, James H. "Defying Social Death: The Multiple Configurations of the African Slave Family in the Atlantic World." *William and Mary Quarterly* 70, no. 2 (2013): 251–72.

———. *Recreating Africa: Culture, Kinship, and Religion in the African-Portuguese World.* Chapel Hill: University of North Carolina Press, 2003.

Sweet, John Wood. *Bodies Politic: Negotiating Race in the American North, 1730–1830.* Baltimore, Md.: Johns Hopkins University Press, 2003.

Taylor, Alan. *The Internal Enemy: Slavery and War in Virginia, 1772–1832.* New York: W. W. Norton, 2013.

Tinsley, Natasha. "Black Atlantic, Queer Atlantic: Queer Imaginings of the Middle Passage." *GLQ* 14, no. 2–3 (2008): 191–215.

Turner, Sasha. *Contested Bodies: Pregnancy, Childrearing, and Slavery in Jamaica.* Philadelphia: University of Pennsylvania Press, 2017.

Wallace, Maurice O. *Constructing the Black Masculine: Identity and Ideality in African American Men's Literature and Culture, 1775–1995.* Durham, N.C.: Duke University Press, 2002.

Warren, Wendy Anne. "'The Cause of Her Grief': The Rape of a Slave in Early New England." *Journal of American History* 93, no. 4 (March 2007): 1031–49.

West, Emily. *Chains of Love: Slave Couples in Antebellum South Carolina.* Urbana: University of Illinois Press, 2004.

West, Emily, with R. J. Knight. "Mother's Milk: Slavery, Wet-Nursing, and Black and White Women in the Antebellum South." *Journal of Southern History* 83, no. 1 (February 2017): 37–68.

Weston, Helen D. "Representing the Right to Present: The 'Portrait of Citizen Belley, Ex-Representative of the Colonies' by A.-L. Girodet." *RES: Anthropology and Aesthetics* 26 (Autumn 1994): 83–99.

White, Deborah Gray. *Ar'n't I a Woman? Female Slaves in the Plantation South.* Revised edition. 1985; New York: W. W. Norton, 1999.

Williams, Heather Andrea. *Help Me to Find My People: The African American Search for Family Lost in Slavery.* Chapel Hill: University of North Carolina Press, 2012.

Williams, Kidada E. *They Left Great Marks on Me: African American Testimonies of Racial Violence from Emancipation to World War I.* New York: New York University Press, 2012.

Winters, Lisa Ze. "'More Desultory and Unconnected Than Any Other': Geography, Desire, and Freedom in Eliza Potter's *A Hairdresser's Experience in High Life.*" *American Quarterly* 61, no. 3 (September 2009): 455–75.

Wood, Betty. "Servant Women and Sex in the Seventeenth-Century Chesapeake." In *Women in Early America,* edited by Thomas A. Foster, 95–117. New York: New York University Press, 2015.

Wood, Marcus. *Slavery, Empathy, and Pornography.* Oxford: Oxford University Press, 2002.

Woodard, Vincent. *The Delectable Negro: Human Consumption and Homoeroticism within U.S. Slave Culture.* Edited by Justin A. Joyce and Dwight A. McBride. New York: New York University Press, 2014.

Woodfin, Maude H., ed., and Marion Tinling, trans. *Another Secret Diary of William Byrd of Westover, 1739–1741.* Richmond: Dietz Press, 1942.

INDEX

Page numbers in italics refer to figures.